DEPLOYING IP MULTICAST IN THE ENTERPRISE

Thomas Maufer

Prentice Hall PTR
Upper Saddle River, NJ 07458
www.phptr.com

ISBN 0-13-897687-2

90000

9 780138 976873

Library of Congress Cataloging-in-Publication Data

Maufer, Thomas
    Deploying IP multicast in the enterprise / Thomas Maufer.
       p. cm.
    Includes bibliographical references and index.
    ISBN 0-13-897687-2
      1. Multicasting (Computer networks)   I. Title.
  TK5105.55.M39   1997
  004.6'6--dc21   97-41591
                                        CIP

Editorial/production supervision: *Joanne Anzalone, Patti Guerrieri*
Cover design director: *Jerry Votta*
Cover designer: *Design Source*
Manufacturing manager: *Alexis R. Heydt*
Marketing manager: *Miles Williams*
Acquisitions editor: *Mary Franz*
Editorial assistant: *Noreen Regina*

Prentice Hall books are widely used by corporations and government agencies
for training, marketing, and resale.

The publisher offers discounts on this book when ordered in bulk quantities.
For more information, contact: Corporate Sales Department, Phone: 800-382-3419;
Fax: 201-236-7141; E-mail: corpsales@prenhall.com; or write: Prentice Hall PTR,
Corp. Sales Dept., One Lake Street, Upper Saddle River, NJ 07458.

All products or services mentioned in this book are the trademarks or service marks of their
respective companies or organizations.

Printed in the United States of America
10 9 8 7 6 5 4 3 2 1

ISBN   0-13-897687-2

Prentice-Hall International (UK) Limited, *London*
Prentice-Hall of Australia Pty. Limited, *Sydney*
Prentice-Hall Canada Inc., *Toronto*
Prentice-Hall Hispanoamericana, S.A., *Mexico*
Prentice-Hall of India Private Limited, *New Delhi*
Prentice-Hall of Japan, Inc., *Tokyo*
Simon & Schuster Asia Pte. Ltd., *Singapore*
Editora Prentice-Hall do Brasil, Ltda., *Rio de Janeiro*

for Deb

CONTENTS

ACKNOWLEDGMENTS

Many people supported and encouraged me while I was writing this book. I doubt I'll be able to remember everyone, and therefore I will apologize now to anyone that I neglect to mention.

The biggest acknowledgment goes to my wife, Deb, for being so patient and supportive during the production of this book. Also many thanks go to my parents, who have encouraged me for my entire life and supported me in all my efforts.

Because parts of this book were based on the RFC I co-authored with Chuck Semeria, entitled "Introduction to IP Multicast Routing," I feel that I must reiterate our extreme appreciation to the RFC's reviewers, who were: Kevin Almeroth, Tony Ballardie, Steve Casner, Jon Crowcroft, Steve Deering, Bill Fenner, Hugh Holbrook, Cyndi Jung, David Meyer, John Moy, Shuching Shieh, Dave Thaler, and Nair Venugopal.

I wish to acknowledge my employer, 3Com Corporation, for giving me permission to write this book. Special thanks goes to Chuck Semeria, a wonderful colleague with whom I have collaborated on many projects over my tenure at 3Com. As a technical writer, Chuck has an absolutely marvelous talent for clearly and appropriately expressing technical material to readers at virtually any level. I would have been thrilled if Chuck could have co-authored this book with me, but his job already involves way too much writing, so taking on this project was out of the question for him. However, he was not uninvolved. I was very lucky to have him as a reviewer, and the book is much better than if he had not been involved.

Speaking of reviewers, I also wish to thank those who helped review this book—you know who you are! I couldn't possibly have accomplished this large project in such a short time period without your valuable input. The finished product is far better due to your assistance, and you have my deepest appreciation and thanks.

I would like to thank NASA's Jet Propulsion Laboratory and SoftBank Forums for agreeing to be spotlighted in the case studies at the end of the book.

Marc Jordan of NASA/JPL was extremely helpful, providing the information for the JPL case study on very short notice. His help was very timely in the information-gathering and first-draft stages of the book, and he provided many useful clarifying comments during the final review process. In both case studies, I tried to accurately convey the technical details and motivation for decisions that have been made regarding deployment issues. Any lingering inaccuracies are entirely my fault, of course.

Finally, I feel the need to acknowledge one of my main sources of technical growth and inspiration over the last three to five years, the InteropNet Network Operations Center (NOC) Team. There is no more knowledgeable group of networking professionals . . . their collective experience is deep, comprehensive, and usually overwhelming. A finer, more talented group probably does not exist on this planet, and it is a real honor to have been associated with them. Steve Hultquist and Jim Martin helped review the case study on the InteropNet at a time when they were both very busy with "retooling" the Interop-Net in preparation for the Atlanta 1997 show. I can't overstate my appreciation for their help during a very busy period in their lives.

Introduction

In the summer of 1995, my company (3Com Corporation) was preparing to ship multicast routing capabilities in one of its router products. At the time, I was part of a team that was responsible for helping our sales force and customers understand this technology and its importance, which often involved writing informational white papers and presentations about the technology with Chuck Semeria. By the end of 1995, we had a paper that introduced people to how multicast routing protocols worked.

After the IETF meeting in Dallas that December, we were encouraged by some fellow Internet Engineering Task Force (IETF) members to publish this document as an IETF informational Request for Comments (RFC). Because multicast routing concepts are unfamiliar to many people, an introductory document was viewed as an important companion to the standards being produced within the IETF.

Over the next 18 months, some of the multicast routing protocols evolved considerably in their predicted operating environments, standardization track, and even some of their internal features and mechanisms. The routing protocols had advanced beyond our original paper, so consequently we wished to delay publishing the RFC until the specifications had stabilized—after all, we didn't want the "Introduction to IP Multicast Routing" to be based on outdated information. Once the majority of these protocols had been finalized, or nearly finalized (circa early 1997), we rewrote the document to reflect the "final" details of the protocols. Just as the protocols had changed during their initial development and standardization phase, it is inevitable that they will continue to evolve over time; in addition, new protocols will be invented. While the document is really only accurate once, it is unlikely that the fundamental concepts will change, and we hope that the RFC will still be useful in the years to come.

Based on an earlier internet-draft version of this developing RFC, Prentice Hall approached us regarding building a book around the foundation laid by the RFC. Given the increasing interest in multicast technology, it seemed like the time was right for such a book. The book introduces the reader to the core ideas of this subject matter, so that they may understand the mechanisms employed, enabling educated decisions on which protocols to deploy in their own unique networks, and allowing them to envision how multicast routing may affect their individual enterprise intranetworks.

Beyond the details provided on the multicast routing protocols, multicast applications are discussed, and also topics which are the subject of active research and intense interest, such as reliable multicast transport protocols. The book concludes with two case studies of existing networks that are already using multicast routing, exploring deployment issues and lessons learned. No two networks are alike, but hopefully the examples chosen will provide interesting reading for those planning to deploy multicast in their own intranets.

A solid multicast routing infrastructure is the key foundation upon which next-generation multicast applications are layered. Applications such as multimedia conferencing, "push-"oriented applications, multipoint data distribution, distance learning, etc., all depend on an efficient multipoint delivery service. Multicast is the key network infrastructure component enabling these and other next-generation applications.

This book is written for anyone that wants to learn about technologies related to multicast IP. It can serve as a quick reference book, giving the broad outlines of the various protocols. Enough details are provided that a reader should be able to understand the internal mechanisms employed by each protocol. Not all protocols are equally applicable to every networking scenario, so understanding how each different multicast routing protocol works is critical to the successful deployment of multicast routing. Knowing the benefits and limitations of each protocol enables network managers to make better-informed decisions about which protocol(s) are appropriate for use in their own networks.

Readers ought to have a basic operational understanding of unicast IP routing. While a basic introduction to unicast routing and addressing is included, it is not intended to be comprehensive, rather a refresher for concepts that are important to the explanation of multicast IP. Also helpful would be a good understanding of the basics of unicast IP applications, especially knowing how they employ the services of the unicast transport layer protocols.

At a minimum, this book will give readers a solid understanding of multicast routing protocols, and the sorts of existing applications that can make use of multicast. In addition, the book can serve as an introduction to more advanced applications enabled by multicast routing technology, including reliable multicast applications. Issues surrounding the use of multicast IP over the Internet are also explored. The case studies serve as proof points that multicast can be used in production networks, and shows what sorts of applications are of interest in these environments.

ROADMAP

This book is not necessarily designed to be read from cover to cover, though a determined reader is welcome to try. Each chapter is designed to be fairly independent of the others, so that it may be used as a concise reference.

The book begins with a overview of the concepts of IP-based "intranets" and moves on to discuss multicast applications, along with a description of the motivation for multicast. Successive chapters place multicast IP in the context of unicast IP, and introduce concepts such as Classless Inter-Domain Routing (CIDR) and subnetting (including Variable-Length Subnet Masking (VLSM)). Before diving in to detailed descriptions of the various different multicast routing protocols, there is a discussion of how to identify and classify multicast applications, leading into a history of the standardization of multicast IP. Multicast "scoping" is discussed, then versions one and two of the Internet Group Management Protocol (IGMP) are explained. IGMP is the protocol that end stations must use to participate in multicast IP sessions.

The routers use information derived from IGMP to help build "trees" so that sources can send traffic to a group without knowing the exact group membership in advance. How the routers determine the shape of these trees is the essence of multicast routing, and all the major algorithms are covered in at least one chapter each. Each protocol takes a different approach to solving this problem, and each chapter includes a short summary of the protocol's tree building techniques and the methods employed to decide how to forward a multicast packet. Once all the existing multicast routing protocols have been covered, there is a discussion of a possible interoperability framework for these protocols, and two fundamental multicast techniques are discussed: expanding-ring searches and the Service Location Protocol.

From this foundation, we move on to introduce the concepts behind reliable multicast transport protocols. A full discussion of this very interesting topic could easily fill a book of its own. I have tried to distill the issues related to reliable multicast transport protocols so that the concepts involved in various techniques can be understood. As I said, a full discussion of the interactions of reliable multicast transport protocols and their associated applications, along with issues surrounding interactions with unicast transport protocols, is beyond the scope of this book. Many of these issues are not yet well understood, and still the subject of active research and debate. The main body of the book concludes with two case studies: Soft Bank's "InteropNet" and NASA's Jet Propulsion Laboratory's campus network.

Finally, the book closes with five Appendices: a Glossary; a detailed discussion of IGMP, including details of all its packet formats; and a history of the development of multicast technology, including the Internet's multicast backbone (MBone). There is a high-level overview of the various multicast routing protocols, and an overview of the two main standards bodies doing work relevant to multicast IP. The book concludes with a list of references, including Requests for Comments (RFCs), some current IETF internet-draft documents, textbooks, and other documents (e.g., Ph.D. theses).

PART I

INTRODUCTION AND PRELIMINARIES

Multicast IP is somewhat different from the more familiar unicast IP, but is growing in importance due to the imminent arrival of next-generation network applications that rely on multipoint delivery. Of the possible ways to implement a multipoint delivery service, network-layer multicast is a technique that minimizes the load on your intranetwork arising from these multidestination applications. If you intend to deploy multipoint applications over your intranet, you need to understand that multicast-based applications can use far less of your intranet's bandwidth. When deployed over a multicast-capable intranet, these applications get the most out of every packet.

We will begin by understanding why multicast is important, and move on to a brief refresher on IP addressing, then an overview of some broad classes of multicast applications.

CHAPTER 1

INTRODUCTION

Multicast IP was developed in the last decade or so to facilitate next-generation applications that can rely on the efficient delivery of packets to multiple destinations across an internetwork. Multicast falls between unicast and broadcast. Unicast is sometimes called singlecast, which is a really awkward name (in the author's opinion) and won't be used again in this book. The unicast mode involves delivery from one source to one destination. At the other extreme, broadcast mode involves indiscriminate delivery from one source to all destinations. Multicast aims to deliver packets to subnetworks only if they contain end stations that have requested the traffic.

To get into the multicast frame of mind, it is even better to view unicast and broadcast as two "degenerate" cases of multicast. Taking this viewpoint, unicast happens when there is only one member of the "multicast group." Similarly, broadcast happens if every end station is a member of the "multicast group."

All stations on any IP subnetwork must receive all (MAC-layer) broadcasts, whereas *only* those stations that have joined a multicast host group will receive packets addressed to that multicast group. A multicast group's receivers may span different subnets, and even different network prefixes, limited only by the administrative policies of the organization which operates a given intranet.

The key difference between broadcast and multicast is that broadcast is indiscriminate about which stations shall receive the packet (all must!), whereas multicast attempts to deliver packets only to end stations that have expressed interest in being members of certain group(s). One important feature of IP multicast's host group model is that senders need not be group members. This has implications for multicast routing protocols, as we will see.

3

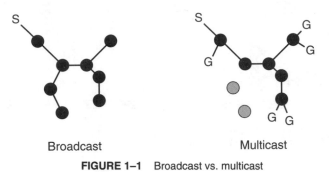

FIGURE 1–1   Broadcast vs. multicast

In Figure 1–1, the S label indicates the source station, and the G labels indicate sub-networks containing group members. Note how broadcast packets are sent everywhere, but the multicasts only follow a tree that leads from the source to the group members.

The use of multicast within an intranetwork enables efficient use of the intranet's available resources (e.g., bandwidth, router forwarding capacity). Multicast helps ensure that applications needing multidestination delivery won't swamp your intranet with (potentially) many extra copies of the same data, replicated once to each of that application's clients.

Multicast enables an application to send each packet of data just once. The application relies on the network to efficiently replicate its packets downstream to the subnetworks containing group members. Downstream is a multicast-specific term meaning the direction away from the source; similarly, upstream refers to the direction toward the source. For an illustration of the upstream and downstream concepts, please see Figure

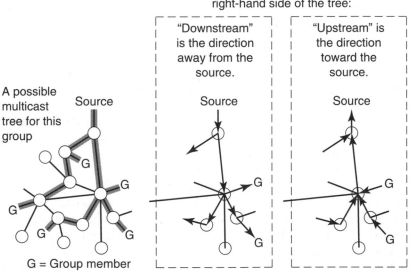

FIGURE 1–2   Upstream vs. downstream

1–2. The key rule of multicast forwarding is that packets are always forwarded *away* from the source. Multicast routing protocols use various techniques to build the trees along which packets are forwarded.

Each group is composed of a set of receivers, which may be arbitrarily distributed across the internetwork. Multicast routing protocols build trees to enable packets to get from the source to the receivers. A very important feature of multicast IP groups is that the source(s) need not be members. These trees, which connect sources to the group's receivers, are called either delivery trees or distribution trees. Different multicast routing protocols use different techniques to build these trees, as we will see later when we discuss the mechanisms of each protocol in detail.

WHAT IS AN INTRANET?

At their essence, intranets are simply IP-based networks operated by private organizations, but there is much more to them than initially meets the eye. Intranets are the current stage in the evolution of enterprise internetworks. The first enterprise networks were terminal-to-mainframe systems based on proprietary protocols such as IBM's Systems Network Architecture (SNA) and, to a lesser extent, DECnet and other protocols.

In the mid- to late 1980s, a grassroots effort to deploy LANs within organizations took place. Partly, this was to put each local organization's applications close to its users, and to give the organization better change control over their applications rather than requesting changes through a centralized Management Information Services (MIS) organization. Whether deserved or not, there was a perception of excessive control by MIS. At a minimum, development cycles for custom applications were much slower in the mainframe era. Local Area Network (LAN) deployment in local organizations may partially have been a reaction to this dominance, a "breaking of the chains" of MIS, if you will. A less cynical view would be that they were simply a useful (and cool) new technology that could be deployed quickly by power users.

These LANs were relatively easy to configure and deploy, which helped foster their popularity. They were typically based on proprietary protocols such as:

- AppleTalk
  - AppleShare
- Novell IPX
  - Netware file and print services
- NetBIOS/NetBEUI
  - 3Com's "3+Open"
  - Microsoft LAN Manager
  - Windows for Workgroups
  - Windows 95 file sharing
  - Windows NT Advanced Server

- TCP/IP
  - Nonproprietary and supported on most operating systems by the late 1980s with varying levels of application support across different platforms
  - Used by "early-adopters" of Internet technology: universities, government labs, certain corporations, and so on.
- XNS
  - 3Com's 3+Share
  - Xerox Network Services

Initially, routers did not support all these protocols, but between the late 1980s and early 1990s most routers became "multiprotocol" routers, able to support all the above protocols and some not listed there, for example, DECnet Phase IV and V, Open Systems Interconnection (OSI) protocols, and tunneling of "legacy" IBM traffic.

The advent of these PC-based LANs did not immediately threaten the mainframe. Virtually all business-critical applications resided on the mainframe; even today, this is still largely true. Undeniably, however, a sea change was occurring. The growth of new mainframe applications had certainly begun to slow down. Toward the end of this era, the demise of the mainframe was predicted, but that has not really happened. Mainframes have adapted to new applications, in some cases acting as massive file servers!

While PC LAN-based networks were supplementing terminal/host mainframe networks, the LANs, which had been deployed earlier in a rather haphazard fashion, began to be interconnected by LAN backbones.

LAN Backbones

For Ethernet LANs, the "backbone" initially may simply have been Ethernet, sometimes based on broadband infrastructure. Token ring shops may have used 4 Mbps token rings for user access and 16 Mbps rings as backbones. As bandwidth demands increased, eventually 10 Mbps Ethernet and 16 Mbps token ring backbones were supplanted by 100 Mbps Fiber Distributed Data Interface (FDDI), 155.52 Mbps ATM, and 100 Mbps Fast Ethernet. Perhaps by early 1998, 1000 Mbps Gigabit Ethernet may begin to enter service as a LAN backbone technology.

A popular network architecture in this era was the router-based "collapsed backbone." This was the heyday of the router as the central device within enterprise network infrastructures, through about 1994 or so.

The distributed applications in each organization began to present an increasingly excessive management overhead, and the next phase began slowly, correlated with the advent of "LAN switching," "server farms," and "flatter networks." The MIS organization, initially not involved with many of the upstart LANs that had been deployed by many organizations, stepped in to assume a role in managing the distributed LANs, the backbone(s) that interconnected them, and especially the centralized "server farms" which began to emerge. Most traffic in this client/server environment was fairly predictable, and LAN switches were deployed to maximize the performance of these networks. Life was good.

In this context, client/server is a broader term than just client/server Structured Query Language (SQL) or other databases. Rather, "client/server" refers to the simple fact that file or print servers have clients accessing these (and other) services. The traffic in such an environment, especially if servers are clustered in "farms," is fairly predictable. Beyond simple file and print service, client/server e-mail packages such as cc:Mail became popular. At about the same time, "groupware" applications such as Lotus Notes emerged, which purported to allow enhanced collaboration between employees. Also, client/server SQL database applications finally began to be deployed to allow LAN-based Graphical User Interface (GUI) front-ends to access SQL- or mainframe-based corporate data.

Then came the explosion of the World Wide Web (WWW) in 1992–94. Free web browsers became available for virtually every combination of hardware platform and operating system. Everyone wanted to use their corporate Internet connection to "surf the web," or urged their corporation to get connected to the Internet for the same reason. Not only was the web fun, there was a lot of great information out there. Organizations saw the potential to reach future customers, and many companies set up first-generation web sites that were little more than electronic versions of glossy brochures and buyer's guides. Eventually, some began offering value-added services, including the ability to purchase items via their web site(s).

The web was arguably the Internet's "killer app." It drove huge increases in traffic volume. These increases in web traffic volume were partially due to the inefficiency of early web browsers and the protocols they used to access web servers. Most of the increase was driven by the staggering increase in the number of users and their associated traffic. For organizations which were newly connected to the Internet, they needed to deploy globally routable IP addresses on their internal networks so their users could access external resources.

Typically, MIS defined addressing and subnetting plans, and operated any centralized address-assignment services such as Reverse Address Resolution Protocol (RARP), the Bootstrap protocol (BOOTP), and later the Dynamic Host Configuration Protocol (DHCP). Naturally, static assignment of IP addresses was also in the domain of MIS' responsibilities. Essentially, MIS was responsible for ensuring that their entire organization was able to use IP, which meant that everyone needed a unique IP address. The bottom line: The explosion of the Internet WWW drove the penetration of IP into the far corners of an ever-increasing number of enterprise networks. Most important for the "intranet revolution," it rapidly put a web browser on each end-user's desktop.

In an echo of the past, many local organizations and even individuals started making their own web servers. The HyperText Markup Language (HTML) is relatively easy to learn, even for nonprogrammers. These local web servers were initially nothing more than personal web sites (here's a picture of my dog/cat/girlfriend/boyfriend/desk/whatever). Departmental web servers may have provided the department's charter, its current project(s) and who was working on them, departmental phone books, common sets of bookmarks of external web sites that were relevant to the department, and so on. Because of the ease of setting up a web server, the number of these local web servers also exploded.

Now, critical mass had been achieved in two areas: IP addresses were virtually universally deployed, and web browsers were on nearly every user's desktop. A number of enterprising startups began using web-based tools to challenge client/server and groupware applications, asserting that web-based front ends could replace expensive "groupware" applications such as Lotus Notes with much cheaper alternatives. Of course, Lotus/IBM reacted by "web-enabling" Notes, and other "threatened" application developers (e.g., Microsoft!) also embraced the web/Internet in a very big way.

One reason that client/server SQL databases had not caught on as much as the early 1990s hype would have suggested was that developing and supporting a common GUI application across multiple computing platforms turned out to be much more difficult than expected. Then, the World Wide Web explosion placed a de facto front end on nearly every desktop. It wasn't long before enterprise database application developers, SQL database application software developers, and others realized this and began planning to take advantage of the web browser in a new role as a front end to corporate data. With mainstream business applications leveraging the existence of web browsers, the dawn of the "corporate intranet era" had arrived.

By 1997, the intranet transition was still far from complete. Clearly, applications based on protocols such as IPX and AppleTalk are waning, while web-enabled applications are enjoying a huge boost, running over IP-based networks. So, an intranet is an IP-based, web-enabled enterprise network. Also, the prediction of the demise of MIS was certainly premature!

HOW IS AN INTRANET DIFFERENT?

Compared to the client/server switched networks that have evolved in recent years, there is the assertion that intranets have less predictable traffic patterns. This idea is founded on the presumption that a popular web server could pop up anywhere within the intranet infrastructure, possibly "drowning" the web server's subnetwork in large quantities of web traffic.

Due to the large numbers of users, traffic levels in this environment are expected to be more unpredictable and quite bursty. It is pretty clear that the old "80/20" rule no longer applies. The 80/20 rule said that usually 80 percent of an organization's traffic was local to it, because of the close proximity of the users to their servers (especially in the early LAN era). The remaining 20 percent of the organization's traffic, then, would correspond to users accessing nonlocal server resources. Accessing remote servers implies that this traffic would need to be carried across the corporate backbone. Intranet web clients will almost certainly be reaching out across the corporate backbone in much larger numbers than before, and to a wider variety of destinations. The implications for increased-performance backbones (at a minimum) is one issue that early intranets have had to face.

Also, due to the geographically distributed, "open protocol" standards-based nature of the intranet, the need for distributed security is far keener than in the past. The ability to enhance collaboration by sharing information widely—to all levels of a corporation—is wonderful, and has proven beneficial in many enterprise networks already. However, there are also corporate resources which are not meant for all eyes. Access to such resources must be restricted to authorized users. Depending on the sensitivity of the data, the exchanges between a secure web server and its client may need to be encrypted. MIS is typically seen as the logical maintainer of a centralized user-authentication database. Such a database will provide common information that the intranet's servers use to authenticate potential users. Such servers may be web servers, dial-up servers, and any other services that interact with users directly.

As router-based collapsed backbone networks yielded to LAN-switched networks, certain scaling problems have become apparent. Broadcasts, multicasts, and unknown-destination packets must be flooded along the switched network's spanning tree so that these packets reach all parts of the switched network. LAN switches are nothing more than multiport bridges that often operate at so-called wire speed. Because they are fundamentally bridges, they must follow bridge forwarding rules set forth in standards such as 802.1d from the Institute of Electrical and Electronics Engineers (IEEE).

Due to the overwhelming drive to deploy higher-performance network infrastructures, switched LANs grew ever flatter and ever larger. The largest switched LANs began to suffer from problems experienced by the earliest bridged networks: excessive broadcasts, broadcast storms, "broadcast radiation," and so on. Many vendors, in their desire to preserve the performance gains of switches, began to develop "virtual LAN" (VLAN) techniques to help segment the switched infrastructure into separate "broadcast domains." Another problem that the VLAN schemes were supposed to solve was the management of moves, adds, and changes, when users changed cubes, buildings, projects, joined or left the company, and so forth.

Today, VLAN standards are emerging out of the IEEE 802.1 committee which will likely begin to appear in products by late 1997 or early 1998. The 802.1Q and 802.1p standards allow two things: a standard way to deploy a VLAN infrastructure over a common layer-two switched internetwork (802.1Q), and an eight-level priority scheme to allow switched LANs to efficiently carry data streams with up to eight classes of service (802.1p). VLANs deployed with these standards will allow the intranet to achieve its full potential, based on a high-performance and extremely adaptable switched infrastructure.

Besides the differentiators we have already examined, intranets are allegedly much more dynamic than the predictable client/server- (i.e., server-farm-) based networks that preceded them. Therefore, intranets must be quickly adaptable to future expansion, increased bandwidth demands, new applications, and new modalities, or ways of working.

In summary, the intranet is seen as the platform for deployment of integrated networking, combining "multimedia" traffic alongside data over a common infrastructure. Multimedia is not simply interactive voice and video, but it also encompasses shared environments, and includes streaming of pre-recorded multimedia content. Also, non-multimedia "push"-oriented applications are ideally suited to operation over multicast-enabled intranetworks.

The future evolution of the intranet, incorporating multicast, layer-three switching, and other new technologies, will be very interesting to watch. Multicast IP is seen as a key enabler of enhanced intranet services due to the perceived ease of deployment and its perceived linkage with multimedia. For now, we'll concentrate on what multicast is and what benefits it can bring to your intranet.

UNDERSTANDING THE NEED FOR MULTICAST

Multicast applications involve data being simultaneously sent to a set of interested end stations, rather than the currently more common case of a packet going to just one destination (unicast) at a time. The motivation for multicast is efficiency. If one assumes that there are interesting and important classes of new applications involving multidestination delivery, then having a network-layer service enabling such applications is a good idea. No matter what technology your intranet is based on, it still has only a finite capacity, which you should not waste gratuitously.

Applications that send many copies of the same data are clearly not beneficial to the health of your intranet. Having different applications, each with its own "solution" to this fundamental scaling problem, would not only cause a bandwidth crunch but would probably also be difficult to manage. At the very least, troubleshooting your intranet would be much more "interesting"!

There are a number of possible techniques for accomplishing multidestination delivery. For comparison, we will discuss broadcast, replicated unicast, and network-layer multicast.

Broadcast

By far the simplest "solution" for multidestination delivery is broadcast. Simply stated, every station on a LAN receives and processes a packet which has been broadcast. Broadcast is a service that is utilized by the network layer, so a server need not have knowledge about all the receivers; it simply sends a packet to the appropriate broadcast address and trusts the intranet's switches and routers to deliver the packet across the correct subnetwork(s). Typically, broadcasts are limited in scope to the LAN on which they were originally transmitted, but in some cases broadcasts can be forwarded across routers. Each router can use its attached subnetworks' native broadcast functionality, where present, to deliver each packet to the appropriate broadcast address.

This solution is inadequate for all but the smallest intranetworks. If there are loops in the intranetwork topology, broadcast storms can render parts of the intranet unusable. Loops are often designed into networks for the sake of resiliency, with redundant backbones being a prime example. Unplanned loops can also arise, in the form of accidental interconnections between leaf subnetworks.

As shown in Figure 1–3, broadcast delivery across routers is nontrivial. Any loops

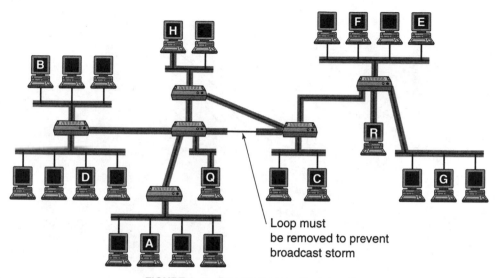

Loop must
be removed to prevent
broadcast storm

FIGURE 1–3   Broadcast across the intranet

in the topology must be detected and removed (from the broadcast forwarding tree) so that broadcast storms do not occur.

A large strike against using broadcast is that each of a subnetwork's end stations must receive a copy of each broadcast packet, despite the fact that only a small number of this subnetwork's end stations are likely to be interested in this application's traffic. It may seem fine that most end stations are not interested in the traffic: they need only receive it and then throw it away. This is exactly the problem, though. These broadcast packets must be received, then checked to see to which layer-three protocol they correspond, and if a given end station is not configured to use that protocol it must then discard the packet. Even if the broadcast matches up with a layer-three protocol in the end station, it is still possible that the packet does not correspond to any application running on this end station.

Thus, there is a secondary cost involved in the use of broadcasts by any protocol in addition to the primary cost of wasted bandwidth. This effect is sometimes called "broadcast radiation." Broadcast radiation wastes the CPU cycles of PCs on the network in inverse proportion to their processing power. Power users need not fear broadcast radiation unless there is a broadcast storm. However, users with 486s or 386s will notice that their machines slow down when the network is busy with broadcast traffic. Even moderate levels of broadcast traffic can waste 5 to 15 percent of a low-end PC's CPU cycles, as shown in Figure 1–4.

Broadcast is a poor solution in several ways. Broadcast storms are more likely with more broadcast traffic on your network. There is also an opportunity cost to broadcast traffic, in that it wastes your intranet's available bandwidth. Finally, broadcast traffic erodes your intranet's collective CPU cycles, more noticeably so as the levels of broadcast traffic are increased.

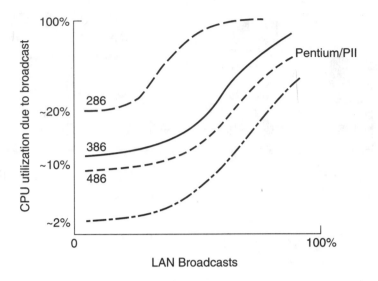

Replicated Unicast

At one end of the spectrum of possibilities exists the "replicated unicast" solution, in which a source sends a copy of the data to each receiver in turn. In order for this solution to work, all interested receivers must preregister with the sender, or the sender must be preconfigured with the receivers' addresses.

This solution may work for small numbers of receivers, but the source must have a priori knowledge of the network address of each receiver. As the number of receivers increases, the source must keep track of ever greater numbers of destinations. If the addresses of the end stations must be statically defined in the source, this application could represent a large management overhead.

Of course, it is possible that client end stations can simply connect to a server to inform it of their interest in receiving certain kinds of data, as in the PointCast™ "push" application. While this relieves the application manager of configuring the server with each receiver's address, it does require that the client receivers be configured with the server's address, or that there be a "server discovery" protocol which clients may use to discover the server's address. One issue with having the clients preregister with the server is that the server becomes the focal point of all the control traffic. This control traffic increases proportionately with the number of clients.

As should be obvious from Figure 1–5, station C's subnetwork sees each of the packets destined for stations A, B, H, Q, R, E, F, and G. This factor inhibits the scalability of this solution, because the packet transmission load on the source's subnetwork increases linearly with the number of destination receivers. LANs have only finite capacity to carry a number of some given size packets per second. Eventually, some number of receivers will require the source's subnetwork to carry more than its maximum number of

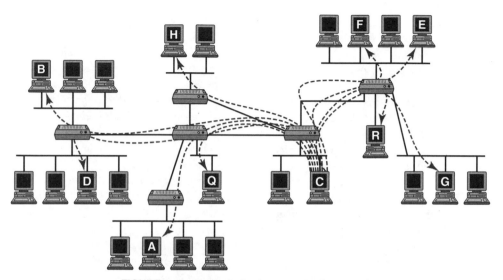

FIGURE 1-5 Replicated unicast across the network

packets per second. Receivers added after this point will exceed the capacity of the source's subnetwork, requiring even more packets to be buffered in the server. As the packet buffers get deeper, parts of the group will experience more and more delays. Similarly, the source itself will gradually use more and more of its CPU resources transmitting even more copies of the same traffic. Of course, if the source's subnetwork is this busy with traffic from one station, the other stations will be starved for bandwidth.

Another issue, not strictly one of scalability, is that of latency across the group. The time it takes to send one copy to one receiver is multiplied by the number of receivers, plus an error factor to allow for the average interreceiver transmission gap. With large numbers of receivers, a substantial amount of time can elapse between sending to the first member of a list and sending to the last. Along with server utilization and network utilization, this latency metric also increases linearly with the number of receivers. Thus, the source server may have to wait a relatively long time before it may begin transmitting the next item of data. This length of time is long compared to the time it takes to transmit one packet to one destination.

Replicated unicast cannot scale up to efficiently deliver traffic to large numbers of end stations (hundreds, thousands, or more), but may be suitable for small numbers of destinations.

Application-Layer Relays

Some applications support application-specific relays (see Figure 1–3) to offload packet delivery from the source station (e.g., PointCast™, CU-SeeMe, H.323-based videoconferencing equipment using a multipoint control unit, or MCU).

For example, assume that 103 clients are naturally clustered in eight groups of 12 and one group of seven stations, and an intranet manager decides to implement this application's relay functionality. The intranet manager clearly does not wish the source to have to send 103 (unicast) copies of each data packet. Besides consuming a large amount of network bandwidth close to the source, this would be a lot of work for the manager: s/he would have to preconfigure the sender with the addresses of all the receivers. Besides the tedious job of initial data entry, over time the manager would have to keep each relay's list of local receivers up-to-date. Besides this clerical work which must be done for each relay, the source must be kept up-to-date with the addresses of all the active relays.

If the manager deployed nine relays, the source server could send just nine copies, one (unicast) copy of the update to each of the nine relays. The relays would then be responsible for unicasting copies of the updates to their local clients, as depicted in Figure 1–6.

It is assumed that the intranet manager will supply the intelligence to place the relays "near" the client receivers, in terms of whatever metric is important to the manager. Also, the intranet manager must configure the potential source(s) with the proper relay addresses, and configure the relays with their local receivers' addresses. None of this is automatic.

Compared with the situation where a single source server sends 103 copies of the same data, using relays is definitely better. But the improvement comes at a cost: more work for the intranet manager!

To summarize: Application-layer relay schemes can make replicated unicast appear to be more efficient. However, they achieve this extra "efficiency" by mak-

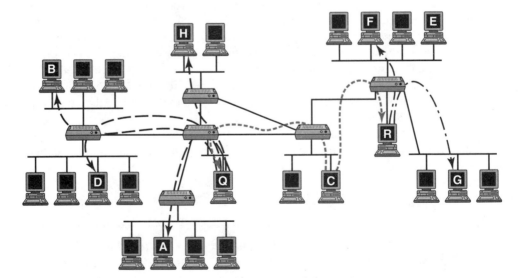

ing the intranet manager's job more difficult. Not only do the managers need to configure the relays and clients appropriately, but the relays have a static topology which cannot reflect group-membership dynamics. These are involuntary receivers, since they can't leave their group.

Replicated unicast has obvious scaling problems. A very bad scenario would occur if many different applications implemented their own slightly different relay schemes. Each additional application having a unique application-layer relay scheme would add gratuitous management overhead and a highly suspect duplication of similar functionality across multiple applications.

A much more scalable idea is to build a replication engine into the network layer and allow multiple applications to leverage that common infrastructure. This is the key idea behind network-layer multicast.

Network-Layer Multicast

For the purposes of this book, the most interesting class of multicast applications use a network-layer-based multicast delivery service. This service enables a source to send a packet to a special multicast IP destination "group address," which identifies an interested set of end stations. The network then delivers the packet to all the group's members. Contrast this with traditional unicast delivery, in which each packet's destination address indicates precisely one receiving end station.

In order for network-layer multicast to deliver packets only to "interested" group members, the end stations must communicate their group membership interest to their local router(s). Given this group membership information, the multicast-aware routers dynamically adjust the shape of each group's "delivery tree" which connects the source's subnetwork to those subnetworks containing interested receivers. Other common names for the delivery tree are "distribution tree" or simply "multicast tree." This tree connects the source to all subnetworks that contain receivers for this group.

The network-layer multicast delivery tree allows a source to reach all receivers without fear of loops (which could lead to multicast storms), excess packet duplication, or additional management overhead. As shown in Figure 1–7, the multicasts do reach all the end stations on each group member's subnetwork, but only group members are "tuned in" to this multicast transmission.

In situations similar to Figure 1–5, in which there are group members on each subnetwork, multicast has clear advantages. No more than one copy of any given packet appears on any subnetwork in the intranet. When the packets ultimately reach the subnetworks with group members, any number of the end stations on that subnetwork may be group members without increasing the load on that subnetwork or the intranetwork—as shown in Figure 1–8. (In contrast, if the number of member stations in Figure 1–5 increased from eight to 23, then 23 packets would need to be transmitted by the source, instead of just one in the multicast scenario.)

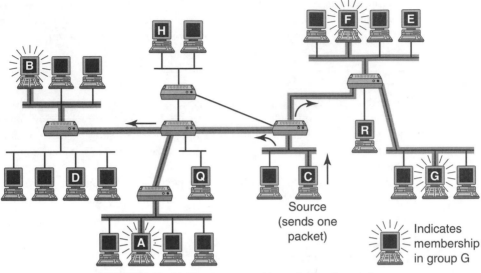

FIGURE 1–7   Multicast compared to application-layer relays

A different way to create the effect of application-layer relays is to use subnet-specific broadcast. For instance, if station D needed to send a packet to station G, a subnet-specific broadcast targeted at G's subnetwork could be used, rather than a unicast to station G. The advantage of this approach is that should any other stations on G's subnetwork want to hear this transmission, they can simply start listening to these broadcasts (which they had previously been ignoring). Subnet-specific broadcast is depicted in Figure 1–9.

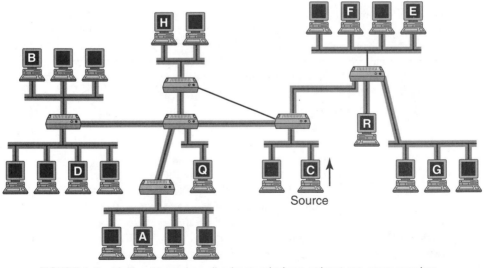

FIGURE 1–8   Multicast tree when all subnetworks have at least one group member

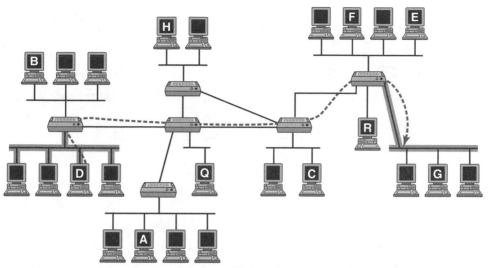

FIGURE 1–9   Subnet-specific broadcast across an intranet

Another advantage of subnet-specific broadcast is that application-layer relays need not be set up and configured. However, the sources' router needs to know where to send the broadcasts, otherwise the source would need to know the receiver's subnet mask(s). Actually, there will be almost as much static configuration in this case. One disadvantage of this technique is that the broadcasts are indistinguishable from each other, and all stations on a subnetwork must receive them. With multicast, each different group may be associated with a different "multicast address." This allows nonmember stations to ignore packets destined for groups in which the stations are not interested.

Multicast applications can take on many forms. The most interesting class of multicast applications is that class of applications which employs multicast delivery at the network layer. Various protocols for multicast routing have already been invented and developed into products, and each has its own unique advantages and disadvantages. Similar to the unicast routing world, there is no universal, or "one-size-fits-all," multicast routing protocol.

CHAPTER 2

IP ADDRESSING OVERVIEW

There are several modes in which IP packets may be delivered among a set of hosts. Table 2–1 summarizes these broad categories.

TABLE 2–1   Modes of IP Packet Delivery

- Unicast (one-to-one)
- Broadcast (one-to-all)
  - Limited broadcast
  - Subnet-specific broadcast
  - All-subnets broadcast
- Anycast (one-to-nearest)
- Multicast
  - One-to-many
  - Many-to-many

THE IP ADDRESS SPACE

IP addresses are 32-bit quantities, most often expressed in "dotted-decimal" notation. In this notation, each address is written as four numbers by taking the first eight bits, the second eight bits, and so on. An 8-bit binary number can take on any value from 0 through 255, so each of the four base-10 numbers must fall between 0 and 255.

For example, here are some IP addresses:

10.177.9.2
129.213.128.100
100.200.1.17
192.1.3.4
199.199.199.199
225.19.20.244
255.255.255.255

The IP address space was broken up into "classes," originally to yield network numbers of different sizes. Initially all defined addresses were unicast, with multicast addresses being defined later, from late 1985 to mid-1986. Classes A, B, and C are unicast, and class D is for multicast.

Here is a list of the address ranges of the IP address classes (note that not all of these addresses are valid, and some are reserved).

Class A	0.0.0.0	to	127.255.255.255
Class B	128.0.0.0	to	191.255.255.255
Class C	192.0.0.0	to	223.255.255.255
Class D	224.0.0.0	to	239.255.255.255

To better understand the relative proportions of these addresses, Figure 2–1 shows that the class A space, while it has only 128 network numbers, consumes fully half of the entire IP address space. The class B space represents one-quarter of the IP address space, but there are just over 16,000 of these. The class C addresses occupy only one-eighth of the total IP address space; even though they are small, they are the most numerous: there are almost 2.1 million class C network numbers.

As depicted in Figure 2–1, the unicast address space accounts for fully seven-eighths (87.5 percent) of the available 32-bit IP address space. In contrast, the multicast

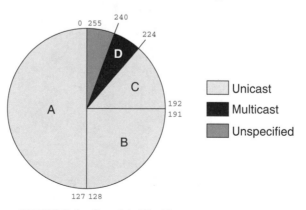

FIGURE 2–1   Complete IP address space

address space represents just 1/16th of the IP address space (6.25 percent). Despite occupying this seemingly small slice of the 32-bit IP address space, there are still over a quarter of a billion possible group addresses (a total of 268,435,456 unique group addresses).

Finally, note that 1/16th of the IP address space is unused. Various proposals over the years have suggested possible uses for this space, but none have caught on.

UNICAST

Unicast delivery is most familiar to users of today's IP-based applications. When one clicks on a hyperlink in a web browser, a series of one-to-one Transmission Control Protocol/Internet Protocol (TCP/IP) connections is made to download the elements of the referenced web page. Each of these connections has precisely one source and precisely one destination. However, as shown in Figure 2–2, the path from S to D may be diffeent than the path from D to S. The Simple Network Management Protocol (SNMP), File Transfer Protocol (FTP), Telnet, Simple Mail Transport Protocol (SMTP), Network News Transport Protocol (NNTP), Post Office Protocol, version 3 (POP3), and others are all designed to use these unicast transmissions. Today, virtually all IP-based applications are based on unicast.

"Classes" of Network Numbers

As we have just seen, unicast addresses originally came in three "classes," depending on the pattern of most significant bits in the four-octet (i.e., 32-bit) IP address. The classes were named A, B, and C, and broke up the unicast IP address space into networks of certain fixed sizes, ostensibly for assignment to organizations of different sizes. But what makes a class A network a class A network? Or a class B network a class B network?

Class A addresses have their highest-order bit set to 0. The remaining seven bits of the most significant octet are the network number. Note that this implies that the lowest

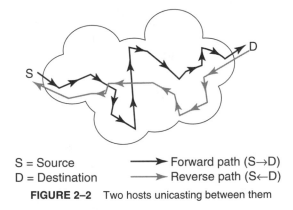

S = Source
D = Destination

⟶ Forward path (S→D)
⟶ Reverse path (S←D)

FIGURE 2–2   Two hosts unicasting between them

possible class A network number is 0000 0001, in binary, which is 1 in decimal, and the highest is 0111 1111, or 127 in decimal. Because network number 0 is reserved, and so is network 127 (as the loopback address), there are 128 − 2 = 126 usable class A network numbers.

The remaining three octets, or 24 bits, make up the "host" portion of the class A IP address; this demarcation between the network portion and the host portion of the address is denoted by a "natural" mask of 255.0.0.0 (1111 1111.0000 0000.0000 0000.0000 0000 in binary, wherein the 1 bits correspond to the network number field of the address, and the 0 bits indicate the host field). A more modern notation that will be used elsewhere in this book represents a mask by its length, expressed as the total number of the mask's 1 bits preceded by a "/". In the case of a class A, it could be expressed as 65.0.0.0 255.0.0.0 or 65.0.0.0/8. For an even more compact notation, this network number can also be written as 65/8.

For class A addresses, this means that there are about 2^{24} possible end-station addresses available, or "host addresses" as they are sometimes called. (Why not exactly 2^{24} addresses? Because there are two reserved bit patterns in the host field of any IP network number or address block: the "all-0s" and "all-1s" patterns. Because these two fixed bit patterns are not available for assignment to end stations, they must be subtracted from the total number of possible combinations. This leaves a maximum of $2^{24} - 2$, or 16,777,214, possible end stations within a class A network number.)

Figure 2–3a illustrates the structure of a class A network address:

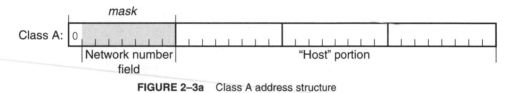

FIGURE 2–3a   Class A address structure

Class B addresses have their two highest-order bits set to 10. The remaining 14 bits of the most significant *two* octets are the network number. Note that this implies that the lowest possible class B network number is **10**00 0000.0000 0001, in binary, which is 128.1 in decimal, and the highest is **10**11 1111.1111 1110, or 191.254.

IP Addresses (Reserved Values)

Generally speaking, in any field of any IP address, the all-0s and all-1s patterns are reserved. In the class A case, this implies that there is no network 0, because the network field is the lower seven of the most significant octet, and that field cannot be all 0s. The fact that a network 127 (0111 1111) exists is an exception: It does, indeed, have all the bits of the network number field set to 1, but network 127 is reserved for use as the "loopback" address, so it can never be assigned to any real network.

This is why the lowest class B network number is not 128.0, and the highest is not 191.255—both of these addresses have either all 0s or all 1s in the network number field of the IP address. (Strictly speaking, the 10-pattern at the beginning is not part of the network number field, since it is a constant.)

Class B addresses have 16 bits left over for the "host" portion of the IP address, so its "natural" mask is 255.255.0.0 (1111 1111.1111 1111.0000 0000.0000 0000 in binary, or a "/16 prefix" in modern notation). Since there are only 14 bits of space in the network number field, and since two bit patterns are reserved (all 0s and all 1s), there are ($2^{14} - 2 = 16,382$) usable class B network numbers. In terms of available host addresses, one class B network number is noticeably smaller than a class A network number, but it is about the right size for most organizations, encompassing at most 65,534 end station addresses ($2^{16} - 2$).

Figure 2–3b depicts the structure of a class B network address:

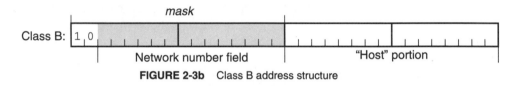

FIGURE 2-3b   Class B address structure

Class C addresses have their three highest-order bits set to 110. The remaining 21 bits of the most significant *three* octets are the network number. Therefore, the lowest possible class C network number is 192.0.1.0 (**110**0 0000.0000 0000.0000 0001.0000 0000 in binary), and the highest is 223.255.254.0 (or **110**1 1111.1111 1111.1111 1110.0000 0000).

Remember, the all-0s and all-1s values in the network number field are reserved, preventing the lowest class C network from being 192.0.0.0, and likewise preventing the highest class C network number from being 223.255.255.0. Thus, the total number of class C network numbers is $2^{21} - 2 = 2,097,150$.

Because 24 bits are used for the network number field (including the class C 110 prefix), only eight bits remain for the "host" portion of the IP address: a class C's "natural" mask is 255.255.255.0 (1111 1111.1111 1111.1111.0000 0000 in binary, or a "/24 prefix" in modern notation). These network numbers are truly tiny compared to class A networks, and even class B networks: There are just 254 ($2^8 - 2$) addresses available for assignment to end stations.

Figure 2–3c shows the structure of a class C network address.

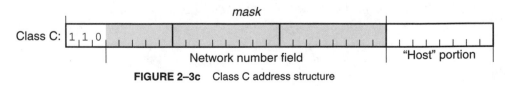

FIGURE 2–3c   Class C address structure

Overview of Subnetting

Subnetting is a way to take the host portion of an IP address and break it up into pieces sized appropriately for your needs. Why would you need to do this? Well, each subnetwork in your intranet needs a unique prefix/mask. If subnetting had not been invented, you'd need a separate IP network number for each subnetwork in your intranet (a LAN, Point-to-Point Protocol (PPP) link, frame relay cloud, etc.)! Wasting an entire class C network number, which can accommodate up to 254 hosts, on a point-to-point link that only requires two addresses—one for each end of the link—is clearly a bad idea. Subnetting gives us a way to carve our allocated network number(s) into appropriate-sized pieces.

If you are lucky enough to possess a class A network, you are quite unlikely to have a single subnetwork with more than 10 million end stations! You probably have lots of subnetworks of various sizes. Through the magic of binary arithmetic, we can successively reduce the size of our host field by half, until the pieces are the right size for us.

First, some terminology:

Natural mask: 8, 16, or 24 bits, depending on the class of network number.

Network number field: See "natural mask."

Subnet field: From 1 to 22 bits, depending on network class. Class A subnet fields can be up to 22 bits long, class B subnet fields up to 14 bits, and class C subnet fields up to 6 bits in length.

Extended network prefix length: The length of the network number field plus the length of the subnet field.

For example, if you start with a class B, you have a natural mask of 16 bits. If you add a one-bit-long subnet field, you have broken the host portion in half. (The extended network prefix in this case is 17 bits.) One of the halves has the 17th bit of the IP address set to 0, the other half has it set to 1. Each of these pieces is half the size of the original address. Actually, we lose two potential end-station addresses each time we halve the subnet size by adding a bit. There are $2 * (2^{15} - 2)$ addresses available now, which is $2 *$ 32,766, or 65,532 addresses in the two combined subnets, two less than the maximum number of addresses within an unsubnetted class B.

Note: Just as with network number fields, host fields within subnets reserve the all-0s and all-1s bit patterns, which mean "this subnet" and "broadcast," respectively.

Routing Considerations for "Special" Subnets

Observe that in this /17 example, the two available subnets are either the all-0s or all-1s subnet: there is only one bit, so it can only be 0 or 1! Strangely enough, whether or not you can use these subnets in your network depends on what kind of routing protocol you are using. IP addressing and routing are very closely interconnected.

These subtleties are best covered in a book devoted to such things, but suffice it to say that if your routing protocol does not advertise a mask along with each prefix, you cannot use the all-0s and all-1s subnets. Routing protocols that prevent you from using the all-0s and all-1s subnets include RIP version 1, Exterior Gateway Protocol (EGP), and cisco's proprietary Interior Gateway Routing Protocol (IGRP), among others. For reasons that will be described later, these protocols are called "classful." Protocols such as Open Shortest Path First (OSPF), Integrated Intermediate System-to-Intermediate System (I-IS-IS or simply IS-IS), Routing Information Protocol (RIP) version 2, and cisco's Enhanced IGRP (E-IGRP) allow usage of the all-0s and all-1s subnets. These routing protocols are called "classless."

If we need two subnets, but must use a classful routing protocol for some reason, we have no choice but to add another bit to the subnet field. A two-bit subnet field has four possible patterns: 00, 01, 10, and 11. Each of these subnets has a little less than one quarter of the address space of the original network.

Now, because we must run a classful routing protocol, we must omit the 00 and 11 subnets, leaving us with the 01 and 10 subnets. Unfortunately, the 00 and 11 subnets represent very nearly half of our available address space, which should motivate us to use a classless routing protocol: we could double the number of available subnets!

Another limitation of classful routing protocols is that you must use the same subnet field size across this entire network prefix, preventing you from efficiently using your address space. You cannot make small subnets for places with fewer hosts, or large subnets for places with many hosts.

The ability to break up your intranet into pieces whose size matches your requirements, instead of a "one-size-fits-one" scheme, is called "variable-length subnet masking," or VLSM. Again, classless routing protocols allow you to use VLSM, which means you can make more efficient use of your address space. This is another good reason to use a classless routing protocol!

Every time we add a bit to the subnet field, we halve the number of available end-station addresses per subnet while doubling the number of subnets. So, three bits of subnetting yields eight subnets ($2^3 = 8$), each about one-eighth the capacity of the whole network. Similarly, four bits of subnetting yields 16 subnets, each about 1/16 the size of the original network. It doesn't matter what class of network you start with, as long as you don't try to use more subnet bits than you have host bits! Table 2–2 shows how many end stations may fit in each size subnet.

So, what do subnets look like? Let's take a class B network for an example, but the class of the network doesn't effect the outcome; this works on any size network prefix.

Class B Subnetting Example (Five Subnets Required)

Let's take a class B network number: 128.42.0.0/16. If we need five equal-sized subnets, we must use a three-bit subnet field. This is because three bits yields eight subnets. We cannot

TABLE 2–2 End-Station Addressing Capacities of All Possible Subnet Sizes

Subnet field length	Available end-station addresses per subnet		
	Class A	Class B	Class C
1	8,388,606	32,766	126
2	4,194,302	16,382	62
3	2,097,150	8190	30
4	1,048,574	4094	14
5	524,286	2046	6
6	262,142	1022	2
7	131,070	510	
8	65,534	254	
9	32,766	126	
10	16,382	62	
11	8190	30	
12	4094	14.	
13	2046	6	
14	1022	2	
15	510		
16	254		
17	126		
18	62		
19	30		
20	14		
21	6		
22	2		

break an IP address block into five equal-sized pieces; we must round up to the nearest power of 2, in this case 8. The next size down, 4, is not enough subnets. A three-bit field has the following patterns: 000, 001, 010, 011, 100, 101, 110, and 111. For safety reasons (unless you *know* you will never have to deploy a classful routing protocol!), you should not use the all-0s and all-1s subnets. Table 2–3 shows the six usable subnets:

TABLE 2–3 Subnet Addresses of a Class B (Assuming 3 Bits of Subnetting)

000	128.42.0.0	(subnet 0, reserved ... all 0s)
001	128.42.32.0	(subnet 1)
010	128.42.64.0	(subnet 2)
011	128.42.96.0	(subnet 3)
100	128.42.128.0	(subnet 4)
101	128.42.160.0	(subnet 5)
110	128.42.192.0	(subnet 6, unused because we only need five subnets)
111	128.42.224.0	(subnet 7, reserved ... all 1s)

How did I know that the subnet numbers would be multiples of 32? It's easy: Of the third octet's 8 bits, 3 have been used for the subnet field, leaving 5 for the host field, and $2^5 = 32$. That's it.

Another way to see this is to write out the binary representation of the third octet:

x y z 0 0 0 0 0

If you set the x y z = 0 0 0, you have the all-zeros subnet. That's easy. If you set x y z = 1 0 1, you have 1 0 1 0 0 0 0 0, which is 128 + 32, or 160. The key pattern to note is the one where x y z = 0 0 1: When you set your subnet field to the value of 1 in binary, you get your "subnet multiplier" to pop out. If we express the entire byte in binary (0 0 1 0 0 0 0 0) we find that it equals 32. Any of the other subnets (x y z patterns) are some multiple of 1 (2 = 2 * 1, 4 = 4 * 1, etc.), so given that 1 maps to 32, 4 maps to 4 * 32, or 128, and so on. Look back to Table 2–3 to see that all the subnet numbers are multiples of 32.

Class B Subnetting Example (478 Subnets Required)

A slightly more challenging example is when the subnet field crosses octet boundaries. Let's assume that we need 478 equal-sized subnets. We must first round to the nearest power of 2, which is 512. $512 = 2^9$, so we need 9 bits in our subnet field. Don't let this throw you off. Think back to the first example. We subtracted 3 from 8 in that case. In this case, we subtract the nine subnet bits from the 16-bit host field, leaving seven bits for the host portion, with $2^7 - 2 = 126$ hosts per subnet.

I don't have room to list all 512 subnets, but we can start the list so you can see how it goes:

0000 0000 0	128.42.0.0	(subnet 0, unused and reserved)
0000 0000 1	128.42.0.128	(subnet 1)
0000 0001 0	128.42.1.0	(subnet 2)
0000 0001 1	128.42.1.128	(subnet 3)
0000 0010 0	128.42.2.0	(subnet 4)
0000 0010 1	128.42.2.128	(subnet 5)
0000 0011 0	128.42.3.0	(subnet 6)
0000 0011 1	128.42.3.128	(subnet 7)
0000 0100 0	128.42.4.0	(subnet 8)

... and so on ...

1110 1110 1	128.42.239.128	(subnet 477)
1110 1111 0	128.42.240.0	(subnet 478)
1110 1111 1	128.42.240.128	(subnet 479, not required)

... and so on ...

1111 1110 0	128.42.254.0	(subnet 508, not required)
1111 1110 1	128.42.254.128	(subnet 509, not required)
1111 1111 0	128.42.255.0	(subnet 510, not required)
1111 1111 1	128.42.255.128	(subnet 511, not required and reserved)

Class B VLSM Example

One final example will show how variable subnetting can work.

Important note: Remember that you cannot use variable subnetting unless you use a classless routing protocol, such as OSPF or Cisco's E-IGRP.

In this example, we will start by assuming you have a subnet you need to break apart. Let's say that our existing subnet is 128.42.64.0/18. Remember that a class B network number equates to a /16 prefix, so an /18 has a mask which is two bits longer. Two additional mask bits effectively slice the class B network number in quarters, because $2^2 =$ 4. If we had two fewer (rather than two additional) mask bits, or a /14 prefix, that prefix would be equivalent to four class Bs, but an /18 is one-fourth of a class B. Keep in mind that longer prefixes are smaller—and shorter prefixes are larger—in terms of how many IP addresses lie within the prefix. Inside this /18 prefix, which is a subnet of our class B network number, there are 14 bits of IP addresses available (because $32 - 18 = 14$), and $2^{14} - 2 = 16,382$.

Let's further assume that we need to allocate three subnets within this /18 prefix. One requires 389 hosts, the second needs 117, and the third needs 195. The first step in defining our variable subnet mask scheme is to round these to the nearest power of 2: 389 rounds to 512 (2^9), 117 rounds to 128 (2^7), and 195 rounds to 256 (2^8). At this point, it is a judgment call as to how many addresses you feel comfortable allocating to each subnet. If you feel that the subnet with 117 is likely to grow, even a little bit, you may decide that you'll need more than 126 addresses in its subnet shortly. You could make the subnet bigger (256 is the next largest power of 2), or you could leave space for growth. I recommend leaving space for growth in places where it looks like you will quickly reach the subnet limit.

Let's sketch out what we need:

Subnet 1: 389 hosts, fits in 512 (2^9)

Subnet 2: 117 hosts, fits in 128 (2^7), but reserve next just in case

Subnet 2': 128 (2^7) hosts, next subnet after subnet 2

Subnet 3: 195 hosts, fits in 256 (2^8)

Summary of required subnet sizes:

512	9 bits
128	7 bits
128	7 bits
256	8 bits

These add up to a total of 1024 IP addresses, or 10 bits of IP address space. If we have 10 bits in the host field of the IP address, there must be 22 bits in the extended-network prefix. In other words, a subnet with 1024 IP addresses is also a /22 prefix. In general, a subnet with 2^n IP addresses is a $/32-n$ prefix. In our example, this implies that we need the following prefixes:

512	9 bits	$/32 - 9 = /23$
128	7 bits	$/32 - 7 = /25$
128	7 bits	$/32 - 7 = /25$
256	8 bits	$/32 - 8 = /24$

A very convenient way to break up those 1024 (2^{10}) addresses is to first take half (2^9) for the biggest subnet, as shown in Figure 2–4. You have two subnets of size 2^9 inside a 2^{10} prefix. One of these may be used for the subnet that needs at least 389 IP addresses. Then the other 2^9 subnet can be broken into two 2^8 subnets. The first of these may be used for the subnet that required 195 addresses. Finally, the other 2^8 subnet may be halved again to yield two 2^7 subnets.

Conveniently, this leaves the "growth subnet" at the top of the range. Remember, the all-0s and all-1s addresses are reserved in any subnet, so there are only 126 available IP addresses in a $/25$ subnet, not 128. Since this subnet is very crowded to start (117 out of 126 addresses used), even a small amount of growth might require that this subnet be enlarged. In the event that this subnet needs more than 126 IP addresses, the end stations on that subnet need to be informed that their mask is now $/24$ instead of $/25$.

Now, we need to fit these subnets into the $/18$ prefix with which we started. We now know that we need a total of 10 bits worth of IP addresses. This is identical to subnetting a class B network number on a six-bit subnet field (that would also leave 10 bits of host addressing in each subnet). The only difference is that in this case we have already broken up our class B, and the piece we are starting with is one quarter of a class B, also written as $/18$.

As we noted earlier, the $/18$ is a rather large subnet, having up to 16,382 hosts ($2^{14} - 2$). The 1024 addresses that we require are a small fraction of this subnet. As long as we have not already used more than 15,357 hosts out of the $/18$ already, we can just take the highest part of the $/18$ for these four new "sub-subnets." We have four bits to play

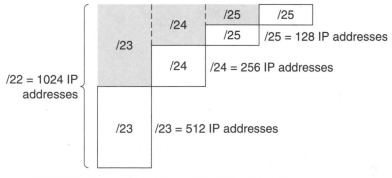

FIGURE 2–4   How to break up a 10-bit IP address block

with: $32 - 10 = 22$, which is 4 more than 18. So, we can *virtually* break up our /18 into 16 pieces and then break up the highest 16th for our 4 subnets. We don't really have to be using these subnets, they are just being created temporarily so we can figure out where the required /22 starts.

The /18 breaks down into sixteen /22s as follows:

128.42.64.0/22	Virtual subnet 1
128.42.68.0/22	Virtual subnet 2
128.42.72.0/22	Virtual subnet 3
128.42.76.0/22	Virtual subnet 4
128.42.80.0/22	Virtual subnet 5
128.42.84.0/22	Virtual subnet 6
128.42.88.0/22	Virtual subnet 7
128.42.92.0/22	Virtual subnet 8
128.42.96.0/22	Virtual subnet 9
128.42.100.0/22	Virtual subnet 10
128.42.104.0/22	Virtual subnet 11
128.42.108.0/22	Virtual subnet 12
128.42.112.0/22	Virtual subnet 13
128.42.116.0/22	Virtual subnet 14
128.42.120.0/22	Virtual subnet 15
128.42.124.0/22	Virtual subnet 16

We now want to break up virtual subnet 16 into the desired subnets:

128.42.124.0/23	Subnet 1, 510 hosts ($2^9 - 2$)
128.42.126.0/23	Not done yet

We could have broken up any of these subnets for this example. The determining factor is whether or not any addresses in a given /22 have been used yet. The second subnet (128.42.126.0/23) is now broken into two /24s:

128.42.126.0/24	Subnet 3, 254 hosts ($2^8 - 2$)
128.42.127.0/24	Not done yet

Again, the second subnet is broken in half:

128.42.127.0/25	Subnet 2, 126 hosts ($2^7 - 2$)
128.42.127.128/25	Subnet 2' (room for growth)

To summarize, we needed three subnets of our /18 for three collections of hosts: 389, 117, and 195, respectively. After identifying how these might fit together in a /22, we needed to decide which of the sixteen /22s that make up our original /18 we wanted to carve up. Once we had decided on the upper /22, it was a straightforward matter to identify the subnets:

128.42.124.0/23:   Our subnet needing space for 389 hosts (about 76.275 percent used; 121 addresses available)

128.42.126.0/24:   The subnet needing space for 195 hosts (about 76.77 percent used; 59 addresses available)

128.42.127.0/25:   The subnet needing only 117 hosts (about 92.857 percent used; only nine addresses available)

128.42.127.128/25: Room for growth if the previous subnet needs more than nine more addresses in the future

In this case, hosts in the /25 part would be reconfigured to think they were in 128.42.127.0/24, which has 254 addresses available for assignment to hosts.

VLSM is a very efficient way to allocate addresses within your intranet. The most important thing to remember is to not assign addresses on decimal boundaries. A common technique is to allocate on octet boundaries, where the addresses are easy for people to deal with. You would do well to avoid the temptation. A /19 or a /23 may be harder to visualize, but your address space is a precious resource, and you will be in a far worse situation if you have not planned ahead and now must readdress large portions of your network to gain back some wasted space.

One other hint: If you do get the chance to lay out an addressing plan for a new network in advance, don't pack the subnets tightly. Allow for growth. And do use VLSM and classless routing, so you can define subnets of the size you really need.

For more details on unicast addressing, including more examples and exercises to help you get better at this, please see the following white paper, available from Prentice Hall: http://www.prenhall.com/allbooks/ptr_0138976872.html

What Is CIDR?

CIDR stands for classless *inter*domain routing. Classful routing has been alluded to above; RIP is classful. Prior to the CIDR era, Internet routing was exclusively "classful," which meant that the interdomain routing protocols did not pass along a mask with each route. Lacking a mask, a router could only infer the mask for a route.

The implication of this is that the granularity of the routing information is at the same level as a network number's class. Thus, if a route's most significant octet lies between 1 and 126, you infer that its mask must be 255.0.0.0. Similarly, routes lying between 128.1 and 191.254 are class B networks, so they are designated with a mask of 255.255.0.0. Class C routes are similarly detected, and their mask is assigned as 255.255.255.0.

Within a network number, VLSM allows chunks of various sizes to be created by using a different mask in each region. To tie all this together, a classless *intra*domain routing protocol was needed. OSPF was a common example of a classless link-state intrado-main routing protocol. Later RIP version 2 was introduced, yielding a classless distance-vector intradomain routing protocol. As we have seen, the VLSM idea is very powerful, allowing address blocks of just the right size to be created. Also, when the address blocks fall on binary boundaries, they are easy to aggregate into routes with shorter masks (fewer subnet bits).

Unfortunately, there was no interdomain routing protocol that carried masks along with network numbers, so classless interdomain routing was not possible until the advent of the Border Gateway Protocol, version 4 (BGP-4). CIDR extends the concepts of VLSM to interdomain routing. This yields several benefits:

1. The concept of "class A/B/C" goes away. A /16 address block is the same size as an old class B network, but you could have a /16 address block in the old class C space. For example, 199.17.0.0/16 is an address block containing 256 /24-sized blocks. The range runs from 199.17.0.0/24 through 199.17.255.0/24.

   CIDR is VLSM applied to interdomain routing. The same math that lets us aggregate 256 /26s (in VLSM) into a single /18 works here. Because $256 = 2^8$, a block of 256 things must have 8 fewer bits in its mask: 256 /30s = one /22, 256 /25s = one /17. To put these numbers in perspective, a /22 is equivalent in size to four consecutive old class C network numbers. A /17 is half of a /16, holding up to 8190 end stations. This is the size of half of an old class B.

2. A single routing advertisement can cover a block of old-style addresses (see Figure 2–5). This helps keep routing tables from growing explosively. Instead of a set of 2048 class C networks being advertised, you could have a single /13 advertisement. This is far more efficient than advertising the 2048 individual routes, and carries the same reachability information—as long as the 2048 "class Cs" are all on one side of

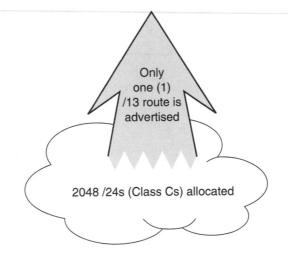

FIGURE 2–5   2048 class Cs being aggregated into a single /13 advertisement

the router advertising the /13. Math explanation: $2048 = 2^{11}$. Thus, a block of 2048 /24s reduces to a single /13 (because $24 - 11 = 13$).

3. Addresses can be assigned hierarchically. This means that large blocks are delegated to large providers, which then break up their allocation, keep some, and delegate smaller blocks to smaller providers. This continues until the smallest allocations are granted to customers. A corporate connection may be granted a /28 or a /27 or a /22, depending on its requirements. A dial-in user gets one IP address, a /32. All these addresses come from the original provider's superblock. The benefit of this hierarchical allocation is that the provider can advertise its superblock as a single shorter-prefix route, thus "covering" the individual routes of hundreds or even thousands of their customers and their customers' customers.

   One of CIDR's biggest problems is that this aggregation is a double-edged sword. The benefit of reducing the excess routing information through aggregation of routes is great, but it only works as long as a provider's customers always stay with them. If the customer leaves the provider, and they insist on keeping their addresses, they must advertise their longer-mask route from their new provider. This has the effect of "punching a hole" in the aggregate that their original provider is still advertising. If all their customers leave and go to other providers, their whole aggregate will have evaporated and the CIDR-derived benefit of hierarchical address assignment with aggregation will be eliminated, at least for this address block.

   Because of this effect, the rules of address ownership have changed. It used to be that customers were assumed to own their addresses. IP addresses were basically free; their only value derived from their being globally unique and routable in the Internet. In today's Internet, however, the core routers have had trouble keeping track of ever-increasing numbers of routes. If the global Internet routing system fails under the weight of some number of routes, everyone's assigned addresses have little value.

   Clearly, CIDR has helped the Internet to remain viable despite a crush of new customers attaching to the Internet. In exchange for CIDR's beneficial impact on the size of routing tables in the core of the Internet, IP users have had to consider their addresses "on loan" from their providers. If they change providers, they can choose to renumber into the new provider's address space, use Network Address Translation (NAT) to translate between their old addresses and their new addresses indefinitely, or do both (i.e., use NAT to enable a smooth transition period, after which NAT is turned off). It turns out that using NAT as a long-term solution only works if the old provider never reuses your old address space. If they do, you will never be able to connect to those IP addresses, because they will appear to be internal addresses to your users.

4. Address blocks can be sized appropriately to fit the requirements of the IP user. If a company attaching to the Internet had more than 254 end stations in the past, it needed a class B network. This caused a severe drain on the class B address space. CIDR helps with this, since a company with 392 end stations can now be assigned a /23-sized address block, which is equivalent to two /24s (i.e., class Cs). NAT can

also provide assistance in this scenario, but a detailed description of NAT is outside the scope of this book.

BROADCAST

Broadcast is a way to send a packet to all stations on an entire subnetwork at once. Many resource-discovery protocols use broadcast techniques at the IP layer in conjunction with MAC-layer broadcast. On an IEEE 802 LAN, such as Ethernet or FDDI, the broadcast (destination) address is 0xFF-FF-FF-FF-FF-FF. MAC-layer broadcast is illustrated in Figure 2–6. Broadcast addresses are not typically used in applications with which end users directly interact.

Some IP-based protocols that use broadcast are:

- Routing protocols (RIP is one example)
- DHCP, in which unconfigured DHCP clients can use an IP broadcast address when the DHCP server's address is not preconfigured

Note: While the Address Resolution Protocol (ARP) uses broadcast at the MAC layer, it is not an IP protocol. ARP has no IP header, so it cannot be using IP-layer broadcast addressing, only MAC-layer broadcast addressing.

Limited Broadcast

The IP "limited" broadcast address is found by setting all 32 bits of the IP destination address to a value of 1. Expressed in dotted-decimal form, this is 255.255.255.255, which is often called the "all-ones" broadcast address. In general, packets addressed to this address are not forwarded off their subnet, regardless of their Time-to-Live (TTL). Many applications that use IP-layer broadcast employ the "limited" broadcast address.

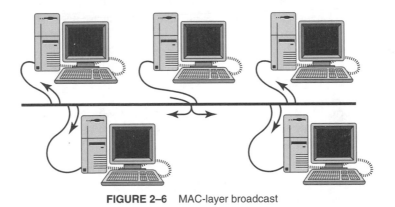

FIGURE 2–6   MAC-layer broadcast

When an IP end station sends any form of broadcast, including this one, the MAC-layer frame on the destination subnet is always sent to the MAC-layer broadcast address. One implication of this is that all devices attached to that data link medium must receive the frame, whether or not they are running IP. Even if all the end stations are running IP, they are not necessarily all running this particular application. For example, RIP packets are broadcast among the routers that are executing the protocol. Despite the fact that perhaps only two or three nodes on the LAN are router interfaces which need to listen to these broadcasts, every IP end station must receive each RIP update. Granted, some end stations do eavesdrop on RIP packets to learn the existence of their "default gateway," as opposed to having the default gateway statically configured. However, most IP end stations will just receive these RIP broadcast packets and then discard them. Worse still, end stations that do not speak IP (e.g., AppleTalk, DECnet, IPX, etc.) also receive these packets and must discard them. This is an example of "broadcast radiation," which will be covered in more detail shortly.

All-Subnets Broadcast

The least used (and coincidentally least useful!) type of broadcast address is the all-subnets broadcast address. It is found by setting the nonnetwork bits of the network address to a value of 1. If we consider the Class B network number 190.45.0.0/16, the all-subnets broadcast address would be 190.45.255.255. The semantics of this address are that an end station within that network address may send a packet to this address for delivery to every IP end station within that network prefix. If a nework address is unsubnetted, this is also the subnet-specific broadcast address, by virtue of the fact that the entire network is only one subnet!

Most routers will not forward such packets by default, but some can be configured to allow them to be forwarded. This can be a bit tricky because in complex topologies it may be difficult to forward exactly one copy of each such packet onto every subnetwork without causing a "broadcast storm." To do this correctly, each router would have to keep a record of each all-subnets broadcast it forwards, and discard subsequent copies after it has fowarded it once. Usage of the all-subnets broadcast has been deprecated by the IETF.

Subnet-Specific Broadcast

Another form of IP-layer broadcast address is the "subnet-specific" broadcast address. For any IP subnetwork, this broadcast address is found by setting the host bits of the address to have a value of 1. For example:

The class B address 190.45.0.0/16 may have a subnet 190.45.104.0/22. The /22 means that the subnet mask consists of 22 left-aligned 1 bits:

```
1111 1111.1111 1111.1111 1100.0000 0000
```

expressed in binary, or 255.255.252.0 expressed in dotted-decimal form. If we examine the octet containing the extended-network-to-host boundary, we find the following bit pattern:

```
252.0 = 111111 00 . 00000000 (third and fourth octets of mask)
104.0 = 011001 00 . 00000000 (third and fourth octets of address)
```

The boundary between the extended-network prefix (network + subnet = extended-network prefix) and the host portion falls after the sixth bit of the third octet. This is because the subnet mask is 22 bits long, and because this is a class B network (with a "natural" 16-bit network prefix length). Therefore, there are six bits in the subnet field (22 − 16 = 6).

The host portion of this subnet is the entire fourth octet, plus the least significant two bits of the third octet, indicated by the ten right-aligned binary zeros above. A host in this subnet will have an address with some combination of the host bits set to nonzero values; for instance,

```
104.77  = 011001 00 . 01001101
105.152 = 011001 01 . 10011000
106.3   = 011001 10 . 00000011
107.107 = 011001 11 . 01101011
```

are all addresses in the 190.45.104.0/22 subnet, despite the fact that not all these addresses have "104" in the third octet.

As indicated earlier, to find the broadcast address for any subnet, we simply set all the bits in the host portion of the address to a value of 1:

```
011001 11 . 11111111
   104 + 3 . 255
=      107 . 255
```

So the subnet-specific broadcast address for the 190.45.104.0/22 subnet is 190.45.107.255, and this address may be used to reach all IP hosts on this particular subnet.

There are two cases in which such an address is usually used:

1. A station on a subnetwork sending to the rest of the stations on that subnetwork. The limited broadcast address of 255.255.255.255 is also commonly used for this application.
2. A station on a given subnetwork sending a packet to all the stations on another subnetwork. For example, 190.45.1.71 sending to all hosts on the 190.45.104.0/22 subnetwork would send to 190.45.107.255.

By default, IP routers might forward subnet-specific broadcast packets beyond the LAN on which they were originally transmitted; however, some routers may not forward such packets without being configured to do so.

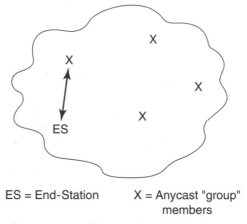

ES = End-Station   X = Anycast "group"
                                    members

FIGURE 2–7   Client sending to anycast address representing routers, connecting to "closest" router

ANYCAST

Anycast techniques are not commonly used in today's IP version 4 networks. There is no separate class of addresses corresponding to anycast. In IP version 6 (sometimes called "IP, the next generation," or "IPng" for short), anycast will be used to facilitate hosts finding their nearest router, and perhaps for other applications that have yet to be defined at the time of this writing. Anycast addresses will look like normal unicast destinations in the routing table, so all IPv6 routers will be able to forward to them.

Anycast is used when you want to communicate with just one, hopefully the closest, of a class of equivalent objects (the closest router, the closest DNS server, etc). See Figure 2–7.

Anycast is unique in that it only delivers a packet to one of a group, whereas multicast delivers packets to the entire group.

MULTICAST

The more familiar unicast addresses are identifiable as part of a class A, B, or C prefix by the pattern of the high-order bits in the first octet:

```
A:  0aaa aaaa
B:  10bb bbbb
C:  110c cccc
```

Each multicast address represents a *group* of arbitrary size, and members of multicast groups may span arbitrary prefixes across the unicast address space. A separate address class has been designated for identifying multicast groups: the class D space.

Now, the list above becomes

```
A:  0aaa aaaa
B:  10bb bbbb
C:  110c cccc
D:  1110 dddd
```

The remaining `dddd` bits in the most significant bit of the class D IP address can take on any value, so the entire class D address space ranges from 224.0.0.0 through 239.255.255.255 (in binary, `1110 0000` through `1110 1111`).

Each of these addresses represents a singular logical entity: a group of IP end stations, also known as a "host group." There is no structure within this address space similar to subnetting in the unicast address space, although the concept of aggregating sets of group addresses has been discussed. Whether or not any structure is eventually imposed on the class D space, it is fundamentally flat. The host group denoted by the address 239.4.17.32 is not necessarily related to any group using the addresses 239.4.17.33, or 239.4.17.31, or 225.1.42.8 for that matter.

Reserved Multicast Addresses

Class D addresses starting with 224.0.0.x and 224.0.1.x have been reserved for various permanent assignments.

RFC-1700, the Assigned Numbers RFC, states:

> The range of addresses between 224.0.0.0 and 224.0.0.255, inclusive, is reserved for the use of routing protocols and other low-level topology discovery or maintenance protocols, such as gateway discovery and group membership reporting. Multicast routers should not forward any multicast datagram with destination addresses in this range, regardless of its TTL.

In this reserved range, which could also be written as 224.0.0.0/24, several assignments have already been made:

224.0.0.0	Base Address (Reserved)
* 224.0.0.1	All Systems on this Subnet
* 224.0.0.2	All Routers on this Subnet
224.0.0.3	Unassigned
* 224.0.0.4	DVMRP Routers
* 224.0.0.5	OSPF All Routers
* 224.0.0.6	OSPF Designated Routers
224.0.0.7	ST Routers
224.0.0.8	ST Hosts
224.0.0.9	RIP2 Routers
224.0.0.11	Mobile Agents

224.0.0.12	DHCP Server/Relay Agent
* 224.0.0.13	All PIM Routers
224.0.0.14	RSVP, ENCAPSULATION
* 224.0.0.15	All CBT Routers
224.0.0.16–224.0.0.255	Unassigned

Reserved addresses marked with * are directly or indirectly related to the operation of existing multicast routing protocols.

There are other permanently assigned multicast addresses for applications not in the categories of "routing protocols and other low-level topology discovery or maintenance protocols." It is useful to have a well-known address for certain applications. A small selection of these reserved "well-known addresses" follows:

224.0.1.1	NTP (Network Time Protocol)
224.0.1.2	SGI-Dogfight
224.0.1.3	rwhod
224.0.1.5	Artificial Horizons—Aviator
224.0.1.20	any private experiment
* 224.0.1.21	DVMRP on MOSPF
224.0.1.22	SVRLOC
224.0.1.23	XINGTV
* 224.0.1.32	mtrace

For a complete listing of all permanent multicast address assignments, see the "Assigned Numbers" RFC (RFC-1700 or its successor), or visit the web site of the Internet Assigned Numbers Authority (IANA), http://www.iana.org/iana/.

The IANA's URL will always reflect the most up-to-date list of assigned numbers available. The Assigned Numbers RFC is simply a snapshot of the data available at the IANA web site, and is guaranteed to be accurate only at the time it is published. Once made, assignments are rarely changed, but new ones are added continuously.

Multicast Address Space

The final reserved multicast addresses are set aside for use within private networks, such as enterprise internetworks, or "intranets." Host groups on the public Internet should not use these addresses, and if private networks employ such addresses, packets destined to such groups should not be forwarded beyond the boundaries of that organization's network infrastructure.

These private multicast addresses range from 239.0.0.0 to 239.255.255.255. You may also hear this referred to as the "administratively scoped" address range. Various techniques for controlling the scope of host groups will be discussed in detail later in the book.

Multicast IP over IEEE 802 LANs

IEEE 802 LANs share a common MAC-layer addressing scheme, using a 48-bit address. The most successful IEEE LAN standards are:

- Ethernet/Fast Ethernet/Gigabit Ethernet (IEEE 802.3)
- Token Ring (IEEE 802.5)
- FDDI
  - Actually an ANSI standard (X3T9.5), but the FDDI MAC layer was designed to fit under the IEEE 802.2 LLC layer

All IEEE MAC-layer technologies support MAC-layer multicast to one degree or another (802.5 has the least sophisticated multicast support). All IEEE 802 LANs have a common MAC address structure, as depicted in Figure 2–8.

If the M-bit is clear (= 0), this is a unicast address; otherwise, the M-bit is set (= 1) and this is a multicast frame.

Note: The MAC-layer broadcast address is composed of 48 consecutive 1 bits (i.e., in hex: 0xFF-FF-FF-FF-FF-FF), so in particular the M-bit in the first byte is set (along with all the rest of the bits!), confirming that the broadcast packet is a multicast, as expected.

To summarize: If a MAC address is multicast, the M-bit is set; and because the M-bit is the least significant bit of the first octet, any multicast MAC address' first octet must be odd. In hex 1, 3, 5, 7, 9, B, D, and F are all valid values for the least significant four bits of a multicast address' first octet.

The L-bit is the universal/local bit. If it is clear (= 0), this is a universally or globally unique MAC address. What ensures this "universal uniqueness"? The IEEE sells "blocks" of MAC addresses to manufacturers of LAN equipment. Each block contains 24 bits of address space (16,777,216 addresses), and each manufacturer typically "burns in" at least one unique ID to each LAN interface it makes. The IEEE is supposed to ensure that no two manufacturers have the same OUI. Similarly, the manufacturers are all supposed to

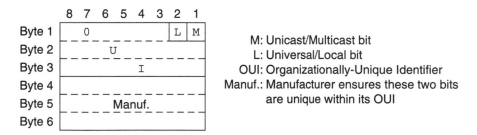

FIGURE 2–8   IEEE 802 MAC address format

ensure that no two devices have the same manufacturer-assigned code within their as-signed OUIs. Assuming that both the IEEE and the manufacturers do their jobs correctly, no two LAN devices should ever have the same MAC address.

In the case of globally unique MAC addresses, the universal/local bit is clear (= 0). There have been occasions, mostly in the early days of the IEEE, that OUIs with the local bit set were assigned to manufacturers. In fact, 0x02-60-8c was one of 3Com's first OUIs, used on many Network Interface Cards (NICs) during the late 1980s and early 1990s. As you can see, since the first byte is 0x02, it has the local bit set, even though it is an IEEE-assigned universally-unique OUI. Technically, the actual OUI in this case is 0x00-60-8c. Luckily, the IEEE never assigned that OUI as well!

Under the IEEE MAC-layer addressing scheme, it is possible to have "locally ad-ministered" addresses, but this is not very common. The most notable examples of locally administered MAC addresses are in 802.5 token ring networks, and in DECnet Phase IV over any IEEE LAN medium. In any situation where locally assigned addresses are in use, it is up to the administering authority to ensure uniqueness. In these cases, the univer-sal/local bit would be set (= 1), not clear.

Note that even though the broadcast address has its local bit set (along with the rest of its bits), it is universally recognized as a special bit pattern meaning "every station on this LAN must receive this frame." So the setting of the L-bit is irrelevant in the case of the broadcast address.

Sending Multicast IP Packets over IEEE LANs

Transmitting IP multicast packets over a LAN is extremely straightforward. For comparison, we will first examine the procedure used to transmit a unicast packet. In the case of unicast, the following seven-step process is used to decide how to forward an IP packet over a LAN:

1. Apply each interface's mask(s) to its IP address(es) so that only the network prefix or extended-network prefix remains. Save these for use every time you need to for-ward a unicast IP packet.
2. Apply each of your interface's masks to the destination IP address.
3. Compare the masked destination address of the packet with each of your interface's prefixes (the results of step 1). If any of these match, proceed with step 4; otherwise skip to step 7.
4. On the interface whose prefix matched the masked destination, check the local ARP cache for the media address of the destination IP address.
5. If the destination IP address is not in the ARP cache, broadcast an ARP request on that interface, asking for the MAC address of the destination IP end station. (If it is in the ARP cache, proceed with step 6, as if you had just received an ARP reply.)
6. Once you have an ARP reply, giving you the desired destination MAC address, you have all the information you need to send the complete Ethernet frame, which will encapsulate the IP packet.
7. In the case of an address which does not fall within any of the end station's inter-face prefixes, the end station must send the packet to the station's default router for

delivery to nonlocal destinations. The station requires the MAC address of the default router in order to forward the packet to it. From the host's configuration or its routing table, the host must extract the IP address of its default router. Steps 4 and 5 may be used to acquire the default router's MAC address and send an Ethernet frame to the default router, which contains this IP packet.

Note that the IP-layer destination of the packet in this case is not the default router; the router is only the destination at the MAC layer, and uses the ultimate IP destination of the packet to deliver the packet hop by hop until it reaches its destination.

Due to the most important parts of this process, it is often called "mask-and-match." These steps, while straightforward, are somewhat involved. While you may have a general familiarity with unicast IP, it may surprise you to discover that it is considerably simpler, even trivial, to send a multicast IP frame over a LAN. Partially, the simplicity derives from the fact that there is no difference between the two cases of sending packets on the LAN versus sending across routers.

There is no multicast equivalent of ARP that works over LANs. A very simple algorithm stands in to make sure that any end station wishing to send to a class D address will always choose the same IEEE MAC-layer multicast address. A sending station extracts the low-order 23 bits of the IP class D destination address and uses them as the low-order bits in a special IEEE MAC-layer prefix containing the IETF's OUI (with the multicast bit set).

The IEEE has assigned an OUI to the IETF: 0x00-00-5E. We must first take the OUI (the most significant three octets of the six-octet MAC address) and make it "multicast" by setting the multicast bit. Thus, the MAC-layer multicast address will begin with the following three octets: 0x01-00-5E. This address format is shown in Figure 2–9.

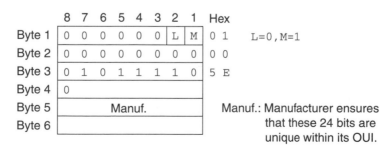

FIGURE 2–9   MAC-layer group addresses under the IETF OUI

As illustrated in the figure, the highest-order bit of the 24 "Manuf." bits is reserved and is always set to zero. This leaves 23 bits in which to carry the least significant portion of the group addresses.

In a class D address, the first four bits are fixed as 1-1-1-0, leaving 28 bits to the group's unique identifier (see Figure 2–10).

In order to map a class D address to a MAC-layer destination address, the first 24 bits are fixed (= 0x01-00-5E), and the next bit is reserved and is always 0. The remaining 23 bits are used to store part of the 28-bit group identifier of the class D address. The choice has been made to employ a one-to-one mapping of the lowest-order 23 bits of the class D address into the available 23 bits in the MAC-layer multicast address.

An example would serve to illustrate this very straightforward mapping.

Assume that an end station needs to send an IP packet to the address 239.147.6.99. This address may be represented in hex and binary, as follows:

```
Decimal:       239          147         6            99
   Hex:         EF           93          6            63
Binary:     1110-1111  · 1001-0011  0000-0110   0110-0011
```

As mentioned earlier, all class D addresses start with `1110`, so, the binary format of this address is

```
(1110) 1111 1001-0011 0000-0110 0110-0011
 . . . . .^^^ ^^^^ ^^^^ ^^^^ ^^^^ ^^^^
```

The low-order 23 bits (indicated by ^ above) are mapped after the IETF OUI, which consists of the following 25 bits for every multicast IP destination:

```
       M
0000-0001 0000-0000 0101-1110 0
```

The "M" indicates the multicast bit. To send the Ethernet multicast frame, now all we must do is concatenate the low-order 23 bits of the destination address with the fixed prefix here:

FIGURE 2–10   Class D address format

```
            M                          |
0000-0001 0000-0000 0101-1110  |  0
                               |  001-0011 0000-0110 0110-0011
                               |  .^^^ ^^^^ ^^^^ ^^^^ ^^^^ ^^^^
```

The result of this operation is the IEEE MAC-layer multicast address, in hex: 0x01-00-5E-13-06-63.

Because this mapping is not one-to-one (the 28-bit group identifier of the IP class D address is mapped into a 23-bit field), there is a possibility that multiple class D addresses will use the same MAC-layer multicast address. Because there are five bits of addresses that are not mapped into the MAC-layer multicast address, up to 32 IP class D addresses may share a MAC-layer multicast group address.

A way to see this ratio of 32 is to consider that because there are 28 bits of class D identifiers, there are 2^{28} (268,435,456) different multicast group addresses. At the MAC layer, there are 23 bits of address space, yielding 2^{23} (8,388,608) possible MAC-layer multicast addresses under the IETF OUI.

Clearly there are more class D group identifiers than MAC-layer multicast addresses available under the IETF OUI.

$$\text{The ratio of } \frac{268,435,456}{8,388,608} = 32$$

Handling Multicasts at the MAC Layer

As with frames to unknown destinations and broadcast frames, multicasts must be flooded across MAC-layer bridges along a spanning tree so that they reach all the segments of the extended LAN. A particular type of bridge that has become extremely popular is the MAC-layer "switch." Switches are extremely fast (often wire-speed) multiport bridges, and thus must flood multicasts out of all their ports. The positive aspect of this flooding is that all interested group members are sure to get a copy of the multicast frame. The bigger negative aspect is that all *non*interested end stations also get a copy of the multicast frame.

LAN NICs must receive broadcasts, but they can be selective about receiving multicasts. Generally, network interface cards have to be specifically programmed to filter multicasts on behalf of the end station. Only multicast frames that pass through the filter will be passed up to the higher-layer software for processing. If you have deployed such multicast-filtering NICs on your extended LAN, there is little or no direct impact on the end stations. They can simply ignore multicast frames unless they are destined for a group to which the end station belongs. The only real impact on the nonmember end stations is that they lose the opportunity to transmit while the multicast frame occupies the wire.

Multicast Summary

We have now described multicast in the context of unicast and broadcast applications, and we have seen that multicast addresses are taken from their own address class, distinct from their unicast cousins. We have also seen that multicast is a network-layer service—a best-effort datagram service—as is unicast delivery.

Now we need to begin to delve into the details to understand how routers decide how to forward multicast datagrams, and to see how hosts inform routers of their interest in participating in certain group(s). In addition, we will see how to deploy multicast in some example scenarios, and look at several real-world networks that have deployed multicast. These case studies will examine the challenges faced in deploying and managing their multicast infrastructure.

CHAPTER **3**

CHARACTERISTICS OF MULTICAST APPLICATIONS

IDENTIFYING MULTICAST APPLICATIONS

True "multicast applications" are those applications requiring the presence of network-layer multicast in order to function. They require the same data to be delivered from one source to many destinations, or from multiple sources to many destinations. The most critical factor in determining if an application is a "multicast application" is whether the application must perform packet replication on its own—either by the sending machine or by application-layer relays—or whether it relies on the network to perform that task. In the case of IP (version 4), you can also tell by looking at the destination addresses of the application's packets: are they "class D" addresses?

It might help to understand what is meant by multicast applications by citing some examples. There are actually a number of existing multicast applications. In fact, some of these have existed for several years: Lecture-mode audio/videoconferences have been used over the Internet's multicast backbone (MBone) since 1992.

- Multiparty videoconferencing
- Multiparty audioconferencing
  - Often used in conjunction with videoconferencing apps
- Shared whiteboards
  - Sometimes used with either one or both of the first two (e.g., to show a presentation while discussing it)

- Proprietary multidestination reliable multicast transport applications
  - StarBurst's mFTP
  - TIBCO's TIB
  - GlobalCast
    - Standard(s) being developed
- Distributed interactive simulations
  - Large military interest here, in fact way beyond the current state of the art (in 1997)
- Networked news/sports/weather/stock tickers and, generically, "push" technology
  - Usenet news maps very nicely to multicast
  - E-mail distribution lists also map nicely to multicast delivery
- Multicast enhancements to Data Link Switching (DLSw)
- IPv6-over-IPv4, an elegant transition scheme to ease deployment of IPv6
- Networked games
  - OK, so games aren't a business application, but at least these aren't broadcast-based, like early versions of Doom over IPX, which melted many corporate networks in the early 1990s
- Many others

Some parameters used to describe multicast applications include:

- The number of (simultaneous) senders to the group
- The size of the group(s) involved
  - Perhaps the number of group members (a.k.a. receivers)
  - Perhaps the geographic extent of the group
  - Perhaps the diameter of the group, measured in router hops
- The longevity of the group
- The number of aggregate packets per second that need to be delivered to the group's members
- The peak/average bandwidth used by the source
- The level of (human) interactivity among the group's members
  - "lecture"-mode conferences versus "group discussion"-mode conferences
  - Unattended database replication or other data-only scenarios

and many other possible metrics.

Multicast ≠ Multimedia

Over the last five years or so, the term "multicast" has been implicitly or explicitly associated with the term "multimedia." However, there is no inherent relationship between multimedia and multicast (except that the two words both begin with the letters m-u-l-t-i). In fact, some of today's most popular multimedia applications do not use (network-layer) multicast at all!

It is certainly possible—maybe even desirable in most cases—to have multimedia applications that are multicast enabled. In fact, many such examples exist already from the Internet's MBone research efforts (vic/vat/wb/etc.). Commercial offerings from companies such as Precept are compatible with these MBone tools.

However, there are many other multicast-based applications that are in no way related to multimedia. Conversely, there are multidestination multimedia applications that don't use multicast IP (e.g., CU-SeeMe).

Multicast Applications Are Not Necessarily Bandwidth-Intensive!

Just as there is no "typical" unicast application, in that some may be very bandwidth-intensive while others may use very little bandwidth, there is also no typical multicast application. Some may use virtually no bandwidth, while others may use more, just as in the unicast case. As the intranet manager, it is up to you to use tools like RMON and RMON2, as well as your knowledge about which applications you have deployed, the number and distribution of your users, and so on in order to ensure that your intranet has the capacity to achieve your business objectives.

It is definitely *not* the case that multicast applications are bandwidth-intensive by default, but by the same token one cannot just deploy new networked applications without investigating the potential consequences!!

Multidestination Applications Don't Always Use Multicast

One has to look at the big picture when evaluating multicast applications. It is a very important point to observe that not all applications having one sender and multiple receivers use network-layer multicast technology. They may simply send the same data multiple times—once for each registered recipient—or use an application-layer relay scheme. Why would a company call their application "multicast" when it was not? Marketing. Today, multicast is a term with a lot of interest. If a vendor wants to attract extra attention, using the latest buzzwords is one way to do that. Caveat emptor: An application that uses "real" (i.e., network-layer) multicast will be a lot easier on your intranet (and on you and your operations staff!) than one which does replication on its own.

Many application developers know that network-layer multicast has not been widely deployed (yet) so they turn to application-layer replication instead. This is not surprising; the developers want to ship a product that has a certain functionality, and they would like to not limit their potential market to the subset of IP networks that are multicast-capable. Thus, they base their applications on the lowest common denominator: unicast (network-layer) packet delivery. However, this choice has implications, and costs, for your network. Figure 3–1 compares replicated unicast and multicast.

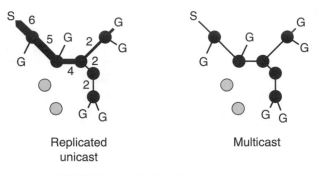

Replicated
unicast

Multicast

FIGURE 3–1   Replicated unicast vs. multicast

As an example, suppose you have a news headline update service that has 47 clients. Suppose that a certain set of news updates requires 26 packets to transmit. Now, in order to get the headline to our 47 receivers, we need to send 26 packets to the first receiver, 26 packets to the second receiver, ..., and 26 packets to the 47th receiver. This has consumed a total of 47 * 26 packets of the intranet's available bandwidth: 1222 packets!! If the average packet size was 200 bytes, and it took 10 seconds to transmit to the 47 stations, then you have used approximately 195,520 bps in each of those 10 seconds.

Another issue is configuration: Each client will need to be configured with the server's address before it can receive any data. Multicast-based solutions use a well-defined protocol between the end stations and the network so that their group membership can be communicated to the network across a standardized interface. If the application uses a well-known address, or can piggyback on a service-advertising protocol, the users can get up and running with far less static configuration than the replicated unicast case. Also, the network manager is free to change the server's address without simultaneously changing that address in each client's configuration.

If this same application were to use network-layer multicast, it would send exactly 26 packets. The network takes care of delivering them to all interested group members; and, what's more, only one copy of any of the 26 packets ever appears on any link of the group's distribution tree, regardless of the number of receivers! That's a savings of 97.9 percent overall, and the more receivers there are, the more you save compared to replicated unicast. In this case, it would take only 10/47 seconds (about 213 ms) to transmit the 26 packets.

Network-layer multicast can be employed to make much more efficient use of your network today, while paving the way for tomorrow's next-generation applications.

MOTIVATION FOR MULTICAST

Efficiency.   Applications that rely on multidestination delivery are emerging at an increasing pace, but they usually do not (yet) work over network-layer multicast. This is partly because multicast is recognized as a very powerful but "new" technology. IP multicasting has actually been around for quite a while, but it is only now that it is starting to be deployed. Today there is a critical mass of multicast routing protocols available from major router vendors that should meet the requirements of most intranets. Also, most modern end-station IP stacks support multicast sending and receiving.

Once application developers see that multicast infrastructure is in place, they will be motivated to support it in their products. All else being equal, applications which support multicast will be favored over those that do not because multicast-based applications will use far less of your network bandwidth to do the same job.

The canonical multicast applications that are mentioned today are video- and audio-conferencing, and some "datacasting" applications, such as delivering stock tickers, news updates, and so on, to the members of a group of interested receivers. Other possible applications include distance learning and training (i.e., watching a lecture with other students who are distributed across an internetwork), "shared whiteboards," and joint document editing by a group. Other applications include audio or video streaming, and "datacasting," the transmission of files to multiple receivers at essentially the same time.

Apparently, none of these applications are multicast's "killer app." If they were, multicast would already have exploded—many of these applications have existed for some time now, and have supported network-layer multicast for their entire existence. Also, many of these apps have been free, so there is no cost to deploy them other than the cost of upgrading (parts of) your intranet to support multicast.

Due to the incredible market penetration of web browsers, a popular browser plug-in that operates over multicast would generate absolutely enormous demand for multicast IP in intranets all over the world. The historically tight linkage between intranets and the web browser, and the emerging web-oriented "push" techniques, seems like a perfect match for multicast delivery. Perhaps a class of killer apps is finally imminent. It is also possible that the killer app for multicast hasn't been dreamed of yet, but there are many useful things you can do with multicast today.

For the remainder of this book, you can assume that any reference to the term "multicast" means IPv4 network-layer multicast unless stated otherwise.

Multicast Videoconferencing and Your Travel Budget

It is somewhat common to hear people make a case for multicast by telling you that deploying such applications in your network will save you money. Their pitch assumes that your company is somewhat dispersed geographically, and posits that multicast videoconferencing will reduce your need to travel, and thus your travel costs. This may, in fact, happen—slightly—but it should not be your driving goal for understanding and deploying multicast in your network. Multicast will save bandwidth compared to sending replicated unicast packets for whatever multicast applications you need or want to deploy.

The major reason that videoconferencing probably won't save you tons of money is very practical and down to earth: time zones. If you have a worldwide presence it is unlikely that there will be any significant overlap between the workdays of your farthest-flung employees. Collaboration across widespread time zones is best facilitated by time-asynchronous applications such as voice mail, e-mail, and file transfer. Also, audio/videoconferences may be recorded for playback later, within a streaming video-on-demand system. If your company happens to span less than a half-dozen time zones, you may be able to enhance your employees' collaboration across geographies. The employees can work together effectively during periods when their workdays overlap.

In the case where your company is in one (or two) time zones (or even operating in several locations in one city), multicast can help enable much more productive use of employees' time. You don't normally think of driving time between buildings or campuses as a travel cost, but there is definitely an opportunity cost associated with this phsyical collaboration: the employees aren't working effectively when they are driving. Multicast-enabled audio/videoconferencing can be very useful if you have several office buildings in a city. Employees can work together more effectively with this technology than if they had to waste time driving across town to meet.

Even in the intracity case, it is not obvious that this improved collaboration will decrease the need to travel, since longer meetings seem to work better face to face. However this capability will probably increase your employees' ability to work well together, which is a very large benefit to their productivity. It will now be feasible to easily have a "face-to-face" multiparty consulation about a pressing issue, which may enable its quick resolution.

The Future of Multicast on Your Intranet

Multicast in your network enables future, as yet uninvented applications, and that intangible is probably the best reason to deploy network-layer multicasting sooner rather than later. There are applications you can use today, but a "killer app" for multicast is not yet on the scene. Web-based "push" applications look like a possible killer app, since "push" is a very good match to multicast's natural abilities.

As the intranet manager, you want to have time to carefully consider a multicast deployment strategy and to do controlled testing to enhance your own understanding, familiarity, and comfort with this new technology. You do not want to have to multicast-enable your entire intranet in less than a month when the "killer multicast app" has your users (and your management) banging on your door!

Business-oriented multicast applications do exist today. If you have an IP-based network in place today, deploying multicast involves simply upgrading the software in selected routers and in those end stations that wish to participate in multicast applications. Although careful planning is recommended before proceeding, enabling multicast routing can be trivial, since perhaps only a handful of commands need to be added or modified in your routers' configurations. Later, as multicast applications need to be deployed over your network, you'll be ready.

The History of IP on Your Intranet

For comparison, consider unicast IP. For years it was in your network, minding its own business. Perhaps it was used for tasks such as network management (ping, traceroute, telnet, SNMP, etc.), or other enterprise-oriented applications such as DLSw or a corporate e-mail backbone. Mundane, workaday stuff; nothing exciting.

Then, all of a sudden, many software vendors started making "intranet" applications: those that took advantage of your existing unicast IP infrastructure, and used newly ubiquitous web browsers as front ends (not to mention the explosive growth of the World Wide Web itself). The web created a strong grass-roots demand to roll out IP to the far corners of your network. The web-enabled intranet vendors helped create top-down pressure as well, no doubt. With an extant IP infrastructure, it was easy to add other applications because everyone already had IP addresses.

The web started out small and grew rapidly to become the most popular application running across the Internet. Near its inception, web traffic measured across the old NSFNet backbone sometimes saw month-over-month growth rates as high as 300,000 percent! This kind of insanely rapid growth was only possible because the infrastructure was already in place to carry the new type of traffic associated with this new application. Despite the fact that the Internet had existed for years prior to the advent of the web, the web was the "killer app" for the Internet, taking it to new levels of market penetration and making it a viable medium for the masses.

Compared to the anarchy of the Internet, which has no central management authority, corporate network managers have much more control over their infrastructure. Due to this tighter level of control, intranet managers are well positioned to capitalize on new applications and technologies quickly—if there is a business justification for them. Another key enabler to deploying new business applications quickly is that the intranet's infrastructure is prepared to support them.

Multicast IP will be an essential building block for the foundation of your current and future intranetwork. Besides videoconferencing and stock tickers, there are many more "business-oriented" applications for multicast technology:

- DLSw scales much more nicely over a multicast-capable infrastructure.
- IPv6 deployment will go much more smoothly if you have not only unicast IPv4 but also multicast IPv4 in place.
- Usenet News is an application that could make effective use of multicast. SMTP mailing lists might also be able to benefit from using multicast.
- The rapid emergence of web-based "push" applications are well suited to future operation over multicast, although they currently often employ a "distributed pull" model where a web client on your machine operates in the background, periodically querying a server to see if there is new data.
  - PointCast™ pioneered this style of application, and others have jumped into this market niche.

There are many other examples, as we will see in the remainder of this book, which should serve to convince you of the usefulness of multicast IP in your intranet.

Multicast Is Not Perfect (Yet) . . .

Multicast in the late 1990s is quite well suited to usage in intranet scenarios, affording intranet owners more efficient bandwidth utilization for applications requiring multipoint delivery.

Unfortunately, multicast is still not sufficiently well developed for Internet-wide use. Researchers are working hard to address these scaling issues, and solutions may begin to appear within two to five years. A later chapter will discuss today's Internet multicast infrastructure (the Multicast Backbone, affectionately known as the MBone) and trends toward a future native multicast-enabled Internet.

PART II

MULTICAST IP TECHNOLOGY OVERVIEW

This section of the book will introduce general multicast IP concepts and architectural details.

First, we will describe the "host group" model of IP multicast, which is the fundamental architecture under which all multicast protocols have developed. Then we will investigate the Internet Group Management Protocol, which is the protocol that hosts implement to inform multicast routers of their group membership interest(s). We will trace the entire history of IGMP, and peer into the future of IGMP to see what new features are being contemplated for addition in the next few years.

In preparation for a rather detailed introduction of all the current multicast routing protocols, we will discuss how to distinguish between multicast routing and multicast forwarding. We'll finish this section with a description of the broad classes of multicast routing protocols that are available today.

CHAPTER 4

MULTICAST IP FUNDAMENTALS

Multicast forwarding is a generalization of unicast forwarding, in which packets are sent to a set of destinations rather than just one, even though each packet is only addressed to one "place," a special address representing a group of end stations. Steve Deering invented several of today's multicast algorithms in his 1991 Ph.D. dissertation, and in August 1989's "Host Extensions for IP Multicasting" (RFC-1112). RFC-1112 has since achieved Full Internet Standard status.

THE LINEAGE OF MULTICAST STANDARDIZATION

In the mid-1980s, Steve Deering and his advisor at Stanford wrote two RFCs that began to develop the ideas which later became RFC-1112. The earlier of these two RFCs was "Host Groups: A Multicast Extension to the Internet Protocol," RFC-966 (with Dr. Cheriton) in December 1985. Then, in July 1986, Deering authored "Host Extensions for IP Multicasting," RFC-988. RFC-988 would be made obsolete in about two years by RFC-1054, also entitled "Host Extensions for IP Multicasting," in May 1988, and again by RFC-1112, of the same name, in August 1989.

"HOST GROUP" MODEL

The core concept in IP multicast is that of the "host group" model. A host group is represented by a single "group address." Packets destined for the group are addressed to its group address, then it is up to the internetwork's routers to determine how to reach the

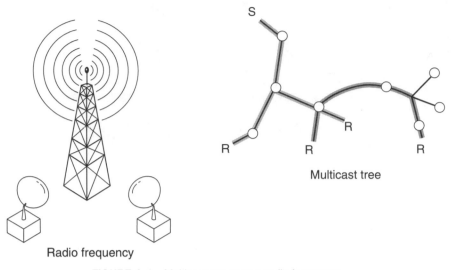

FIGURE 4–1   Multicast tree versus radio frequency

group's members. Host groups may have any number of members, deployed in arbitrary ways throughout the internetwork topology. Groups can theoretically have any shape, size, or geographical extent, and end stations can join or leave groups at will; whether or not to be a member of a group is a local decision. One very important feature of host groups is that senders need not be members of the group(s) to which they send traffic.

Probably the single most important feature of the host-group model is that group membership is receiver initiated. When senders emit traffic, it is up to the network to deliver to any known receivers. If there are no receivers, the sender's local routers do not accept the traffic for further processing, and the traffic never leaves the sender's local subnetwork.

Receiver-initiated join has good scaling properties: As the group grows, it is ever more likely that new receivers will be able to splice onto a nearby, already active branch of the distribution tree. Consider how differences in group scale, distribution of members, and so on will affect how true this statement is. It is more likely to apply well to campus intranets than large, distributed WANs.

As depicted in Figure 4–1, a host group is similar to a radio frequency: Anyone with a transmitter may send on that channel, and anyone with a receiver may tune in. The difference is that a radio frequency is a passive broadcast medium, while an internetwork must actively discover paths (tree branches) between senders and receivers.

CONTROLLING THE SCOPE OF MULTICAST FORWARDING

There are several mechanisms available for controlling how far, in terms of router hops, your multicast transmissions may propagate. The two main ways of doing this are administrative scoping and TTL-based scoping. It is possible to use one or the other of these methods, and it is even possible to use both together. In addition, certain group addresses are implicitly scoped.

Implicit Scoping

Implicitly scoped groups are generally reserved multicast addresses, which are TTL-limited to the subnet on which they were originally transmitted. Besides the fact that end stations or routers are required to originate packets to certain reserved groups with a TTL of 1, routers are supposed to know that certain ranges of multicast addresses are not to be forwarded, regardless of their TTL. (This is an additional safety mechanism to protect against broken implementations that may not send such packets with a TTL of 1.) The implicitly scoped addresses are sometimes referred to as "link-local" addresses, and are taken from the range 224.0.0.0/24. These reserved address assignments were discussed in more detail in Chapter 2.

TTL-Based Scoping

Table 4–1 lists the conventional values used on multicast routers to control multicast forwarding. These are usually configured on intranet border routers which connect the intranet to the global multicast infrastructure.

For example, under this convention, a packet must have a TTL ≥ 16 to get outside of a site. Any intranet manager is free to choose values that make sense to them—including defining what a site and region mean in their case—as long as their users' applications are configured properly and only send internally destined multicast packets with small enough TTLs so that they cannot leak out onto the Internet. Note that this leakage does not pose too great a threat, because even if a packet had a sufficient TTL to leave the corporate intranet, it is unlikely that there would be anyone outside who would have known which group to join. Even if there were such a person, the packet's TTL would not necessarily be sufficient to reach an interested outsider.

A multicast router will only forward a multicast datagram across an interface if the TTL field in the IP header is greater than the TTL threshold assigned to the interface. (As with unicast packets, each time a router forwards a packet, its TTL is decremented by 1.)

TABLE 4–1   Conventional TTL Scope Control Values

TTL	Scope threshold
0	Restricted to the same host
1	Restricted to the same subnetwork
15	Restricted to the same site
63	Restricted to the same region
127	Worldwide
191	Worldwide; limited bandwidth
255	Unrestricted in scope

The TTL threshold does not change this behavior. If the packet's TTL is greater than the interface's threshold, its TTL is still only decremented by 1 when crossing the router. The unconfigured threshold for a unicast or multicast packet is 1. If a packet's TTL is not at least 1, it will not be forwarded.

TTL-based scoping is not sufficient for every application. Conflicts arise when trying to simultaneously enforce limits on topology, geography, and bandwidth. In particular, TTL-based scoping cannot handle overlapping regions, which is a necessary characteristic of administrative regions. In other words, if an interface has a TTL threshold of 37, it is applied to *all* multicast IP groups wanting to cross this interface.

It is often desirable to have overlapping regions, but TTL scoping is indiscriminate; all groups are treated equally. Also, TTL-scoped boundaries only affect packets with a TTL of less than the threshold. Any packets, regardless of group address, will go through if their TTL is high enough (i.e., greater than the threshold). Despite its limitations, TTL-based scoping has been popular throughout the life of the MBone. As you can see from Table 4–1, the TTL limit conventions are related to bandwidth limits. Packets with larger TTLs are supposed to represent lower-bandwidth streams because their TTLs are large enough for them to be forwarded across the entire MBone.

TTL scoping can be aided by the sender being preconfigured with different TTL limits for each group. For instance, a sender could limit its transmission's scope to 10 router hops by setting the TTL to 10 in all of its multicast packets, or just in packets destined for certain groups. Alternatively, it could set each group's initial TTL to 14 as they are transmitted, which should keep the packets inside the same site. The senders are then leaving it to the routers to decrement TTLs and discard packets that don't exceed the imposed thresholds.

Besides all the problems listed above, another problem with using the TTL to control forwarding scope is that it requires the source to know how far away authorized receivers are. If a new subnet is created that is one hop further away than the TTL limit but still within your administrative domain, the packets won't make it onto this new subnet without informing the source station that packets can now "legally" go one hop further than before.

Even if the hosts know how large or small a TTL to use, you still may not want all subnets within a diameter of N hops to be able to receive this source's traffic; however, with TTL scoping, you cannot be selective about which subnets within that diameter may have legitimate receivers. We have not covered multicast routing protocols yet, but some protocols will periodically broadcast traffic across the network to test for new receivers. If such protocols are in use, some packets will be delivered onto each subnetwork within the sender's TTL radius. Not all routing protocols behave this way, so it may not always be an issue.

TTL scoping is limited because of several factors:

1. It is essentially impossible to have overlapping scope regions if the only administrative metric is the TTL.

2. The TTL field in the IP header is semantically overloaded. It is simultaneously used for three completely unrelated purposes:

    a. Limits the lifetime of a packet

    b. Packet confinement due to bandwidth

    c. Packet confinement for administrative reasons (group address reuse, privacy, etc.).

3. It requires arbitrary choices of TTL ranges to be effective as a tool for building multicast regions, but it is difficult to use except at the very edge of a network.

4. The responsibility for enforcing the scope is divided between two separate entities: the intranet manager, who configures TTL thresholds in multicast routers, and the users controlling the source station(s) in each region. It is all too easy for a user to send packets with TTLs greater than the administrative thresholds, thus rendering them ineffective.

    The users must be trusted to configure their end stations' applications to send multicasts with TTLs such that their transmissions stay within the defined scope regions. The intranet manager must monitor their transmissions to ensure compliance with the organization's policies.

Except in small networks with well-understood topologies and well-managed user communities, the source station is definitely not a convenient place to enforce desired scope boundaries for your intranet. A given source may want to send to several different groups, each with unique scoping requirements. If the source has to keep track of all this, it is sure to be an added administrative burden, or at least too difficult for the typical user to handle.

Ideally, the source should not need to be aware of the TTL limits imposed by the routers, but the routers cannot easily distinguish between various sources or groups. In summary, TTL thresholds are a blanket parameter applied to every packet needing to be forwarded across an interface, regardless of the packet's source or its destination group.

In a perfect world, a packet would never be trying to cross a threshold unless an end station on the other side of that threshold had joined the group. In this case, the group member has extended the delivery tree across that threshold. Were the group member not present in this location, the packet would never have been forwarded in the direction of this router's TTL threshold. So, in a perfect world, it is not entirely unsafe that a source end station may send traffic with a larger TTL than their policy says they should. Multicast packets are only supposed to go where there are interested receivers.

In Figure 4–2, the source station is eight hops from the receiver, so it would need to use a TTL of at least 9 in its unicast or multicast IP packets to reach this receiver. However, the router on the edge of this region may have a TTL threshold of 7, or the source may be using a TTL of less than 9. Either of these conditions would mean that this receiver, despite its interest in being a group member, will never receive a packet from this source. First, the source's TTL is insufficient to reach this receiver. Second, the TTL-scoped region's router is blocking the source's traffic on its way to this receiver.

Unfortunately, this is not a perfect world. Certain routing protocols, the mechanics of which will be discussed a bit later, use broadcast techniques to expose potentially interested end stations to new multicast sessions. If your multicast routing protocol uses these so-

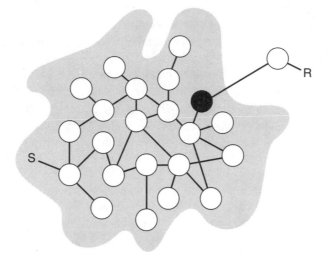

FIGURE 4–2   Wrong side of the tracks

called broadcast-and-prune techniques, your sources' TTLs will affect the diameter of the broadcast, possibly extending the packet's reach well beyond its set of known receivers.

TTL thresholds are not per-source, per-group, or per-(source, group), so TTL scoping ends up being practical only as a safety net: At the edge of your intranet, you may set a TTL threshold that all packets leaving your network must be able to cross. If you can ensure that no source within your network can originate packets with TTLs greater than, for example, 32, then a threshold of 64 at the edge of your network will ensure that no internally sourced and internally destined packets will leak onto the Internet. Of course, for global sessions you originate, you would set the TTL as appropriate to reach all your receivers, including those outside your intranet.

Administrative Scoping

In light of the challenges in using TTL as the only administrative metric, "administrative" scoping was originally presented to a working session of the IDMR working group at the 30th IETF (July 1994 in Toronto, Canada). The idea behind administrative scoping is to provide a way to do scoping based on multicast address. A portion of the class D address was then reserved to accommodate this form of scoping.

Besides providing a mechanism for well-defined boundaries (which may overlap), administrative scoping also allows for privacy and address reuse within the class D address space by multiple administrative domains. Certain addresses would only be usable within a given administrative scope (e.g., a [portion of a] corporate internetwork) but would not be forwarded beyond the scoped boundaries.

The range from 239.0.0.0 to 239.255.255.255 has been reserved for administrative scoping within corporate intranets or any other private organization's network. A shorthand way to refer to this part of the class D address space is 239.0.0.0/8, or simply 239/8.

Packets destined to 239/8 are not to be forwarded outside an organization's network; their edge routers must be configured to enforce this restriction. Also, as an added level of protection, ISP routers should not accept packets destined for any group address within 239/8 from any of their customers.

As an example, suppose that two organizations are using the organization-local scope (239.192.0.0/14). Figure 4–3 shows that there is no conflict in this case.

Each side need not use all of the 239/8 space, but each can use as much as they like. The only requirement is that each of their routers must block packets destined for 239/8 from leaving their site (and from arriving at their site!). Also, under no circumstances shall ISPs ever forward packets destined for these addresses.

Even though the administratively scoped addresses represent only a small portion of the multicast address space (1/16), there are still plenty of addresses to be used inside an organization's network. 239/8 contains $2^{24} = 16,777,216$ group addresses, which should be more than enough for even the largest organization's needs. Remember, this address space encompasses only those groups which are currently active or already reserved (scheduled) for a future time.

While administrative scoping has been available and in limited use since 1994 or so, it has yet to be widely deployed. The IETF MBoneD working group is developing a formal definition of, and attempting to encourage deployment of, administrative scoping. For additional information, please see the work in progress: `draft-ietf-mboned-admin-ip-space-01.txt`, or its successor entitled "Administratively Scoped IP Multicast."

In one way, reserving a set of group addresses for local use is similar to the "Address Allocation for Private Internets" (RFC-1918) scheme for reusing parts of the unicast address space within organizations; however, the motivations are very different. RFC-1918 is trying to conserve unicast addresses, or make it easy to change providers without renumbering (via Network Address Translation), while multicast administrative scoping is trying to allow any organization to control its local multicast group usage under a com-

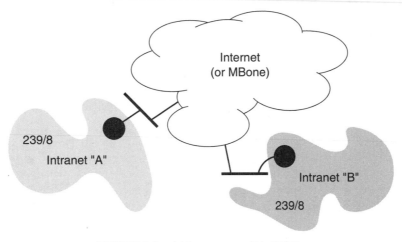

FIGURE 4–3   Address reuse within 239/8

mon administrative framework. In the unicast case the private addresses are intended to still be accessible from the global Internet. Multicast address reuse provides a way for groups to be truly local, with no chance of any packet leaking out, even if (1) a broadcast-and-prune protocol is in use and (2) the packet's TTL is high enough.

Within your network you may have other, more specific boundaries. You may have a teleconference among your top executives, or some managers may be conducting wage review on-line. If you pick local group addresses from within 239/8, you can allow any multicast router to be a potential enforcer of an administrative scope boundary. If you always pick addresses from within 239/8 you can be sure that they will not go where they ought not, provided the intranet's boundaries are defined appropriately for your needs.

One key benefit of administratively scoped regions is that they may overlap. It is extremely difficult to get TTL-scoped regions to overlap.

The two LANs in Figure 4–4 which are in both regions may receive packets destined for any part of 239.193/16 or 239.255/16. However, since boundary definitions are bidirectional, packets will not be able to flow between the administratively scoped regions.

Suggested Structure for the Admin-Scoped Addresses

In order to ensure consistency in the use of the 239/8 space (and to align as closely as possible with IPv6 multicast address structure, which embeds the forwarding scope in the group address' prefix), a set of suggestions has been made on how to use the administratively scoped address space.

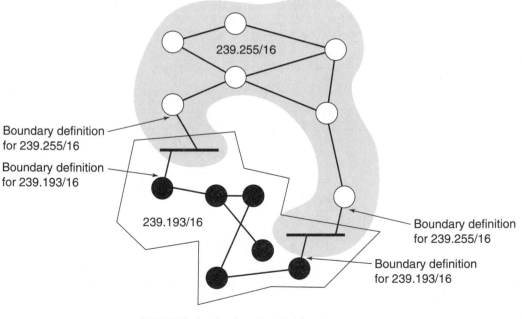

FIGURE 4–4 Overlapping administrative groups

Table 4–2, excerpted from the admin-scoping internet draft, outlines the partitioning of the IPv4 multicast space, and gives the mapping to IPv6 SCOP values [RFC-1884].

TABLE 4–2   RFC-1884 Scope Definitions

IPv6 Scope	RFC 1884 Description	IPv4 Prefix
0	Reserved	
1	Node-local scope	
2	Link-local scope	224.0.0.0/24
3	(Unassigned in IPv6)	239.255.0.0/16 (admin "local" scope)
4	(Unassigned in IPv6)	239.254.0.0/16
5	Site-local scope	239.253.0.0/16
6	(Unassigned in IPv6)	
7	(Unassigned)	
8	Organization-local scope	239.192.0.0/14
A	(Unassigned in IPv6)	
B	(Unassigned in IPv6)	
C	(Unassigned in IPv6)	
D	(Unassigned in IPv6)	
E	Global scope	224.0.1.0 through 238.255.255.255
F	Reserved	
	(Unassigned in IPv6)	239.0.0.0/10
	(Unassigned in IPv6)	239.64.0.0/10
	(Unassigned in IPv6)	239.128.0.0/10

Items 3, 5, and 8 are the administratively scoped addresses, summarized in Table 4–3, below.

Table 4–3   IPv4 Administrative Scopes

"local"	239.255.0.0/16	Packets destined for locally scoped groups may not cross any administratively scoped boundary, whether or not this address range is listed in an interface's boundary definition.
site-local	239.253.0.0/16	Represents 65,536 group addresses
organization-local	239.192.0.0/14	Four times as many as that, equivalent to the following /16s: 239.192.0.0/16 239.193.0.0/16 239.194.0.0/16 239.195.0.0/16

These are only recommendations, but it is likely that many implementations will adopt these as default values. As administrative scoping becomes more widely available, it is possible that the administratively scoped space guidelines could be expanded or refined to match evolving practice. Intranet managers may create a scope region whenever a unique multicast scope is required. It is possible, perhaps even desirable in some cases, to configure overlapping scope regions.

As shown in Table 4–3, 239.255.0.0/16 is the "local scope" for IPv4 multicast. As stated earlier, pertaining to the local scope, there is one final rule: The local scope must not span any other boundary. Any scope boundary is a boundary for the local scope. Therefore, setting any boundary on an interface (for any prefix/mask) implicitly sets that interface with a boundary for the local scope. Packets sent to groups in the 239.255.0.0/16 range must not be forwarded across any link with any scoped boundary defined (even if the local scope is not explicitly listed in the interface's scoped address list).

Usage Guidelines for Administrative Boundaries

An administratively scoped IP multicast region is a region with a fixed boundary, defined by one or more routers having common boundary definitions. A boundary definition is part of the router's configuration consisting of a (list of) prefix/mask(s), indicating that a router must not forward packets across or receive packets from an interface if their destinations fall within these defined admin-scoped range(s). Each interface may have its own boundary definition list.

The local scope is special, in that packets destined for locally scoped addresses can never cross any scope boundary. It is up to each intranet manager to decide what "local" means in the context of their network.

All administratively scoped and TTL-scoped regions must have the following properties:

- They must be "convex."

  This means that there must be no path between any two points in the bounded region which crosses a region boundary. In Figure 4–5a, each router interface to a link which leaves the region must have a list of "boundary defnitions." These boundary definitions restrict some blocks of the administratively scoped addresses to the depicted regions.

- They must be "connected," or "compact."

  In other words, an arbitrary path between any two nodes within any bounded region must not leave the region, as shown in Figure 4–5b.

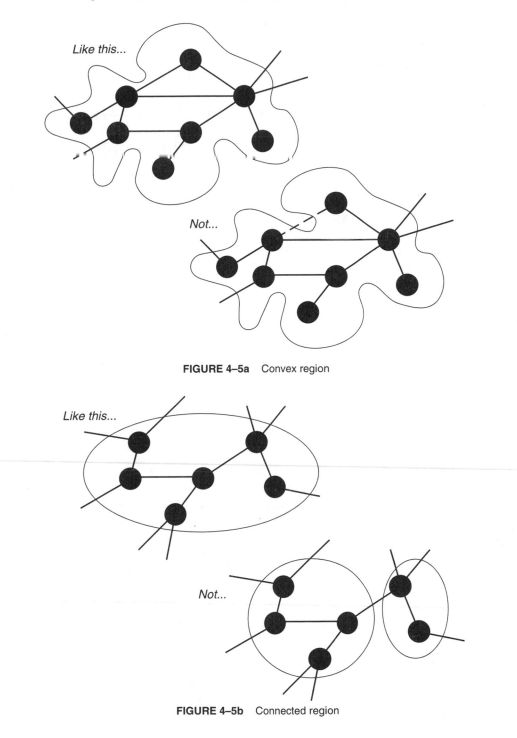

FIGURE 4–5a Convex region

FIGURE 4–5b Connected region

CHAPTER 5

OVERVIEW OF THE INTERNET GROUP MANAGEMENT PROTOCOL

Multicast IP delivery is selective: Only interested end stations are supposed to receive traffic for any given group. In order to build these selective distribution trees which only reach group members, it is a basic requirement that members must tell the routers where they are, and what group(s) interest them.

The Internet Group Management Protocol (IGMP) is the signaling protocol that end stations use to signal their group membership interest. IGMP is only locally significant; IGMP packets are not forwarded by routers. Besides allowing end stations to join and maintain membership in multicast groups, IGMP also allows routers to explicitly query subnetworks for members of any group.

IGMP is an integral part of IP, as is the more familiar Internet Control Message Protocol (ICMP). IGMP has been designed, deployed, and improved in an iterative cycle over the last decade or so. In a sense, IGMP is the most important protocol relative to multicast IP: without it, nothing else works. We will examine all the versions of IGMP to see the jobs IGMP was designed to do, as well as the improvements that have been made over the years. Finally, we will examine the future directions in which IGMP is likely to evolve.

There have been two versions of IGMP so far, and since version 2 is virtually ubiquitous at this time, we will concentrate on that version after understanding the essentials of IGMPv1. The features of version 1 are still present in version 2, with some enhancements to improve efficiency.

IGMP VERSION 1

IGMPv1 Protocol Overview

IGMPv1 was specified in RFC-1112, Appendix one. According to the specification, one multicast router per LAN must periodically transmit Host Membership Query messages to determine which host groups have members on the Querier's directly attached networks. IGMP Query messages (see Figure 5–1) are addressed to the all-hosts group (224.0.0.1) and have an IP TTL = 1. This means that Query messages sourced from a router are transmitted onto the directly attached subnetwork but are not forwarded by any other multicast routers.

When an end station receives an IGMP Query message, it responds with a Host Membership Report for each group to which it belongs, addressed to each group to which it belongs. This is a very important point: While IGMP Queries are sent to the "all hosts on this subnet" class D address (224.0.0.1), IGMP Reports are sent to the group(s) to which the host(s) belong. IGMP Reports, like Queries, are sent with the IP TTL = 1, and thus are not forwarded beyond the local subnetwork.

Why Send IGMP Reports to the Group Being Reported?

The design choice of sending Host Membership Reports to the reported group's class D address implies that all multicast routers must promiscuously receive and process all multicast frames.

Another choice could have been to send Reports to the "All routers on this subnet" (224.0.0.2) address, and include the group being reported somewhere in the IGMP header. This technique would have allowed a router to only listen for one MAC address (thus one IP address) for all IGMP reports. Why was this not chosen?

In order to function as a multicast router, the router already must promiscuously listen to all possible class D addresses, so they can receive multicast traffic from the LAN and forward it elsewhere (if necessary). Given this fact, IGMP's design did not make the router's job any more difficult. In retrospect, it certainly would have been nicer for layer-two switches if the IGMP Report address were predictable (for instance, if IGMP had

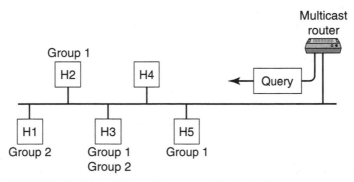

FIGURE 5–1   Internet Group Management Protocol—Query message

used the All-Routers group address, 224.0.0.2). IGMP Snooping could have been done in hardware at very low cost. Given that LAN switches did not exist when IGMP was invented, it is not surprising that IGMP's design did not accommodate them!

Note that next-generation LAN switches will likely have sufficiently powerful hardware to perform IGMP snooping in an entry-level switch. Also on the horizon is IGMPv3, which *may* change IGMP's behavior so that Reports would be sent to the all-routers address (224.0.0.2). IGMPv3 is a long way from being completed, and there is no guarantee that this new feature will survive the design process.

The IGMP Report Supression Technique

In order to avoid a flurry of Reports from every group member, a Report supression technique is employed. Each end station starts a randomly chosen Report delay timer for each group to which it belongs. During each group's delay period, if any end station is heard to issue a Report, every other end station in that group resets its timer to a new random value. This procedure minimizes Report traffic for each group by spreading Reports out over a period of time. This technique avoids requiring each member end station to send a report (each Query could result in an explosion of IGMP Reports if there are many active receivers). It is only important that each router knows that there is at least one member of a group on a LAN. How many members, and exactly what the members' IP addresses are, is not important.

If there is only one group member, the Report-cancelling algorithm still ensures that its Report will be heard; if there are 2, 20, or 200 group members, it ensures that Report traffic is kept to a minimum. Each group member restarts its random Report timer (between 0 and [maximum Response Time] seconds, in units of tenths of seconds), and every time one of the end stations sends a report, the others again reinitialize their random report timers. This report suppression mechanism depends on the group members hearing each other's Reports, another reason why Reports are sent to the group itself.

It should be noted that multicast routers do not need to be directly addressed since their interfaces are required to promiscuously receive all multicast IP traffic. In comparison, unicast packets are addressed to their ultimate destination at the IP layer, but are addressed to the next-hop router at the MAC layer. In contrast, multicast packets are addressed to their class D group address at the IP layer, and an IEEE-802 representation of that address at the MAC layer. Also, a multicast router is not required to maintain a detailed list of which hosts belong to each multicast group; the router only needs to know that at least one group member is present on a given interface.

Detecting Group Membership Changes

Multicast routers periodically transmit IGMP Queries to refresh their knowledge of the group members present on each network interface. This process updates its local group database. Eventually, the router should be able to detect that no members of a group are present on an interface any longer and—if possible—remove itself from the multicast delivery tree for this group. If the router does not receive a Report from any members of a group after a number of Queries (the exact number is not specified in RFC-1112), the router assumes that no group members are present on a particular interface. When a router is just starting up, or if multicast routing has just been enabled, a router may (in order to quickly learn which groups have local members) send several IGMP Queries in rapid succession.

Assuming this is a leaf subnet (i.e., a subnet with at least one group member but no multicast routers connecting to additional group members which are further downstream and reachable via this interface), this interface is removed from the delivery tree(s) for this group. Multicasts will continue to be sent on this interface only if the router can tell (via multicast routing protocols) that there are additional group members further downstream which are reachable via this interface. Only one multicast router on a subnetwork is active as a Querier at any time. IEMPv1 required that the routing protocol elect a Querier. IEMPv2 includes a Querier-election algorithm within IGMP.

End Stations and "Join Latency"

When an end station first joins a group, it does not wait for a router's Query; it immediately transmits a Report for the group. This reduces the "join latency" for the first host to join a given group on a particular subnetwork.

"Join latency" is measured from the time an end station's first IGMP Report is sent until the transmission of the first packet for that group onto that host's subnetwork. Obviously, if the group is already active on this LAN, the join latency is approximately zero: the host will receive the traffic whether or not it sent an IGMP Report! Another way of saying this is that if the LAN is already part of the group's distribution tree, the join latency is zero. Conversely, if this LAN is not on this distribution tree, and we assume that the group is currently active elsewhere on the internetwork, then the join latency is how much time it takes to attach this LAN, along with any necessary intermediate upstream links and their intervening routers, to this group's distribution tree.

IGMP VERSION 2

IGMPv2 was distributed along with the Distance Vector Multicast Routing Protocol (DVMRP) implementation (`mrouted`) source code, versions 3.3 through 3.9. IGMPv2 incorporated design improvements based on deployment experience using IGMPv1 in the field. IGMPv2 was enhanced to help multicast routing scale better.

Initially, there was no detailed specification for IGMPv2 other than this source code. The specification has recently been published in the internet draft `draft-ietf-idmr-igmp-v2-07.txt`, which is not a finished protocol specification but a work in progress (as are all internet drafts). When a future version of this draft is finally published as an RFC, it will update the IGMPv1 specification, found in the first appendix of RFC 1112. IGMPv2 extends IGMPv1 while maintaining backward compatibility with version 1 hosts.

Usage of IGMPv1 has probably all but died out—all "modern" IP multicast implementations support IGMPv2 by default. (Microsoft Windows 98 allegedly will, though

Windows 95 does not. IGMPv2 is available for most flavors of UNIX™, and also Microsoft's Windows NT 4.0, and the Apple Macintosh). The only support for IGMPv1 that you may see is in multicast routers, because the IGMPv2 specification requires routers to interoperate with any old IGMPv1 implementations that may be present.

IGMPv2 Querier Election

IGMPv2 defines a procedure for election of the multicast Querier for each LAN. In IGMPv2, the multicast router with the *lowest IP address* on the LAN is elected the multicast Querier. The Querier election algorithm works as follows: Every multicast router initializes itself to believe that it is the multicast Querier on each of its interfaces for which it is configured as a multicast router. At boot time, or when multicast routing is enabled, the router transmits Query messages as defined by the IGMPv2 specification. Later, if the router hears a Query that is sourced from a numerically lower IP address, it ceases to act as a Querier on that interface.

Contrast this with IGMPv1, in which Querier election was determined independently by each multicast routing protocol. Multiple Queriers could have been elected in cases where several multicast routing protocols were active on the same LAN. This does little real harm other than slightly increasing the amount of IGMP traffic. Due to the Report supression technique employed by IGMP, the number of Host Membership Reports would probably not increase much in the presence of multiple Queriers, if at all.

IGMPv2 New Messages

IGMPv2 defines a Leave Group message to help lower IGMP's "leave latency." Whenever any end station wishes to leave a group, it transmits a Leave Group message to the all-routers group (224.0.0.2) with the group field indicating the group being left.

IGMPv2 also defines a new type of Query message: the Group-Specific Query. Group-Specific Query messages allow a router to transmit a Query pertaining to a specific multicast group. IGMPv1 Host Membership Queries and IGMPv2 General Queries allow a router to discover at least one member of *every* group residing on a directly attached subnetwork.

IGMPv2's two new messages are related. In response to a Leave Group message, the elected Querier begins transmitting Group-Specific Query messages on the interface from which it received the Leave Group message.

"Leave Latency" and IGMPv2

Definition: "Leave latency" is measured between two points in time:

1. The LAN's last group member sends its last Report.
2. The router stops forwarding traffic for that group onto this LAN.

"Leave latency" is measured from a router's perspective. In IGMPv1, leave latency was the time from a router hearing the last Report for a given group until the router aged out the interface from the delivery tree for that group (continuing to assume that this is a leaf subnet). How could an IGMPv1 Querier tell that this was the LAST group member? The only way was for it to wait for several Query intervals to pass without hearing a Report from any member of this group. Typically, a minimum of three Query intervals must elapse, taking on the order of minutes.

IGMPv2 reduces this time interval by allowing an end station to explicitly indicate that it has lost interest in traffic destined for a certain group. This explicit mechanism allows a more effective response than the implicit method IGMPv1 used. The IGMPv2 Querier has no doubt that an end station definitely wants to leave the group, it just doesn't know if this is the group's last member.

Under IGMPv2, the process is considerably more deterministic. The end station is able to directly inform the router that it is leaving (using the Leave Group message). Then the router asks the LAN if there are any other group members present (using the Group-Specific Query). If this end station was the last group member present, the router will not hear any Host Membership Reports in response to its Group-Specific Query messages. If this is a leaf subnet, this interface is removed from the delivery tree(s) for this group. Multicasts will continue to be sent on this interface only if the router can tell (via multicast routing protocols) that there are additional group members further downstream reachable by transmitting across this interface.

The Benefit of Lowering the Leave Latency

IGMPv2, with the addition of the Leave Group message, allows a group member to immediately inform the router that it no longer wishes to be a member of a group.

In response to this message, the Querier then sends out a series of Group-Specific Queries in order to determine whether there are any other group members still present on the LAN. If there are, [at least] one of them should respond to these queries. This slightly increased amount of control traffic on the LAN (due to the Group-Specific Queries) is presumed to be considerably less than the wasted bandwidth incurred during the waiting period used by IGMPv1, during which the group's data continues to flow where it is not wanted.

IGMPv2 also responds better on LANs with rapidly varying group membership. The timely group membership information available with IGMPv2 allows multicast routers to quickly adapt the group's delivery trees to only provide data onto LANs containing active receivers.

Thus, the benefit of lowering the leave latency is that the router can remove itself from the group's delivery tree as soon as possible once the last member host has dropped out of the group. This is far better than waiting for several (minutes worth of) Query intervals to pass. Despite the last end station's new state of indifference toward this group's traffic, the traffic continues to be forwarded by the router onto this LAN. If a group is experiencing high traffic levels, it can be very beneficial to stop receiving data for this group as soon as possible.

Lowering the leave latency saves bandwidth in two ways. First, bandwidth is saved on the branches of the delivery tree leading to this router. If any of the links along the branch to this router are expensive, slow, or highly utilized WAN links, it is extremely beneficial to eliminate this group's traffic from that branch. Second, bandwidth is saved on the LAN that no longer has any group members, and therefore no longer needs to experience this group's traffic. This gives other LAN stations more opportunities to transmit.

IGMPv2 Summary

Queries and Reports

When an IGMP Querier interrogates the LAN, all the multicast IP end stations hear the Query because it is addressed to the "All Systems on This Subnet" class D address (e.g., 224.0.0.1).

"All Systems on This Subnet"

All multicast-capable end stations must "join" this group, but this joining is not an explicit process. Multicast-capable end stations must simply listen for multicasts with this destination, as if they had explicitly joined that group. In the same way, OSPF router implementations are written so that they use the multicast addresses 224.0.0.5 and 224.0.0.6 for certain operations. It is a requirement that they implicitly "join" these groups on each LAN interface for which OSPF is enabled.

No multicast routing infrastructure is required for this to work, since these packets must never be forwarded beyond the subnetwork onto which they were originally transmitted. Remember the rule that any packet destined to addresses within 224.0.0.0/24 must not be forwarded; they are treated as if their TTL was 1, regardless of whether it actually was.

Upon hearing the IGMPv2 Query, each group's hosts on the LAN must report their status, but there is a mechanism to help prevent an explosion of Report traffic. As discussed earlier regarding IGMPv1, each Report* for a group is sent to the group's class D

---

*Reports are sent with their TTL = 1 so that they cannot be forwarded beyond the LAN. This is a sort of safety net, because multicast routers are not supposed to forward packets destined for addresses within 224.0.0.0/24 regardless of the value of the TTL.

Additionally, all IGMPv2 messages are sent with the IP Router Alert option appended to the IP header (see the detailed packet headers in Appendix B, so the routers are sure to notice them for this reason as well. This IP option is designed to help routers take note of packets that need special processing. Since IGMP packets are addressed to a multicast address at the MAC layer and also at the IP layer, the router may not notice an IGMP packet if it is very busy with other tasks.

The "Router Alert" IP option, described further in the appendix on IGMP, is designed to ensure that the router notices the packet. In general, IP options take routers out of their highly optimized "quick path" forwarding code, thus making them examine the packet more closely (which is desirable in this case). If the router does not recognize this IP option, at least it had to carefully parse the packet to get to that point, so the IGMP parts of the packet are less likely to be missed than if the option was not present. If the router does recognize this option, the option just tells the router to pay attention to the contents of the packet.

The IP Router Alert option helps the router notice IGMP Reports. RSVP packets use this technique as well. (There is an IPv6 Router Alert hop-by-hop extension header as well, and it exists for the same reason.)

address. If other group members are present on the LAN, they will hear the Report of the first group member that successfully transmits its Report. Upon hearing that Report, they assume that the Querier has also heard the Report, so they suspend sending a Report at this time and reinitialize their random Report timers, ranging between 0 and the maximum Response Time in units of tenths of seconds.

Leaving a Group

The final component of the protocol concerns leaving a group. If an end station wishes to leave a group, it sends a "Leave Group" message. This message is sent to the "All Routers on This Subnet" class D address (224.0.0.2). Upon receiving such a message, the Querier is responsible for determining if this end station was the last group member or not. To do this, a series of Group-Specific Query messages is transmitted onto this LAN. The Querier expects that any remaining group members will send Host Membership Reports in response, according to the Report supression technique.

IGMPV2 AND IGMPV1 COEXISTENCE RULES

Rules for IGMPv2 End Stations

If an IGMPv2 end station hears another end station send an IGMPv1 Report for one of its member groups, it must allow this group's random Report generation timer to be reinitialized by either IGMPv1 Reports or IGMPv2 Reports.

IGMPv2 Host Membership Reports use a value of 6 (0110) in the Type field, while IGMPv1 uses a value of 2 (0010) in its Report messages. This is how IGMPv2 Reports may be distinguished from IGMPv1 Reports, which are depicted in Figure 5–2 from RFC-1112.

As you can see in the figure, which describes the header format of IGMPv1, the IGMPv2 field now used for establishing the maximum Response Time was "Unused" in IGMPv1. IGMPv1 end stations were expected to set this field to a value of zero when transmitting it, and to ignore any nonzero value in this field upon receiving IGMPv1 packets. In IGMPv1, all implementations understood the Maximum Response Time to be 10 seconds (this was hard-coded into the implementations).

IGMPv2 allows the Querier to set a smaller (or larger) Maximum Response Time. In IGMPv2, this feature allows the volume of IGMP traffic to be tuned on a per-subnetwork basis. An intranet manager could use this functionality to control how responsive IGMPv2 will be to changes in group membership. A smaller Maximum Response Time will allow IGMPv2 routers to more quickly establish that group members have departed; a longer Maximum Response Time will lessen the amount of IGMPv2 control traffic, at the expense of reducing IGMPv2's sensitivity to inactive groups. However, the default Maximum Response Time is still 10 seconds, indicated by a default value of 100 in the Query's Maximum Response Time field (0x64 in hex).

```
                         1                   2                   3
 0 1 2 3 4 5 6 7 8 9 0 1 2 3 4 5 6 7 8 9 0 1 2 3 4 5 6 7 8 9 0 1
+-+-+-+-+-+-+-+-+-+-+-+-+-+-+-+-+-+-+-+-+-+-+-+-+-+-+-+-+-+-+-+-+
|Version| Type  |    Unused |            Checksum               |
+-+-+-+-+-+-+-+-+-+-+-+-+-+-+-+-+-+-+-+-+-+-+-+-+-+-+-+-+-+-+-+-+
|                          Group Address                        |
+-+-+-+-+-+-+-+-+-+-+-+-+-+-+-+-+-+-+-+-+-+-+-+-+-+-+-+-+-+-+-+-+
```

Version

> This memo specifies version 1 of IGMP. Version 0 is specified
> in RFC-988 and is now obsolete.

Type

> There are two types of IGMP message of concern to hosts:
>
> 1 = Host Membership Query
> 2 = Host Membership Report

Unused

> Unused field, zeroed when sent, ignored when received.

Checksum

> The checksum is the 16-bit one's complement of the one's
> complement sum of the 8-octet IGMP message. For computing
> the checksum, the checksum field is zeroed.

FIGURE 5–2   IGMPv1 header format

An IGMPv2 end station may choose to omit sending Leave Group messages on a LAN which has an IGMPv1 Querier. Further details of IGMPv2's rules for coexistence with IGMPv1 follow.

Rules for Routers

IGMPv2 Routers in the Presence of IGMPv1 End Stations

If an IGMPv2-capable router hears an IGMPv1 Report for some group(s), the router must treat *these groups* on the attached LAN as if all their members spoke IGMPv1. At the same time, other groups on this LAN could be purely IGMPv2 speakers. The router is expected to treat groups appropriately depending on their IGMP version composition, even if a LAN has a mixture of IGMP versions present.

The router sets a timer applicable to each of the group(s) for which it has heard IGMPv1 Reports. If no IGMPv1 Reports are heard within IGMPv1's usual Group Membership Interval, the router may again operate as an IGMPv2 router on this LAN for these groups, if they are still active.

Since the router may be operating in IGMPv1 mode for selected groups on an interface, any Leave Group messages related to such groups must be ignored. In other words, no Group-Specific Queries may be sent for those groups which include IGMPv1 members. Again, an IGMPv2-capable router may be operating in IGMPv1 mode for one list of groups, and in IGMPv2 mode for another list of groups—on the same physical interface! The router must maintain state for each group on each interface so that it can remember which version of IGMP to use for each group.

IGMPv1 Routers in the Presence of IGMPv2 End Stations

IGMPv2 packets that are transmitted by hosts (Host Membership Report and Leave Group messages) are unrecognizable to IGMPv1 router implementations, and should be ignored by IGMPv1 routers. IGMPv1-compliant routers, therefore, should be unaffected by the presence of IGMPv2 end stations. Any IGMPv2 messages from end stations will be sent before the end station has learned that the Querier is running IGMPv1.

Once an IGMPv2-capable end station discovers that the Querier is speaking IGMPv1, it should revert to IGMPv1 operation.

An IGMPv1 Querier may be detected as follows:

- IGMPv2 end stations expect any [General] Query's Maximum Response Time field to contain some nonzero value between 1 and 100 (i.e., 0x01 through 0x64). IGMP Queriers set this field to zero because it is an Unused field in IGMPv1.
- IGMPv1 Query packets will lack the IP Router Alert option. All IGMPv2 packets use this IP option. See Appendix B for a discussion of IP options and IGMPv2's use of the IP Router Alert Option.

Mixing IGMPv1 and IGMPv2 Routers

In IGMPv1, each routing protocol was responsible for its own Querier election process. Since IGMPv2 elects a Querier itself, it is a requirement that IGMPv2 routers be configurable to operate in IGMPv1 mode.

If an IGMPv2-capable Querier receives either version 1 or version 2 Queries from another router, it must log these events. If an IGMPv2 Querier hears an IGMPv2 Query from a numerically lower IP address, it must relinquish Querier status. This is the IGMPv2 Querier election process.

Of course, if an IGMPv1 Querier receives an IGMPv1 Query from another router, it is definitely an error condition of which the intranet manager should be made aware. Presumably, IGMPv1 implementations would be written to identify this as an error scenario. Certainly, IGMPv2 implementations operating as IGMPv1 Queriers should be smart enough to recognize this.

Similarly, if an IGMPv2 router is not explicitly configured to operate as an IGMPv1 speaker, but hears an IGMPv1 Query, it must also log this event.

IGMP VERSION 3 (FUTURE)

IGMP version 3 is a preliminary work in progress that was originally published as draft-cain-igmp-00.txt; it has since expired, but work on this protocol is being resurrected in late Summer 1997. IGMP version 3 will introduce support for Group-Source Report messages so that an end station can elect to receive traffic only from specific sources sending to a multicast group.

An Inclusion Group-Source Report message allows an end station to specify the IP addresses of the specific sources from which it wants to receive traffic for this group. An Exclusion Group-Source Report message allows an end station to explicitly identify the sources from which it does *not* want to receive traffic for this group. Using IGMP versions 1 or 2, if an end station wanted to receive *any* traffic for a group, it must have received traffic from *all* the group's sources.

IGMP version 3 will help conserve bandwidth by allowing an end station to select the specific sources from which it wants to receive traffic. Troublesome hecklers within the session may be effectively silenced by tuning them out. Multicast routing protocols will be able to make more informed tree-building decisions using this information.

Finally, support for Leave Group messages first introduced in IGMPv2 will be enhanced to support Group-Source Leave messages. This feature allows an end station to leave an entire group or to specify the specific IP address(es) of the (source, group) pair(s) it wishes to leave. Note that at this time not all existing multicast routing protocols have mechanisms to support such requests from group members. This is one issue that will be addressed during the ongoing development of IGMP version 3.

IGMPv3 is still very early in its development, and it is difficult to predict what features will ultimately be included when it is completed. It is possible that it will operate very differently from the older versions of IGMP. For instance, discussions are currently evaluating whether to transmit IGMPv3 Reports to the All-Routers multicast address (224.0.0.2) instead of the class D address of the group being reported. Much debate, simulation, development, and implementation remains before IGMPv3 will be as mature as today's IGMPv2.

CHAPTER 6

INTRODUCTION TO MULTICAST ROUTING AND FORWARDING

Multicast routing protocols are used by multicast routers to discover delivery paths (trees) that enable the forwarding of multicast datagrams across an internetwork. Multicast forwarding is done based on information derived from multicast routing protocols.

Here are definitions of some multicast routing terms:

Multicast routing: Activities performed by IP routers in order to determine how to forward multicast IP packets, either from some particular source to a group, or from any source to a group.

Distribution tree: A set of routers and subnetworks that allows a group's member(s) to receive traffic from a source. Depending on the algorithm in use by the multicast routing protocol, the tree may be rooted at a source or at some central point in the network.

Upstream: For any router on each source's distribution tree, the direction known as "upstream" is the "best" direction from this router toward that source. Packets must never be forwarded back toward the tree's source, only away from it.

Downstream: On the other hand, for any router on a source's distribution tree, downstream is any direction that is not upstream. Downstream interfaces are the subset of all possible nonupstream interfaces that lead away from this tree's source to active receivers, which are reached via this router. (Any router that is on an active

branch of a multicast delivery tree will have one upstream interface and at least one downstream interface.)

Multicast forwarding: For each multicast IP packet received, a forwarding decision
must be made. Typically, each packet must arrive on a
specific upstream interface (i.e., incoming interface), and
then be copied onto a (set of) downstream "outgoing inter-
face(s)."

As with unicast IP routing, there are many choices for multicast routing protocols.
At the time of this writing, the following list of five multicast routing protocols are in
some stage of research, development, or deployment (in alphabetical order):

- Core-Based Trees (CBT)
  - Nearly ready for experimentation
- Distance-Vector Multicast Routing Protocol (DVMRP)
  - Deployed on the Internet's Multicast Backbone (MBone)
- Multicast Extensions to Open Shortest Path First (M-OSPF)
  - Standards track protocol that leverages OSPF
- Protocol-Independent Multicast—Dense Mode (PIM-DM)
  - Nearly ready for experimentation
- Protocol-Independent Multicast—Sparse Mode (PIM-SM)
  - Actively being deployed and experimented with

Of the protocols in the previous list, only DVMRP incorporates its own internal
"unicast" routing protocol. To be clear, the purpose of this unicast routing protocol in
DVMRP is to determine the best cost route to each source subnetwork. DVMRP uses
knowledge of the source subnetwork's location, relative to each router, to determine how
to forward packets; remember, packets must never be forwarded back toward the source,
to prevent loops from forming. A later chapter in the book will be devoted to a detailed
examination of DVMRP, including how the protocol evolved, how it works, and its scaling and deployment issues.

The Future of Multicast Routing over IPv6

---

*It is highly unlikely that there will ever be a version of DVMRP for IPv6. OSPF is
being defined for IPv6, and M-OSPF will work similarly to the way it does with
IPv4. PIM (either flavor) is easily modifiable to support IPv6, as is CBT, because
both CBT and PIM only require that there be a unicast IP routing table present in
the router.*

In the future, it is likely that more multicast routing protocols will be developed. In
particular, an interdomain hierarchical multicast protocol is essential to the future deployment of "native-mode" multicast forwarding in the Internet. In 1995, Steve Deering and

Ajit Thyagarajan proposed a protocol then called "Hierarchical DVMRP," or H-DVMRP. The precise approach taken in this proposal has been abandoned due to technical difficulties related to its scaling properties. However, the key attributes of H-DVMRP must be built into a future hierarchical multicast routing protocol. H-DVMRP has served to bring the issues to the forefront, despite there being no currently proposed protocol which incorporates all the desirable features of H-DVMRP in a workable specification.

At the time of this writing, there is extremely active work underway to specify a multicast routing protocol that can operate on the scale of the Internet. Some form of policy-based hierarchical routing is required for true Internet-scale operation; ideally, a two-level hierarchy in which intranets execute a multicast interior gateway protocol, and providers use a multicast exterior gateway protocol to facilitate routing at the ISP level. Whatever exterior multicast protocol(s) emerge from the standards process, are implemented in routers, and—most important—are deployed by ISPs will finally enable multicasting on a truly global scale.

Finally, although it is not really a "multicast routing protocol," there is one other protocol that is essential to the operation of multicast IP: the "Internet Group Management Protocol" (IGMP).

In some sense, IGMP is to multicast what ICMP (and ARP) is to unicast: IGMP is the protocol by which control messages pertaining to multicast IPv4 are transmitted. While ICMP mostly functions as an informational message and error-reporting protocol for unicast IP, IGMP is simply concerned with exchanging group-membership information between hosts and routers; it has no end-to-end error reporting component as ICMP does.

IPv6 note

The functions of ICMP, ARP, IGMP, and more (Router Discovery, Prefix Discovery, Parameter Discovery, Address Autoconfiguration, Next-hop determination, Neighbor Unreachability Detection, Duplicate Address Detection), are all folded into ICMPv6. There is no separate protocol known as IGMPv6.

MULTICAST ADDRESS ALLOCATION

How Are Class D Addresses Assigned?

There are two broad classes of group address assignment. By far, most addresses will be assigned dynamically. A few addresses are reserved for special functions and permanently assigned to certain functions.

Clearly, the Internet Assigned Numbers Authority (IANA) is the assignment mechanism for the few applications that are important enough or unique enough to require permanent assignments. By far, most class D addresses are available for use by transient groups, and thus are assigned and used dynamically. The Session Advertising Protocol (SAP) used in the MBone Session Directory tools (sd [SAP version 0] and sdr [SAP version 1]), allows extremely efficient dynamic allocation of group addresses within the unallocated portions of the class D address space.

The SAP itself reserves a block of multicast addresses for its own operation:

```
224.2.127.254    SAPv1 Announcements
224.2.127.255    SAPv0 Announcements (deprecated)
224.2.128.0/17   SAP Dynamic Assignments
```

The IETF Multiparty Multimedia Session Control (mmusic) working group has been working on issues pertinent to multicast address allocation since the early 1990s. The Session Announcement Protocol (SAP) and Session Description Protocol (SDP) are implemented in a program called `sdr`. Another possible method uses a web-based front end to allocate addresses for intranet conferences from an available pool of addresses. For integration with wide-area users, `sdr` data can be imported into the web server for access by web-based clients. It is also possible for a web-based client to create a global group which can then be advertised via SAP/SDP. Precept is one example of a company that sells such products.

Allocation of multicast addresses is an important function to which multicast applications must have access. The problem of multicast address assignment is at least a three-dimensional one: (1) How does one get an address? (2) How can you make sure the allocation is unique? (3) What is the policy for usage of allocated addresses? (e.g., How long can it be reserved? When can you start using it? What scope is associated with it? Is it part of a block of addresses?)

The method used by `sdr` is an adaptive method that uses educated guesses to efficiently grab unused addresses out of the available multicast address space. The "conventional wisdom" is that `sdr`'s technique depends on there being few active groups relative to the total number of available groups. In simulation, `sdr` has been able to work well until the address space was quite saturated.

There have also been proposals to use DHCP to allocate multicast addresses, which may or may not be standardized in the future. Also, for small numbers of users and sessions static assignment is possible, although this technique is clearly not scalable.

BRIEF OVERVIEW OF ROUTING TECHNIQUES

The primary means of classifying multicast routing protocols is by noticing how senders "meet" receivers. The basic job of a multicast routing protocol is to build a distribution tree so that traffic may be efficiently delivered to all the active receivers which are members of this group, from any source.

There are two common types: "broadcast and prune" and "shared trees." In multicast routing protocols that exist today, broadcast-and-prune-oriented protocols build source-based trees. It may not be much of a surprise that shared-tree protocols build shared trees. However, there is one protocol that builds source-based trees, but uses explicit-join mechanisms. Yet another protocol uses shared trees by default, but can have a delivery tree that incorporates both shared and source-based trees.

Broadcast and Prune

Broadcast-and-prune protocols make a key assumption: that the multicast data traffic itself is a convenient way to control the construction of the tree. Periodically, the data is reliably broadcast from the source to the extremities of the internetwork, effectively "testing the waters" in a search for active group members. Broadcast-and-prune protocols are also called "data-driven," since they use the data itself to control the building of the tree.

Forwarding State and Multicast Flows

Forwarding state at the network layer for multicast flows is often identified by the flow's source along with the group to which traffic is addressed. A shorthand notation for these flows is a (source, group) pair. It is possible for protocols to have forwarding state based only on the destination group.

In broadcast-and-prune protocols, the first packet for a "new" multicast data flow is broadcast to the edges of the internetwork (see Figure 6–1). At the internetwork's extremities, the edge routers consult their IGMP-derived local group databases. If there are no local members of this group, the router may remove itself from the delivery tree by sending messages upstream. In an analogy to the maintenance of real live trees, the router is said to have "pruned" itself from the branch (see Figure 6–2). The idea is to ultimately have the tree only include branches that lead to active group members, as shown in Figure 6–3. Such branches are called "active branches." The process of pruning continues upstream (toward the source), thereby removing this inactive branch from the delivery tree.

In order to keep prunes from building up in router memory forever, the prune lifetime is kept relatively short (typically on the order of minutes to hours). Once the prunes expire, any traffic for multicast flows that have no prune state is rebroadcast to the edges of the internetwork. If the flow has ceased within the last prune lifetime, no further packets for this flow will be seen, and thus no further "prune state" will need to be created in the routers.

FIGURE 6–1 Broadcasting procedure

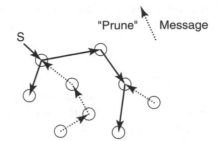

FIGURE 6–2   "Prune" messages travel upstream

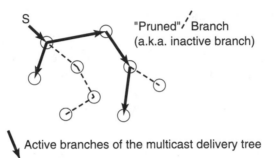

Active branches of the multicast delivery tree

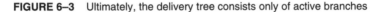

FIGURE 6–3   Ultimately, the delivery tree consists only of active branches

Examples of Broadcast-and-Prune Multicast Routing Protocols

As we will see later, the Distance Vector Multicast Routing Protocol (DVMRP) and Protocol-Independent Multicast—Dense Mode (PIM-DM) are data driven, using the data to probe the edges of the network for active receivers. Edge routers with no receivers then prune their branch of the distribution tree hop by hop upstream, until the nearest active branch of the tree is reached.

Clearly, DVMRP and PIM-DM routers are either on the distribution tree for a multicast flow or not. If they are on the tree, they have a forwarding cache entry for this (source, group) pair, which lists the expected incoming interface for packets from this source and the required outgoing interface(s) onto which packets must be copied in order to reach group members that are known to be active. Routers that are not on the tree must have prune state. As the number of active sources and groups increases, the demands for storage of state information increases for all routers in the internetwork.

The broadcast-and-prune technique's key disadvantage is that it is designed to waste bandwidth when periodically broadcasting traffic to the edges of the internetwork. Also, off-tree routers are required to store "prune state." Ideally, an off-tree router should not have to know anything about a (source, group) pair. Despite these two disadvantages (wasted bandwidth due to the broadcasting procedure and excess "prune state" in off-tree routers), data-driven protocols can work acceptably well in some smaller environments.

First, there must be enough available bandwidth (good deployment scenarios are campus LANs and MANs) to support the broadcasting procedure. Of course, this is relative. If there are a few groups with high-bandwidth streams, the broadcasting procedure could be a real drain on the internetwork's available bandwidth. Even if the average per-group bandwidth is small relative to the common link speeds in this network, if there are a large number of these groups, the bandwidth consumed by the broadcasting procedure could still be excessive. Another disadvantage of having large numbers of groups is that the prune state in off-tree routers increases as the number of sources and groups increases.

Second, the group members should be relatively densely distributed. This does not necessarily mean that there are a lot of group members, just that it is likely that a significant fraction of the edge LANs will have group members. In this case, a high percentage of the routers will be on the delivery trees, so overhead due to carrying "prune state" will be minimized. Also, assuming a dense distribution of receivers implies that the broadcasting technique will often reach edge routers with attached group members.

Shared Trees

Another class of protocols uses shared trees, which have a central point to which all receivers attach. All traffic destined for the group emanates from this central point. The key difference between the data-driven broadcast-and-prune protocols and shared tree protocols is that shared trees must be joined prior to the flow of data; otherwise, the central point knows of no downstream receivers, and data stops there.

Join Styles

In this respect, these protocols not only employ shared trees, but they are also **explicit-join** *protocols. If the center of the tree observes that no one has joined the tree for a group, it concludes that no one must want this traffic.*

By default, a broadcast-and-prune protocol can deliver packets to the entire internetwork—at the expense of the bandwidth consumed by the broadcasting process. In contrast, if a shared tree has not been set up for a group in advance, no traffic flows.

You may want to think of broadcast-and-prune protocols as "implicit-join," since they assume that everyone wants the traffic for every group, and expect others to drop off the tree.

Among the protocols we have briefly touched on so far, there has been a pattern. The implicit-join protocols have constructed source-based trees, while the explicit-join protocols have employed shared trees. There is a protocol that uses source-based trees, but is not an implicit-join protocol: the Multicast extensions to Open Shortest Path First (MOSPF). MOSPF is an explicit-join protocol that builds source-based trees. Figure 6–4 is a matrix of tree and join styles.

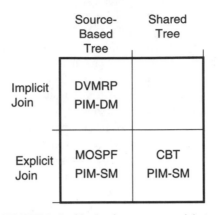

FIGURE 6–4   Matrix of tree types vs. join types

Shared trees are not data driven, as are the source-based trees built by broadcast-and-prune multicast routing protocols. Shared tree protocols use the concept of a group-specific "center" that distributes traffic sent to (preregistered) group members. Inside a shared tree routing domain, it is possible that there is only one center serving all the groups, or there may be multiple centers, each in use by a different set of groups. However, each group receives its traffic over the same delivery tree, regardless of the source.

Unlike broadcast-and-prune algorithms, which build a separate tree from each source to their target group(s), shared tree algorithms construct a single delivery tree that is shared by all members of a group.

Shared versus Source-Based Trees

A tree is shared in the following sense: From the center to the routers serving active group members, the tree is essentially fixed (only dynamic changes in group membership or unicast routing topology changes affect its shape). Each source must find a way to reach the center. The sources rely on the center to deliver their packets to all the active receivers. In this sense, all sources share the same delivery tree (from center to receivers), although all the sources probably took very different paths to reach the center (see Figure 6–5).

In contrast, the source-based tree protocols build separate trees for each source to all the group members. Thus, each source has its own tree to reach the active group members. These source-based trees are often called "shortest-path trees."

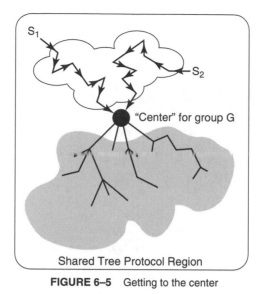

FIGURE 6–5   Getting to the center

Shared Tree Operation and Benefits

A shared tree involves a single router, which is the "root" of a multicast delivery tree.

Similar to other multicast forwarding algorithms, shared tree algorithms do not require that the source of a multicast packet be a member of a destination group in order to send to a group.

In terms of scalability, shared tree techniques have several advantages over source-based trees. Shared tree algorithms make efficient use of router resources since they only require a router to maintain state information for each group, not for each source or each (source, group) pair. Remember that source-based tree techniques require all routers in an

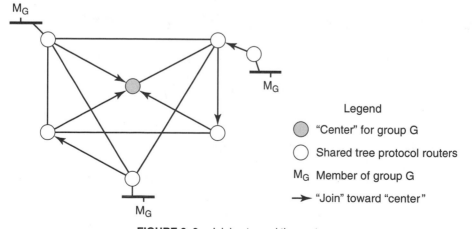

FIGURE 6–6   Joining toward the center

internetwork to either (1) be on the delivery tree for a given source or (source, group) pair, or (2) have prune state for that source or (source, group) pair. Thus, the entire internetwork must participate in the source-based tree protocol. Using a shared tree that is explicitly joined improves the scalability of applications with many active senders since the number of source stations is no longer a scaling issue. Also, shared tree algorithms conserve network bandwidth since they do not require that multicast packets be periodically broadcast across all multicast routers in the internetwork. This can offer significant bandwidth savings, especially across low-bandwidth WAN links or when receivers sparsely populate the domain of operation, or even in resource-rich campus environments with more than a few medium- to high-bandwidth streams. Because receivers are required to explicitly join the shared delivery tree, data only ever flows over links leading to active receivers.

Limitations of Shared Trees

Despite these benefits, there are still several limitations to protocols based on a shared tree algorithm. Shared trees may result in traffic concentration and bottlenecks near the center since traffic from all sources traverses the same set of links as it approaches the center. Shared trees may not be perfectly optimal compared to source-based trees, which are shortest-path trees from the source to the group's receivers. In simulations, some test cases had about 10 percent worse latency than a comparable shortest-path tree. In many cases, this difference in latency may be unimportant, but if an application requires very low latency it may require either careful placement of the center router or use of a different multicast routing protocol.

Finally, expanding-ring searches probably will not work as expected inside shared tree domains. The searching host's increasing TTL will cause the packets to work their way up the shared tree, and while a desired resource may still be found, it may not be as topologically close as one would expect. A later chapter will examine expanding-ring searches in more detail.

MULTICAST FORWARDING VERSUS MULTICAST ROUTING

While multicast routing protocols establish or help establish the distribution tree for a given group, thus enabling multicast forwarding of packets addressed to the group, multicast forwarding is the act of using the information derived from the multicast routing protocols to determine how to forward any given multicast packet.

Unicast versus Multicast Forwarding

In the case of unicast, routing protocols are also used to build a forwarding table which is commonly (confusingly?) called the routing table. Unicast destination networks in the routing table are associated with some metric (e.g., hops, cost) and a next-hop router toward the destination.

Multicast routing protocols use the same sort of routing table data in the opposite sense. Rather than looking for next hops to a destination, they interpret the data as "previous hops" from a source. In other words, the unicast routing table is interpreted as listing "go-to" information, and the multicast routing table is interpreted as listing "comes-from" information.

The key difference between unicast forwarding and multicast forwarding is that unicast routing protocols facilitate the forwarding of packets *toward* a destination, while multicast packets must be forwarded *away from their source.* If a packet is ever forwarded back toward its source, a forwarding loop could be formed, possibly leading to a multicast "storm."

In the scenario depicted in Figure 6–7, two loops have formed. As a packet arrives from the source, it is forwarded downstream. In the course of being forwarded, two copies are returned to the beginning of the loops. Then each of the two copies goes through the process again, and now there are two copies of each of those two copies. Now four copies reenter the loops, yielding eight copies, and so on. Note that after each pass some of the copies leak downstream, and this extra traffic just increases. The only thing that eventually stops the loop is the fact that the looping packets' TTL is gradually being decremented. The left loop decrements the TTL by 5 on each pass, the right loop by 4.

Multicast Forwarding Procedure

Once a tree has been constructed for a group by a multicast routing protocol, each router knows at most these two facts about a group's delivery tree (see Figure 6–8):

- The incoming interface (a.k.a. "iif") on which packets from each source will arrive
- Which outgoing interfaces (a.k.a. "oiflist") onto which packets must be copied in order to reach active group members

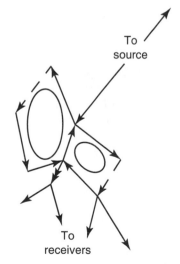

FIGURE 6–7   Multicast forwarding loop(s)

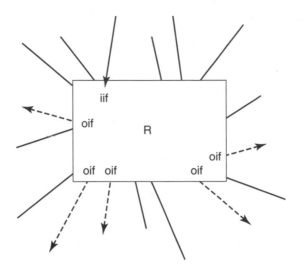

FIGURE 6–8   Multicast forwarding state inside a router

Not all multicast routing protocols keep source-specific state. All do follow the rule that traffic is forwarded away from the source. Again, this is called the "downstream" direction.

The multicast routing table and multicast forwarding table are two different tables. Most multicast routing protocols don't build a separate routing table, they just use whatever unicast routing table exists. That is sufficient to find the way toward the source. The multicast routing table is used to help build the multicast forwarding table, along with control messages that are particular to each protocol.

Multicast Routing Protocols: Scalability and Routing Policy Issues

It is thought that protocols which keep forwarding state only for groups are probably the most scalable. To see why, one first assumes that multicast will be ubiquitously deployed on the Internet someday (the largest possible scale...). In this scenario, there will likely be lots of small groups with lots of sources (family videoconferences, interactive games, etc.). If routing protocols must not only keep track of forwarding information for all groups, already a lot of state, but for each group must also track all of its sources as well, the memory requirements within routers may be excessive under those protocols. Given that we are still in the early deployment phase of multicast, it is rather difficult to imagine the exact operational stresses to which a future multicast-enabled Internet will be subjected.

The research community has thus far created a number of multicast routing protocols, each of which may be applicable in different scenarios; however, no "one-size-fits-all" multicast routing protocol has yet been invented. One feature notably absent from multicast protocols developed so far is any mechanism to express—and enforce—multicast routing and forwarding policies among peer Internet service providers.

In the unicast world, the policies between peers are a direct representation of the business arrangements they have made with each other. Also, their policies reflect their own technical requirements to ensure that they control the routing of packets in a way which makes sense for their infrastructure. The lack of policy control mechanisms is one big reason that multicast routing in the Internet has not yet caught on: providers feel that the existing protocols are inadequate for widespread deployment. Current multicast routing protocols don't have sufficient handles to allow them to control the routing and forwarding of multicast traffic.

However, the providers' requirements are very different than those of intranet managers. The existing protocols are usable within intranets to deploy multicast services that can benefit intranet users today.

PART **III**

INTRANET MULTICAST ROUTING TODAY

Three multicast routing protocols are available today in many vendors' hardware: the DVMRP, MOSPF, and PIM. To differing degrees, these protocols have been rather widely deployed already and have had bugs found and design improvements made. Intranet managers can safely assume that all the fundamental bugs in these protocols have been or are being worked out.

There are other multicast routing protocols that are also available today, but have not been tested as extensively due to the simple fact that they are much newer and haven't had the time to acquire real-world experience yet. This will change gradually, as more vendors support a wider list of multicast routing protocols and more intranet managers deploy them, giving vendors feedback on any difficulties encountered. Also, any industry interoperability testing will help improve the production quality of many vendors' implementations. The following multicast routing protocols' designs are suited to deployment on intranets, however.

CHAPTER 7

EVOLUTION OF REVERSE-PATH MULTICASTING (RPM)

Reverse-path multicasting is a forwarding technique around which several multicast routing protocols have been built. It is instructive to examine the evolution and operation of this algorithm not only because it, or variants of it, have been incorporated into real-world protocols, but also because the ideas embodied in this algorithm are useful background when examining other mechanisms employed by multicast routing protocols. Before examining RPM in detail we briefly look at a trivial multicast "routing" protocol: flooding.

FLOODING

Multicast extensions to various protocols were suggested by Deering in his Ph.D. thesis. Flooding is one algorithm that can be used to build an unsophisticated multicast routing protocol. Flooding is primitive in that it tends to either waste bandwidth or require a large amount of computational resources within the multicast routers involved. This technique may work only in small networks with very few senders, groups, or routers, and does not scale well to larger numbers of senders, groups, or routers.

Conceptually, a flooding algorithm is one of the simplest techniques one can envision for delivering multicast datagrams to all routers (and thus all potential receivers) in an internetwork. The flooding procedure begins when any router receives a packet that is addressed to a multicast group (really, *any* multicast group; they are all treated the same by the flooding algorithm).

Each router employs a protocol mechanism to determine whether or not it has seen this particular packet before. For example, it could record—for every multicast packet— the source, destination, and a message digest of the packet, or some other set of data that would enable it to uniquely identify every packet it has seen "recently." If this is the first reception of the packet, it is forwarded on all interfaces except the one on which it arrived. This guarantees that every multicast packet will reach all routers in the internetwork.

Looping is prevented by discarding packets the router has seen before. Without this loop avoidance mechanism, any loops in the topology would lead to geometrically increasing multicast storms. (All multicast routing algorithms must have some mechanism to prevent loops from forming.)

A flooding algorithm is very simple to implement since a router does not have to maintain a routing table and only needs to keep track of the most recently seen packets. However, flooding does not scale for Internet-wide (or even intranet-wide) applications since it generates a large number of duplicate packets and uses all available paths across the internetwork instead of just a limited number. Also, any flooding-based protocols would make inefficient use of router memory resources since each router is required to maintain distinct table entries for all "recent" packets. It would be difficult to estimate the number of recent packets to remember. Certainly, a router with faster interfaces would need to have a longer table.

REVERSE-PATH BROADCASTING (RPB)

Reverse-path broadcasting has a long history. In the late 1970s, there was interest in developing a network-layer broadcast service. The RPB technique was used as the starting point for the development of reverse-path multicasting. One can view RPM as a refinement of RPB. As we said earlier, multicasting is selective while broadcasting is indiscriminate about who shall receive packets.

Reverse-Path Broadcasting: Operation

The fundamental algorithm to construct these source-based trees is RPB, which was first described by Dalal and Metcalfe in 1978. The RPB algorithm is actually quite simple. For each source, if a packet arrives on a link that the local router believes to be on the shortest path back toward the packet's source, then the router forwards the packet on all interfaces except the incoming interface. If the packet does not arrive on the interface that is on the shortest path back toward the source, then the packet is discarded. The interface over which the router expects to receive multicast packets from a particular source is referred to as the "parent" link. The outbound links over which the router forwards the multicast packet are called "child" links for this source.

This basic algorithm can be enhanced to reduce packet duplication. The enhancement requires each router to determine whether a neighboring router on a potential child link is "downstream." In plain RPB, all nonparent links are child links. In this enhancement to RPB, only those links that have downstream neighbors are considered child links. A given router "D" is "downstream" of some other router "U," if router "D" sees router

"U" as being on the shortest path back toward some source. You should observe that an interface may not be a child interface for packets from every source.

If a link does, in fact, have a downstream neighbor, the packet is multicast across this child interface; otherwise, the packet is not forwarded on this nonparent link. The packet need not be forwarded because the neighboring router will just discard the packet; it will have arrived on a nonparent link for the source. Figure 7–1 illustrates the RPB forwarding algorithm.

In order to make this downstream decision, a routing protocol must be used. Each router needs to know "how far" it is from each packet's source. The information to make this "downstream" decision is relatively easy to derive from a link-state routing protocol, since each router maintains a topology database for the entire routing domain. If a distance-vector routing protocol is employed, there are at least two possible ways to convey the information necessary to make this decision. One method would be for every router to advertise its previous hop for each source subnetwork as part of its routing update messages. Another method would be for a router to "poison reverse" the source subnetwork's route on each source's parent interface. Either of these techniques enables a router to determine if one of its child interfaces is some other router's parent interface back toward this source.

Please refer to Figure 7–2 as we describe the basic operation of the enhanced RPB algorithm.

Note that the source station (S) is attached to a leaf subnetwork directly connected to router A. For this example, we will look at the RPB algorithm from router B's perspective. Router B receives the multicast packet from router A on link 1. Since router B considers link 1 to be the parent link for the source, it forwards the packet on link 4, link 5,

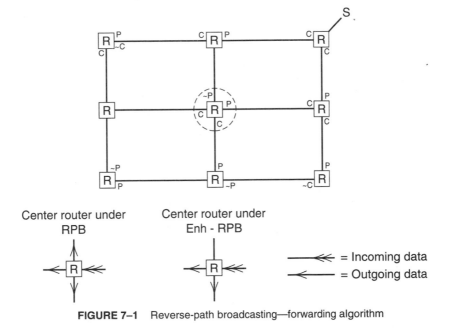

FIGURE 7–1   Reverse-path broadcasting—forwarding algorithm

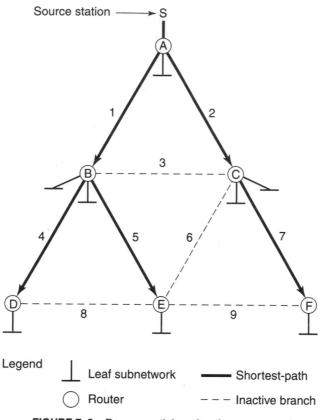

FIGURE 7–2   Reverse-path broadcasting—an example

and the local leaf subnetworks if they contain group members. (Before we use the term anymore, a leaf subnetwork is attached to only one router; thus, no neighboring routers could be attached.) Router B does not forward the packet on link 3 because it knows from routing protocol exchanges that Router C considers link 2 its parent link for the source's subnetwork.

This may seem somewhat obvious by examination. To reach this source's subnetwork, router C needs to choose between crossing two intermediate routers to reach the source (router B, then router A), or simply using link 2, a direct connection to router A from router C. A distance-vector protocol would always choose the direct path (one hop to the source's subnetwork) over a path with more than one hop, assuming hop count was the only metric in use.

However, if a link-state protocol is in use, it is definitely possible that the path cost for C_B_A could be less than the cost of C_A. Consider a scenario in which the link C_A is a 56 kbps leased line, but the links C_B and B_A are both 10 Mbps

> *Ethernets. Even though the costs for C_B and B_A are added together, their com-*
> *bined cost could still be far less than the cost for C_A. In this case, the path with*
> *more router hops is actually "cheaper."*

Router B knows that if it were to forward the packet across link 3 it would be discarded by router C—the packet would not be arriving on router C's parent link for this source. This means that, as far as router B is concerned, link 3 is not a child interface since it has no downstream neighbors.

RPB: Benefits and Limitations

The key benefit to reverse-path broadcasting is that it is reasonably efficient and easy to implement. It does not require that the router know about the source's entire spanning tree; nor does it require a special mechanism to stop the forwarding process (as flooding does). In addition, it guarantees efficient delivery since multicast packets always follow the "shortest" path from the source station to the destination group. Finally, the packets are distributed over multiple links, resulting in better overall network utilization since a different tree will be computed for each source.

Because the RPB algorithm is creating a broadcast delivery service, it does not take into account (multicast) group membership when forwarding packets from a source. RPB is designed to ensure that all subnetworks will receive traffic from any source. As a result, broadcast datagrams are almost certain to be forwarded onto subnetworks that have no interested receivers. Just as undesirably, the datagrams will consume bandwidth across links leading to these uninterested receivers.

Further enhancements to RPB were needed to better suit it for use as a multicast routing protocol. A multicast service should be more cognizant of where receivers actually are, so that traffic is only sent along links leading to them. Truncated RPB does not meet this goal completely. It only uses group membership information to decide whether or not to forward traffic onto a leaf subnetwork.

TRUNCATED RPB (TRPB)

Truncated reverse-path broadcasting (TRPB) was developed to overcome one of the limitations of RPB. Using group membership information provided by IGMP, multicast routers can determine whether or not to forward datagrams onto a leaf subnetwork. If a leaf subnetwork does not contain at least one member of a given destination group, then no traffic for this group is forwarded onto the LAN. Thus, the delivery tree is "truncated" by the router if a leaf subnetwork has no group members.

Figure 7–3 illustrates the operation of the TRPB algorithm. In this example the router receives a multicast packet on its parent link for the Source. The router forwards the datagram on interface 1 since that interface has at least one member of G1. The router

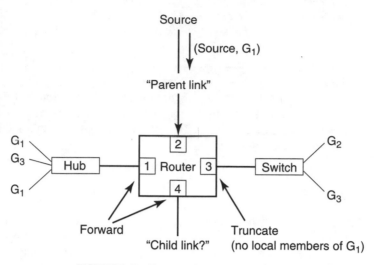

FIGURE 7–3   Truncated reverse-path broadcasting

does not forward the datagram to interface 3 since this interface has no members of G1. The datagram is forwarded on interface 4 if and only if some neighbor router considers this subnetwork to be its "parent link" for this source.

TRPB solves only part of the problem. It eliminates unnecessary traffic on leaf sub-networks, but it does not consider group memberships when building the branches of the delivery tree. If we could determine a way to keep traffic from flowing all the way to a leaf subnetwork's router, we would save even more bandwidth.

REVERSE-PATH MULTICASTING

Reverse-path multicasting (RPM) is an enhancement to RPB and TRPB.
RPM creates a delivery tree that includes only:

- Subnetworks with group members
- Routers and subnetworks along the shortest path from the source to each of these subnetworks with group members

RPM allows the source-based "shortest-path tree" to be "pruned" so that datagrams are only forwarded along branches that lead to active members of a destination group. As we will see, the RPM algorithm is effectively bootstrapped by RPB, which provides for the broadcasting of data to the edges of the network. Some people refer to this broadcasting process as "flooding," but flooding is not exactly what is going on. It is better to use the term broadcasting, since it is more accurate.

Operation

When a multicast router receives a packet for a (source, group) pair, the first packet is forwarded following the TRPB algorithm across all routers in the internetwork. Routers on the edge of the network (which have only leaf subnetworks) are called leaf routers. The TRPB algorithm guarantees that each leaf router will receive at least the first multicast packet. The leaf router will transmit the packet onto those subnetworks which have at least one group member (see Figure 7–4).

If none of the leaf router's subnetworks contain members of this group, the leaf router may inform the upstream router. This information tells the upstream router to not forward packets from this particular source to this particular group toward this leaf router. A shorthand notation for representing traffic to a group from some source is "(source, group) pair." This process is called "pruning." RPM's prune messages are sent just one hop back toward the source. An upstream router receiving a prune message is required to store the prune information in memory for a time.

Under what circumstances may the upstream router send its own prune message even further upstream? First, just as with the leaf router, the upstream router must have no recipients on local leaf subnetworks. Since it has interfaces with other routers attached, it

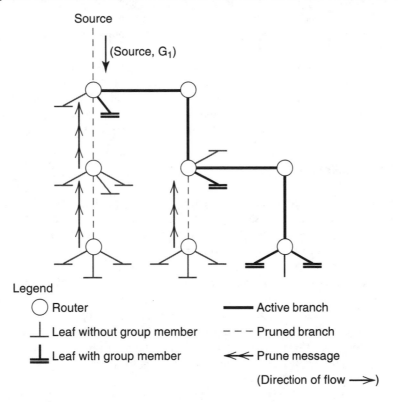

Source

$(Source, G_1)$

Legend

◯ Router

⊥ Leaf without group member

⊥ Leaf with group member

▬▬▬ Active branch

– – – Pruned branch

≪ Prune message

(Direction of flow ⟶)

FIGURE 7–4   Reverse-path multicasting

must also have received prune messages from each downstream neighbor on each of the child interfaces for this source. If both of these conditions are true, then the upstream router does not need to receive additional packets for the (source, group) pair. Therefore, the upstream router itself can generate a prune message, traveling one hop further back toward the source. This cascade of prune messages results in an active multicast delivery tree, consisting exclusively of "live" branches (i.e., branches that lead to active receivers).

As indicated earlier, prune information is only held for a certain lifetime. As each prune message expires, routers purge it from their memory. If this source is still sending to this group, then the next packet for the (source, group) pair is broadcast across all downstream routers. This allows "stale state" (prune state for groups that are no longer active) to be reclaimed by the multicast routers.

Grafting

What happens if a prune has been sent upstream, indicating that no receivers for this group are present along some branch, and then later a member of this group appears? The router immediately adjacent to the new group member remembers that it has sent a prune related to this group, and it knows the previous-hop router for the source. The router sends a graft message upstream, one hop back toward the source, as it deletes its own prune information.

This process continues until an active branch of this (source, group) pair's delivery tree is reached. This formerly inactive branch is now added to this (source, group) pair's delivery tree, and data flows toward the new group member. Figure 7–5 illustrates the RPM grafting process. Each graft message is sent reliably, so a downstream router can be sure that its previous hop (toward this particular source) has received it.

RPM's Limitations

Despite the improvements offered by the RPM algorithm, there are still several scaling issues that need to be addressed when attempting to develop an Internet-wide (or even a large-scale) multicast delivery service. The first limitation is that multicast packets must periodically be broadcast across every router in the internetwork. This is wasteful of bandwidth (until the updated prune state is constructed).

This "broadcast and prune" paradigm is very powerful, but it wastes bandwidth and does not scale well, especially if there are receivers at the edge of the delivery tree which are connected via low-speed technologies (e.g., dialup ISDN [Integrated Services Digital Network] or modem, or low-speed leased lines, such as 56 kbps). Remember that data for *every* active group is periodically broadcast; if there are many groups, or if any of the groups use a relatively large amount of bandwidth, the broadcasting will have a larger impact on the internetwork.

Also, note that every router participating in the RPM algorithm must either have a forwarding table entry for a (source, group) pair or have prune state information for that

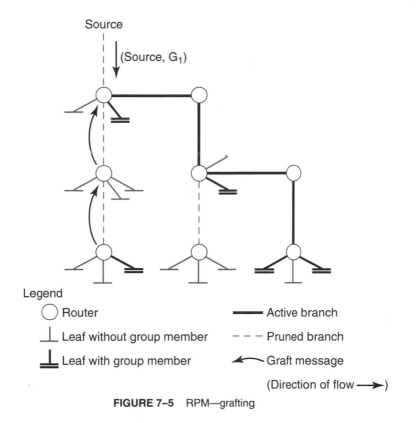

FIGURE 7–5 RPM—grafting

(source, group) pair. As the number of active sources and groups increases, it is clearly wasteful to place such a burden on routers that are not on every (or perhaps any) active delivery tree. Shared tree techniques are an attempt to address these scaling issues, which become quite acute when most groups' senders and receivers are sparsely distributed across the internetwork. By sparse, we do not necessarily mean that a group has few members, rather that a group's consituent subnetworks are widely scattered across the internetwork.

Two multicast routing protocols have been developed using RPM. The first, which will be discussed next, is the Distance-Vector Multicast Routing Protocol (DVMRP). Later, we will discuss Protocol-Independent Multicast—Dense Mode (PIM-DM), which is also based on RPM.

CHAPTER 8

DISTANCE-VECTOR MULTICAST ROUTING PROTOCOL

The Distance-Vector Multicast Routing Protocol (DVMRP) is a distance-vector routing protocol designed to support the forwarding of multicast datagrams through an internetwork. DVMRP constructs source-based multicast delivery trees using the reverse-path multicasting (RPM) algorithm. Originally, the entire MBone ran only the DVMRP. Today, the DVMRP is still the MBone's core routing protocol.

The DVMRP was first defined in RFC-1075. The original specification was derived from the Routing Information Protocol (RIP) and employed the truncated reverse-path broadcasting (TRPB) technique. The major difference between RIP and the DVMRP is that RIP calculates the next hop toward a destination, while the DVMRP computes the previous hop back toward a source. Since mrouted 3.0, the DVMRP has employed the RPM algorithm. Thus, the latest implementations of the DVMRP are quite different from the original RFC specification in many regards. There is an active effort within the Internet Engineering Task Force's (IETF's) Inter-Domain Multicast Routing (IDMR) working group to completely document version 3 of the DVMRP.

The current DVMRP v3 internet-draft, representing a snapshot of this work-in-progress, is available from the internet-drafts shadow directory near you, as `draft-ietf-idmr-dvmrp-v3-05.txt`, or `draft-ietf-idmr-dvmrp-v3-05.ps`.

PHYSICAL AND TUNNEL INTERFACES

The interfaces of a DVMRP router may be either a physical interface to a directly attached subnetwork or a tunnel interface to another multicast-capable island. All interfaces are configured with a metric specifying cost for the given interface, and a TTL threshold that limits the scope of a multicast transmission (packets must have a TTL larger than the interface's TTL threshold in order to be forwarded across the interface). In addition, each tunnel interface must be explicitly configured with two additional parameters: the IP address of the local router's tunnel interface and the IP address of the remote router's interface.

A multicast router will only forward a multicast datagram across an interface if the TTL field in the IP header is greater than the TTL threshold assigned to the interface. Figure 8–1 lists the conventional TTL values that are used to restrict the scope of an IP multicast packet. By this convention, a multicast datagram with a TTL of less than 16 is restricted to the same site and should not be forwarded across an interface to other sites in the same region. These numbers are recommendations, and you are free to define your own values and meanings within your intranet, as long as you are careful to ensure that packets with a TTL large enough to leave your intranet are supposed to be able to do so!

TTL-based scoping is not always sufficient for all applications. Conflicts arise when trying to simultaneously enforce limits on topology, geography, and bandwidth. In particular, TTL-based scoping cannot handle overlapping regions, which is a necessary characteristic of administrative regions.

Another problem with TTL thresholds on multicast router interfaces is that they interfere with RPM's broadcasting mechanism, which affects both the DVMRP and PIM-DM (to be discussed in the next chapter). Ideally, if a packet has a certain starting TTL in its header, RPM's broadcasting procedure should carry the packet away from its source to all subnetworks within a hop-count radius defined by the packet's original TTL. If a packet cannot cross some router interface's TTL threshold, the packet cannot reach all the leaf subnetworks within the radius of the packet's original header TTL. Due to this artificial limit, the multicast tree cannot be built across a TTL threshold—unless the packet's TTL is large enough to cross the threshold. In this way, TTL limits can adversely impact the effectiveness of expanding-ring searches.

Despite problems with TTL scoping, scoping is still a desirable feature to have within the multicast routing infrastructure. Managers of enterprise networks and other private intranetworks need tools to help them control where their multicasts go. Since scoping is desirable, researchers were motivated to develop a better system than purely using TTLs. As a result of this effort, "administrative" scoping was created in 1994, to provide a way to do scoping based on multicast address. Certain addresses would be usable within

TTL	Scope threshold
0	Restricted to the same host
1	Restricted to the same subnetwork
15	Restricted to the same site
63	Restricted to the same region
127	Worldwide
191	Worldwide; limited bandwidth
255	Unrestricted in scope

FIGURE 8–1   TTL scope control values

a given administrative scope (e.g., an enterprise internetwork, or part of one) but would not be forwarded onto the global MBone. This allows for privacy and address reuse within the class D address space. The range from 239.0.0.0 to 239.255.255.255 has been reserved for administrative scoping.

> **IPv6 Note**
>
> IPv6 supports administrative scoping quite naturally, since part of the multicast (destination) address includes a field defining the forwarding scope for this address. In short, scoping is an internal attribute of an IPv6 multicast address. Interestingly, in this scheme addresses that differ only in their scopes are *actually different addresses*, and must be joined separately, if desired.
>
> Contrast this with IPv4, in which the addresses have no inherent scope meaning. For a given IPv4 multicast address, its scope is determined by the router configurations across which the packet is forwarded; thus, the IPv4 multicast scope is an external attribute.

Administrative scoping has been in limited use since 1994 or so, but has yet to be widely deployed. The IETF MBoneD working group is working to encourage the deployment of administrative scoping. For additional information, please see `draft-ietf-mboned-admin-ip-space-01.txt` or the successor to this work in progress, "Administratively Scoped IP Multicast."

BASIC OPERATION

The DVMRP implements the RPM algorithm. According to RPM, the first datagram for any (source, group) pair is broadcast across the entire internetwork (provided the packet's TTL and router interface thresholds permit this). Upon receiving this traffic, leaf routers will transmit prune messages back toward the source if there are no group members on their directly attached leaf subnetworks. The prune messages remove the branches that do not lead to group members, leaving a source-based shortest path tree.

After a period of time, the prune state for each (source, group) pair expires to reclaim stale prune state, left over from (source, group) pairs that are no longer in use. If those groups are actually still active, a subsequent datagram for the (source, group) pair will be broadcast across all downstream routers. The broadcast happens because there is no longer any prune state to prevent this! This broadcasting will result in a new set of prune messages, serving to regenerate the source-based shortest path tree for this (source, group) pair. In implementations of the DVMRP prior to `mrouted-3.9`, prune messages are not reliably transmitted, so the prune lifetime must be kept short to compensate for the possibility of lost prune messages.

The DVMRP also implements RPM's mechanism to quickly "graft" back a previously pruned branch of a group's delivery tree. If a router that has sent a prune message for a source discovers new group members on a leaf network, it sends a graft message to the previous-hop router for this source. When an upstream router receives a graft message, it cancels out the previously received prune message. Graft messages cascade (reliably) hop by hop back toward the source until they reach the nearest "live" branch point on the delivery tree. In this way, previously pruned branches are quickly restored to a given delivery tree.

DVMRP ROUTER FUNCTIONS

In Figure 8–2, router C is downstream and may potentially receive datagrams from the source subnetwork from router A or router B. If router A's metric to the source subnetwork is less than router B's metric, router A is dominant over router B for this source.

    This means that router A will forward any traffic from the source subnetwork and router B will discard traffic received from that source. However, if router A's metric is equal to router B's metric, the router with the lower IP address on its downstream interface (child link) becomes the dominant router for this source. Note that on a subnetwork with multiple routers forwarding to groups with multiple sources, different routers may be dominant for different sources, depending on which router is closest to each active source subnetwork.

DVMRP ROUTING TABLE

The DVMRP process periodically exchanges routing table updates with its DVMRP neighbors. These updates are independent of those generated by any unicast Interior Gateway Protocol.

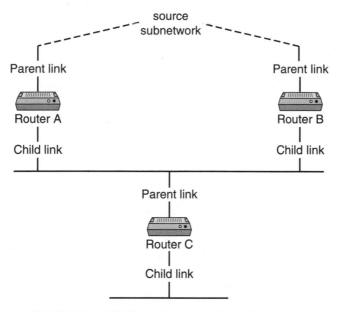

FIGURE 8–2 DVMRP dominant router in a redundant topology

Since the DVMRP was developed to route multicast and not unicast traffic, a router will probably run multiple routing processes, at least one to support the forwarding of unicast traffic and another to support the forwarding of multicast traffic. (This can be convenient in firewalled environments: A router can be configured to only route multicast IP, with no unicast IP routing.)

Again, consider Figure 8–2. There are two types of routers in this figure: dominant and subordinate; assume in this example, for a given source, that router B is dominant, router A is subordinate, and router C is part of this source's downstream distribution tree. A subordinate router is one that is *not* on the shortest path tree back toward a source. The dominant router can tell this because the subordinate router will "poison-reverse" the route for this source in its routing updates which are sent on the common LAN (i.e., router A sets the metric for this source to "infinity").

The dominant router keeps track of subordinate routers on a per-source (and per-interface!) basis; it never needs or expects to receive a prune message from a subordinate router. Only routers that are truly on the downstream distribution tree will ever need to send prunes to the dominant router. Note that IGMP also must have told it that there are no local members of any group from this source subnetwork.

A sample routing table for a DVMRP router is shown in Figure 8–3. Unlike the table that would be created by a unicast routing protocol such as the RIP, OSPF, or the BGP, the DVMRP routing table contains source prefixes and from gateways instead of destination prefixes and next-hop gateways.

The forwarding table represents the shortest path (source-based) spanning tree to every possible source prefix in the internetwork: the RPB tree. The DVMRP routing table does not represent group membership or received prune messages.

The key elements in the DVMRP routing table include the following items:

Source prefix— A subnetwork that is a potential or actual source of multicast datagrams.

Subnet mask— The subnet mask associated with the source prefix. Note that the DVMRP provides the subnet mask for each source subnetwork (in other words, the DVMRP is classless).

From gateway—The previous-hop router leading back toward a particular source prefix.

Source prefix	Subnet mask	From gateway	Metric	Status	TTL
128.1.0.0	255.255.0.0	128.7.5.2	3	Up	200
128.2.0.0	255.255.0.0	128.7.5.2	5	Up	150
128.3.0.0	255.255.0.0	128.6.3.1	2	Up	150
128.4.0.0	255.255.0.0	128.6.3.1	4	Up	200

FIGURE 8–3   Sample DVMRP routing table

TTL— The time to live is used for table management. It indicates the number of seconds remaining before an entry is removed from the routing table. This TTL has nothing at all to do with the TTL used in TTL-based scoping.

DVMRP FORWARDING TABLE

Since the DVMRP routing table is not aware of group membership, the DVMRP process builds a forwarding table based on a combination of the information contained in the multi-cast routing table, known active groups, and received prune messages (prune state). The forwarding table represents the local router's understanding of the shortest path source-based delivery tree for each (source, group) pair (i.e., the source's RPM tree for this group).

The forwarding table for a sample DVMRP router is shown in Figure 8–4.

The elements in this display include the following items:

Source prefix— The subnetwork sending multicast datagrams to the specified groups (one group per row).

Multicast group—The class D IP address to which multicast datagrams from this source have been addressed. Note that a given source prefix may contain multiple source end stations.

InIntf— The parent interface for the (source, group) pair. A 'Pr' in this column indicates that a prune message has been sent to the up-stream router (the from gateway for this source prefix in the DVMRP routing table).

OutIntf(s)— The child interfaces over which multicast datagrams for this (source, group) pair are forwarded. A 'p' in this column indicates that the router has received a prune message(s) from a (all) down-stream router(s) on this interface.

DVMRP TREE BUILDING AND FORWARDING SUMMARY

As we have seen, the DVMRP enables packets to be forwarded away from a multicast source along a group's RPM tree. The general name for this technique is reverse-path forwarding, and it is used in some other multicast routing protocols, as we shall see later.

Source prefix	Multicast group	InIntf	OutIntf(s)
128.1.0.0	224.1.1.1	1 Pr	2p3p
	224.2.2.2	1	2p3
	224.3.3.3	1	2
128.2.0.0	224.1.1.1	2	2p3

FIGURE 8–4 Sample DVMRP forwarding table

Reverse-path forwarding was described in Steve Deering's Ph.D. thesis, and was a refinement of early work on RPB done by Dalal and Metcalfe in 1978. As a broadcasting algorithm, RPB was wasteful if employed to deliver multicast datagrams, because all nodes received a (single) copy of each packet, whether or not there were any interested receivers. No effort was made in RPB to prune the tree to only include branches leading to active receivers. After all, RPB was a technique for implementing broadcast, not multicast.

Truncated RPB added a small optimization so that IGMP was used to tell if there were listeners on the LANs at the very edge of the RPB tree. If there were no listeners, the packets were stopped at the leaf routers and not forwarded onto the edge LANs. Despite the savings of LAN bandwidth, TRPB still sends a copy of each packet to every router in the topology.

RPM, used in the DVMRP, takes TRPB one step further. The group membership information derived from IGMP is used to generate control messages upstream (i.e., toward the source subnetwork) in order to "prune" the distribution tree. This technique trades off some memory in the participating routers (to store the prune information) in order to gain back the wasted bandwidth on branches that do not lead to interested receivers.

In the DVMRP, the RPM distribution tree is created on demand to describe the forwarding table for a given source sending to a group. The forwarding table indicates the expected inbound interface for packets from this source, and the necessary outbound interface(s) for distribution to the rest of the group. Forwarding table entries are created when packets to a "new" (source, group) pair arrive at a DVMRP router. Initially, the packets are forwarded over all the child interfaces for this source subnetwork. The packets are not broadcast onto all nonincoming interfaces (that was how the flooding algorithm worked). Once pruning happens, only a subset of this source's child interfaces at any given router will be left leading to active group members. After pruning is complete, the list of outbound interfaces to reach a given group will be limited to only those child interfaces that lead to active group members. As each subsequent packet is received, its source and group are matched against the appropriate row of the forwarding table. If the packet was received on the expected inbound interface (this source subnetwork's parent interface), it is forwarded downstream on the appropriate outbound interfaces for this group.

DVMRP's tree-building protocol is called "broadcast-and-prune" because the first time a packet for a new (source, group) pair arrives, it is transmitted toward all routers in the internetwork. Then the edge routers initiate prunes. Unnecessary delivery branches are pruned within the round-trip time from the top of a branch to the furthest leaf router, typically on the order of tens of milliseconds or less; thus, the distribution tree for this new (source, group) pair is quickly trimmed to serve only active receivers.

The validation check that DVMRP routers do when a packet arrives is called the "reverse-path check." The first thing a router must do upon receipt of a multicast packet is determine that it arrived on the "correct" inbound interface. For packets matching (source, group) pairs this router has already seen, there will already be a forwarding table entry indicating the expected incoming interface.

Once the incoming interface and valid downstream child interfaces for this (source, group) pair are determined, a forwarding table entry is created to enable quick forwarding of future packets for this (source, group) pair. A multicast packet must never be forwarded back toward its source; this would result in a forwarding loop.

WEAKNESSES IN DVMRP

DVMRP has several design flaws which prevent it from operating across an internetwork of the Internet's scale. While it is not infinitely scalable, it is useful in certain applications. Before we discuss some possible applications of DVMRP, we need to fully understand what DVMRP's limitations are.

1. Distance-vector routing protocol:
   a. Slow to adapt to topology changes (i.e., slow to converge).
   b. Limited network diameter: 15 hops.
2. Must maintain source-specific state when *not* on-tree:
   a. Keeping state in off-tree routers is a waste of valuable router memory.
   b. Source-specific state doesn't scale well as the number of sources increases.
3. Multicast traffic is periodically broadcast across the entire internetwork.

DEPLOYING DVMRP

The DVMRP is really not suitable for use on a wide scale, whether a large intranet or the Internet. Despite its inscalability, it has been used on the MBone since its inception (at the time there was no other protocol to choose from). As the MBone has continued to grow, the fielded DVMRP implementations have had to stretch to keep the MBone together. The MBone is now a sizable network, with many thousands of member subnetworks. As many MBone-connected networks have deployed other multicast routing protocols, the DVMRP has remained the MBone's core routing protocol. Effectively, it is now being used as an interdomain multicast routing protocol, although there is no real hierarchy in place, and logically the MBone is still one (extremely) large, flat routing domain.

The DVMRP suffers from RPM's well-understood scaling problems, and certainly would not be the core routing protocol of the MBone today if it were being built from scratch. Despite the DVMRP's limitations, which prevent its use on a truly global scale, some people may consider it to be useful for some intranet applications.

"Native" DVMRP Intranet

Depending on the size of your intranet, it may be possible to just run DVMRP. If you have relatively few sources and groups, and relatively abundant bandwidth, you can probably deploy DVMRP without fear. In this scenario, you need to first enumerate which of your subnetworks will support multicast forwarding. Then, you must notice which router(s) on each of these subnetworks will form the edge of your DVMRP internetwork. Lastly, you must ensure that this network edge is fully interconnected across your backbone by enabling DVMRP routing on selected core router interfaces until you have connected all the edge subnetworks across your intranet's backbone. One reason that this scenario may be attractive to some people is that the DVMRP is supported by virtually all vendors of multicast-capable routers.

Backbone between Domains Running Other Multicast Routing Protocols

In large, multicampus intranets, the interior gatway protocol called Open Shortest Path First (OSPF) and the exterior gateway protocol called Border Gateway Protocol (BGP) are often used together to help the intranetwork scale to very large-size regimes. Because of the DVMRP's presence as the backbone routing protocol of the Internet's MBone, all other protocols have specifications detailing how to attach a domain running multicast routing protocol X to a backbone running DVMRP.

Fortuitously for the intranet manager, if multiple domains need to be knitted together, DVMRP is a proven solution: virtually all multicast routers implement it. Moreover, if the multicast router supports other routing protocols, it is likely to support interoperability tecniques to allow DVMRP to be used as a backbone protocol. Essentially, a miniature MBone can be built within the intranet.

Connecting to the Internet's Multicast Backbone

One obvious place where you'll be very likely to employ the DVMRP is at the edge of your intranet, where you attach to the Internet's MBone. A future Internet that supports delivery of native (i.e., non-tunneled) multicast packets will not use the DVMRP as its core routing protocol. Even before the multicast-capable Internet is reached, it is possible that the DVMRP could be supplanted as the MBone's core routing protocol. That day is probably not near, given the size of the MBone. It is difficult to make large-scale changes to something as large as the MBone, especially given that it has no central administrative authority.

As in today's Internet, where RIP is sometimes used by ISPs to advertise a default route to a customer and learn which customer networks are reachable, the DVMRP may be used for similar functions. On the other hand, new multicast routing protocols based solely on the unicast routing table, or on entirely different mechanisms, may make the DVMRP obsolete outside of local intranets. In today's world, it is very simple to configure the DVMRP to attach to the MBone: Simply define the local and remote tunnel endpoint addresses, and wait a few minutes for the routing tables to converge.

CHAPTER **9**

PROTOCOL-INDEPENDENT MULTICAST—DENSE MODE

PROTOCOL-INDEPENDENT MULTICAST OVERVIEW

The Protocol-Independent Multicast (PIM) routing protocols are being developed by the Inter-Domain Multicast Routing (IDMR) working group of the IETF. The objective of the IDMR working group is to develop one—or possibly more than one—standards-track multicast routing protocol(s) that can provide scalable multicast routing across the Internet.

"PIM" is actually two protocols: PIM—Dense Mode (PIM-DM) and PIM—Sparse Mode (PIM-SM). In the remainder of this overview, any references to "PIM" apply to either of these; however, there is no intention to imply that there is only one PIM protocol. While PIM-DM and PIM-SM have similar names, and they do have related control messages, they are really independent.

PIM receives its name because it is not dependent on the mechanisms provided by any particular unicast routing protocol. Remember that the DVMRP had a built-in unicast routing protocol to facilitate locating source subnetworks relative to any router, and to help determine which interfaces were children with respect to any source. However, any PIM implementation requires the presence of a (set of) unicast routing protocol(s) to provide routing table information and to adapt to topology changes. Any combination of existing unicast routing protocols will suffice for this purpose: OSPF, Integrated IS-IS, RIPv1, RIPv2, BGP-4, IGRP, E-IGRP, and so on.

PIM makes a clear distinction between a multicast routing protocol designed for so-called "dense" environments and one designed for "sparse" environments. Just as "sparse" does not refer to the number of group members being few, dense does not imply a large number of group members. What it describes is a domain of operation in which group members occupy a significant fraction of the available subnetworks. Also, typically domains that are suited to dense-mode protocols have rather plentiful amounts of bandwidth (campus LANs and MANs).

Many people, including the designers of PIM-SM, observe that PIM-DM, the DVMRP, and MOSPF (which will be discussed in the next chapter) are not well suited for multicast topologies in which group members and senders are sparsely distributed. PIM-DM, DVMRP, and MOSPF do not provide the most efficient multicast delivery service, in the sense that they use more bandwidth or router resources than might be necessary in a protocol designed for the "sparse" case. These protocols deliver packets efficiently once they have built their trees, but the tree-building process is inefficient. The DVMRP periodically broadcasts multicast data packets over many links that do not lead to group members, while MOSPF spreads group membership information across links that do not lead to senders or receivers.

PIM—DENSE MODE (PIM-DM)

While the PIM architecture was primarily driven by the need to provide efficient, scalable sparse-mode delivery trees (across WANs, which demand efficiency), PIM also defined a new dense-mode protocol. It is envisioned that PIM-DM would be deployed in resource-rich environments such as campus LANs, where group members densely occupy a large percentage of the subnetworks, and bandwidth is likely to be readily available. By design, PIM-DM's control messages are similar to PIM-SM's.

PIM-DM is based on the reverse-path multicasting (RPM) algorithm, as is the DVMRP v3. Notably absent from PIM-DM is an embedded routing protocol. PIM-DM and -SM, as mentioned earlier, rely on the presence of a unicast routing table so that they may execute their RPF check.

Besides this difference with respect to routing protocols, another difference between PIM-DM and DVMRP is that PIM-DM simply forwards multicast traffic on all non-incoming interfaces until explicit prune messages are received, unlike the DVMRP, which calculates a set of child interfaces for each source pair. PIM-DM is willing to accept some excess packet duplication to simplify routing protocol dependencies, and to avoid the overhead inherent in determining the parent/child relationships. Figure 9–1 illustrates this difference between PIM-DM and the DVMRP.

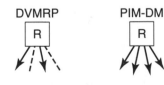

--- Child interface

FIGURE 9–1   PIM-DM vs. DVMRP broadcasting

For those cases where group members suddenly appear on a previously pruned branch of the delivery tree, PIM-DM, like the DVMRP, employs (reliable) graft messages to reattach the previously pruned branch to the delivery tree.

PIM-DM TREE BUILDING AND FORWARDING SUMMARY

Dense-mode PIM builds source-based trees. It is based on the RPM algorithm, as is the DVMRP; thus, PIM-DM is a data-driven protocol that broadcasts packets to the edges of its domain and expects prunes to be returned on inactive branches. A minor difference from DVMRP is that PIM-DM floods packets for new (source, group) pairs on all non-incoming interfaces. PIM-DM trades off a bit of extra flooding traffic for a simpler protocol design.

Pruning in PIM-DM only happens via explicit Prune messages, which are multicast on broadcast links (if there are other routers present that hear a prune, and they still wish to receive traffic for this group to support their own active downstream receivers, these other routers must multicast PIM-Join packets to ensure they remain attached to the distribution tree). Finally, PIM-DM uses a reliable graft mechanism to enable previously sent prunes to be "erased" when new downstream group members appear after a prune is sent.

Since PIM-DM uses RPM, it implements a reverse-path check on all packets it receives. Again, this check verifies that received packets arrive on the interface which the router would use if it needed to send a packet toward the source's subnetworks. Since PIM-DM does not have its own routing protocol (as opposed to the DVMRP), it uses the existing unicast routing table to orient itself with respect to the source(s) of multicast packets it has seen.

CHAPTER 10

MULTICAST EXTENSIONS TO OSPF (MOSPF)

Version 2 of the Open Shortest Path First (OSPF) routing protocol is defined in RFC-2178. OSPF is an interior gateway protocol (IGP) that distributes unicast topology information among routers belonging to a single OSPF "autonomous system." OSPF's routing table is calculated based on link-state algorithms, which permit rapid route calculation while consuming a minimum of bandwidth due to routing protocol traffic. In addition to efficient route calculation, OSPF is an open standard that supports hierarchical routing, load balancing, and the import/export of external routing information.

The Multicast Extensions to OSPF (MOSPF) are defined in RFC-1584. MOSPF routers maintain a current image of the network topology through the unicast OSPF link-state routing protocol. The multicast extensions to OSPF are built on top of OSPF Version 2, so that a multicast routing capability can be incrementally introduced into an OSPF Version 2 routing domain. Routers running MOSPF will interoperate with non-MOSPF routers when forwarding unicast IP data traffic. MOSPF does not support tunnels.

INTRA-AREA ROUTING WITH MOSPF

"Intra-area routing" describes the basic routing algorithm employed by MOSPF. This elementary algorithm runs inside a single OSPF area and supports multicast forwarding when a source and all destination group members reside in the same OSPF area, or the entire OSPF autonomous system is a single area (and the source is inside that area). The following discussion assumes that the reader is already familiar with OSPF.

Figure 10–1 depicts an OSPF autonomous system which has been subdivided into five areas.

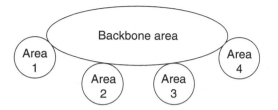

FIGURE 10–1   OSPF autonomous system divided into five areas

Local Group Database

Similar to all other multicast routing protocols, MOSPF routers use the Internet Group Management Protocol (IGMP) to monitor multicast group membership on directly attached subnetworks. MOSPF routers maintain a "local group database" which lists directly attached groups and determines the local router's responsibility for delivering multicast datagrams to these groups.

On any given subnetwork, the transmission of IGMP Host Membership Queries is performed solely by the OSPF designated router (DR). However, the responsibility of listening to IGMP Host Membership Reports is performed by not only the DR but also the backup designated router (BDR). Therefore, in a mixed LAN containing both MOSPF and OSPF routers, an MOSPF router *must* be elected the DR for the subnetwork. This can be achieved by setting the OSPF RouterPriority to zero in each non-MOSPF router to prevent them from becoming the (B)DR.

The DR is responsible for communicating group membership information to all other routers in the OSPF area by flooding Group-Membership LSAs. Group-Membership LSAs are flooded into the backbone area from the area in which they were created, but not from the backbone into any other area.

Datagram's Shortest Path Tree

The datagram's shortest path tree describes the path taken by a multicast datagram as it travels through the area from the source subnetwork to each of the group members' subnetworks. The shortest path tree for each (source, group) pair is built "on demand" when a router receives the first multicast datagram for a particular (source, group) pair.

When the initial datagram arrives, the source subnetwork is located in the MOSPF link-state database. The MOSPF link-state database is simply the standard OSPF link-state database augmented by Group-Membership LSAs. Based on the Router- and Network-LSAs in the OSPF link-state database, a source-based shortest path tree is constructed using Dijkstra's algorithm. Because the locations of this group's members within the topology are known, the tree is built through this router such that its branches lead only to subnetworks containing members of this group. The output of these algorithms is a source-based tree rooted at the datagram's source.

To forward multicast datagrams to downstream members of a group, each router must determine its position in the datagram's shortest path tree. Figure 10–2 illustrates the

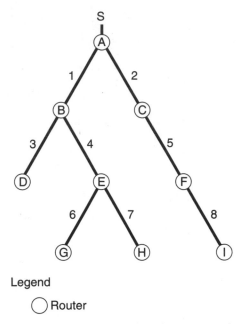

Legend

◯ Router

FIGURE 10–2   Shortest path tree for a (source, group) pair

shortest path tree for a given (source, group) pair. In this example, router E's upstream node is router B, and there are two downstream interfaces, one connecting to subnetwork 6 and another to subnetwork 7.

Note the following properties of the basic MOSPF routing algorithm:

- For a given multicast datagram, all routers within an OSPF area calculate the same source-based shortest path delivery tree. Tie-breakers have been defined to guarantee that if several equal-cost paths exist, all routers agree on a single path through the area. Unlike unicast OSPF, MOSPF does not support the concept of equal-cost multipath forwarding.

- Synchronized link state databases containing Group-Membership LSAs allow an MOSPF router to build a source-based shortest path tree in memory, working forward from the source to the group member(s). Unlike the DVMRP, this means that the first datagram of a new transmission does not have to be flooded to all routers in an area. However, all routers in an area do need to store all the Group-Membership LSAs, whether or not any source is even sending to this group.

- The "on-demand" construction of the source-based delivery tree has the benefit of spreading calculations over time, resulting in a lesser impact on participating routers. Of course, this may strain the CPU(s) in a router if many new (source, group) pairs appear at about the same time, or if there are a lot of events which force the MOSPF process to flush and rebuild its forwarding cache. In a stable topology with long-lived multicast sessions, these effects should be minimal.

Forwarding Cache

Each MOSPF router makes its forwarding decision based on the contents of its forwarding cache. Contrary to DVMRP, MOSPF forwarding is not RPF-based. The forwarding cache is built from the source-based shortest path tree for each (source, group) pair and the router's local group database. After the router discovers its position in the shortest path tree, a forwarding cache entry is created containing the (source, group) pair, its expected upstream interface, and the necessary downstream interface(s).

The forwarding cache entry is now used to quickly forward all subsequent datagrams from this source to this group. If a new source begins sending to a new group, MOSPF must first calculate the distribution tree so that it may create a cache entry which can be used to forward the packet. Figure 10–3 displays a simulated forwarding cache for an example MOSPF router.

The elements in the display include the following items:

Destination group—A known (destination) group address to which datagrams are currently being forwarded, or to which traffic was sent "recently" (i.e., since the last topology or group membership or other event which [re-]initialized MOSPF's forwarding cache).

Source—The datagram's source host address. Each (destination group, source) pair uniquely identifies a separate forwarding cache entry.

Upstream—Datagrams matching this row's destination group and source must be received on this interface.

Downstream—If a datagram matching this row's destination group and source is received on the correct upstream interface, it is forwarded across the listed downstream interfaces.

TTL—The minimum number of hops a datagram must cross to reach any of the destination group's members. An MOSPF router may discard a datagram if it can see that the datagram has insufficient TTL to reach even the closest group member.

The information in the forwarding cache is not aged or periodically refreshed; it is maintained as long as there are system resources available (e.g., memory) or until the next topology change. The contents of the forwarding cache will change when:

Destination group	Source	Upstream	Downstream		TTL
224.1.1.1	128.1.0.2	11	12	13	5
224.1.1.1	128.4.1.2	11	12	13	2
224.1.1.1	128.5.2.2	11	12	13	3
224.2.2.2	128.2.0.3	12	11		7

FIGURE 10–3 An example MOSPF forwarding cache

- The topology of the OSPF internetwork changes, forcing all the shortest path trees to be recalculated. Once the cache has been flushed, entries are not remembered and immediately rebuilt. If another packet for one of the previously active (destination group, source) pairs is received, a "new" cache entry for that pair will be created.
- There is a change in the Group-Membership LSAs indicating that the distribution of individual group members has changed.

INTERAREA ROUTING WITH MOSPF

Interarea routing involves the case where a datagram's source resides in a different OSPF area than some of its destination group members. It should be noted that the forwarding of multicast datagrams continues to be determined by the contents of the forwarding cache, which is still built from each area's local group database and the datagram's source-based trees. The major differences are related to the way in which group membership information is propagated and how the interarea source-based tree is constructed.

Interarea Multicast Forwarders

In MOSPF, a subset (usually just one) of an area's area border routers (ABRs) functions as "interarea multicast forwarders." An interarea multicast forwarder (MABR) is responsible for the forwarding of group membership information and multicast datagrams between areas. Configuration parameters determine whether or not a particular ABR also functions as an interarea multicast forwarder (see Figure 10–4).

Interarea multicast forwarders summarize their attached areas' group membership information to the backbone by injecting their area's Group-Membership LSAs into the backbone area. Note that the summarization of group membership in MOSPF is asymmetric. This means that group membership information from non-backbone areas is distributed into the backbone, but group membership from the backbone (or from any other non-backbone area) is not flooded into any non-backbone area(s) (see Figure 10–5).

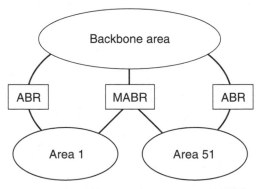

FIGURE 10–4   Multiple ABRs and one MABR

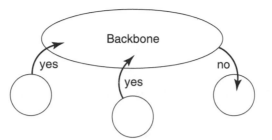

FIGURE 10–5 Asymmetric summarization of group membership information

To permit the forwarding of multicast traffic between areas, MOSPF introduces the concept of a "wildcard multicast receiver." A wildcard multicast receiver, shown in Figure 10–6, is a router that receives all multicast traffic sourced within in an area. In non-backbone areas, all interarea multicast forwarders operate as wildcard multicast receivers. This guarantees that all multicast traffic originating in any non-backbone area is delivered to its interarea multicast forwarder, and then if necessary into the backbone area. If any other area, or the backbone area, has a member of this group, the interarea multicast forwarder simply multicasts the packet into the backbone area.

Since the backbone knows group membership for all areas, the datagram can be forwarded to the appropriate location(s) in the OSPF autonomous system, provided it is forwarded into the backbone by the source area's multicast ABR. As shown in Figure 10–6, the area's wildcard multicast receiver is included in the delivery tree for each (source, group) pair, whether or not any group members are present outside the source's area. A future enhancement to MOSPF is being designed to allow the wildcard multicast receiver to remove itself from the intra-area distribution tree, provided it can determine that there are no group members outside the source's area. You could think of this as a pruning mechanism for MOSPF.

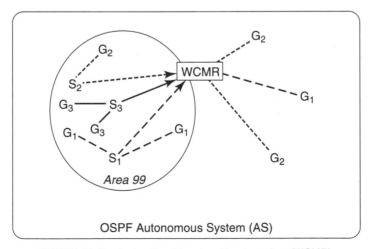

FIGURE 10–6 An area's wildcard multicast receiver (WCMR)

An Interarea Datagram's Shortest Path Tree

In the case of interarea multicast routing, it is usually impossible to build a complete shortest path delivery tree. Incomplete trees are a fact of life because each OSPF area's complete topological and group membership information is not distributed among all the other OSPF areas. Topological estimates are made through the use of wildcard receivers and OSPF Summary-Links LSAs.

If the source of a multicast datagram resides in the same area as the router performing the tree-building calculation, it must carefully ensure that branches leading to other areas remain within the tree. As in the intra-area case, those branches leading to subnetworks with no group members are omitted from the tree (in the source's home area). Branches containing wildcard multicast receivers must be included in the tree since the local routers do not know whether there are any group members beyond these wildcard receivers (e.g., residing in other areas); see Figure 10–7.

If the source of a multicast datagram resides in a different area than the router performing the tree-building calculation, the precise topological details describing the source station's local topology are not known. However, this information can be estimated using information provided by Summary-Links LSAs for the source's subnetwork.

In this case, the base of the tree (outside this area) begins with branches directly connecting the source subnetwork to each of its home area's interarea multicast forwarders. The tree continues across the backbone area (any router within the backbone knows which areas have members of this group, and therefore which ABRs need to receive this packet) into this area. The packets are then distributed along a tree from the area's multicast ABR to all the group members within the area, as shown in Figure 10–8.

Since each interarea multicast forwarder is also an ABR, it must maintain a separate link-state database for each attached area. Thus, each interarea multicast forwarder is required to calculate a separate forwarding tree for each of its attached areas. The trees within each area are "glued" together to connect the source, wherever it is within the OSPF routing domain, with all the group members.

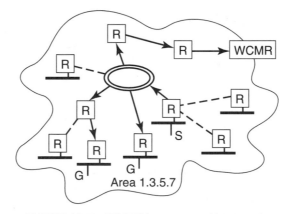

FIGURE 10–7   MOSPF intra-area multicast tree

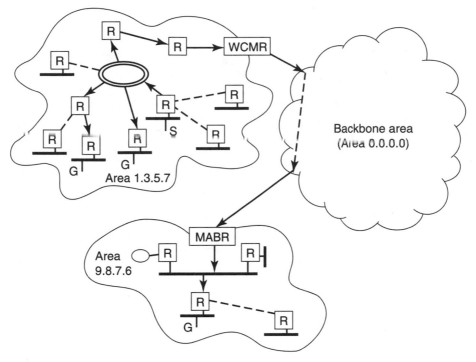

FIGURE 10–8   An MOSPF inter-area multicast tree

INTER-AUTONOMOUS-SYSTEM MULTICASTING WITH MOSPF

Inter-autonomous-system multicasting involves the situation where a datagram's source or some of its destination group members are in different OSPF autonomous systems. In OSPF terminology, "inter-AS" communication also refers to connectivity between one OSPF routing domain and another, which could be within the same autonomous system from the perspective of an exterior gateway protocol such as BGP-4.

To facilitate inter-AS multicast routing, selected autonomous system boundary routers (ASBRs) are configured as "inter-AS multicast forwarders." MOSPF makes the assumption that each inter-AS multicast forwarder executes an inter-AS multicast routing protocol which forwards multicast datagrams in a reverse-path forwarding (RPF) manner. Since the publication of the MOSPF RFC, a term has been defined for such a router: "multicast border router." (See Chapter 15 for an overview of MBR concepts.) Each inter-AS multicast forwarder is a wildcard multicast receiver in each of its attached areas. This guarantees that each inter-AS multicast forwarder remains on all pruned shortest-path trees and receives all multicast datagrams.

The details of inter-AS forwarding are very similar to interarea forwarding. On the "inside" of the OSPF domain, the multicast ASBR must conform to all the requirements of

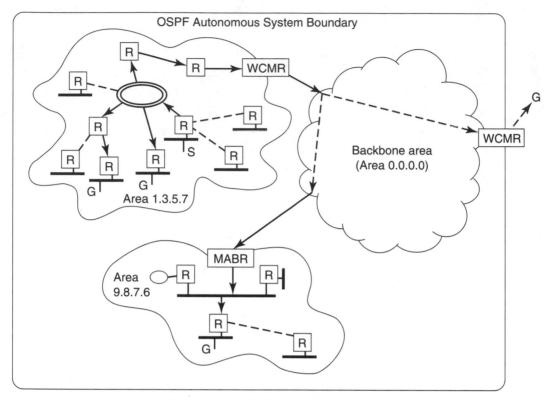

FIGURE 10–9   MOSPF inter-AS multicast tree

intra- and inter-area forwarding. Within the OSPF domain, group members are reached by the usual forward path computations, and paths to outside sources are approximated by a reverse-path source-based tree, with the multicast ASBR standing in for the actual source.

When the source is within the OSPF AS, and there are external group members, it falls to the inter-AS multicast forwarders, in their role as wildcard receivers, to make sure that the data gets out of the OSPF domain and is sent off in the correct direction. Figure 10–9 illustrates this case, with a source in the MOSPF region and external group members.

MOSPF TREE BUILDING AND FORWARDING SUMMARY

MOSPF builds a separate tree for each (source, group) combination. The tree is rooted at the source, and includes each of the group members as leaves. If the (M)OSPF domain is divided into multiple areas, the tree is built in pieces, one area at a time. These pieces are then glued together at the (multicast) area border routers which interconnect the various areas.

Sometimes group membership of certain areas (or other ASes) is unknown. MOSPF forces the tree to extend to these areas and/or ASes by adding their area border routers/AS boundary routers to the tree as "wildcard multicast receivers."

Construction of the tree within a given area depends on the location of the source. If the source is within the area, "forward" costs are used, and the path within the area follows the "forward path," that is, the same route that unicast packets would take from the source to any given intra-area group member's subnetwork. If the source belongs to a different area, or a different AS, "reverse costs" are used, resulting in reverse path forwarding (RPF) through the area. (RPF is less preferred, but is forced because OSPF Summary LSAs and AS-External LSAs only advertise costs in the reverse direction).

MOSPF's tree-building process is data-driven. Despite having Group-Membership LSAs present in each area's link-state database, no trees are built unless multicast data is seen from a source to a group (of course, if the Link State Database indicates no Group-Membership LSAs for this group, no tree will be built since there are clearly no group members present in this area). Because of this feature, MOSPF is an explicit-join protocol, not a broadcast-and-prune protocol (despite being data-driven).

If a packet arrives for a (source, group) pair which has not been seen by this router before, the router executes the Dijkstra algorithm over the relevant links in the link-state database. The Dijkstra algorithm outputs the "source-rooted" shortest path tree for this (source, group), as described earlier. The router examines its position in the tree, caching the expected inbound interface for packets from this source and listing the outbound interface(s) that lead to active downstream receivers. Subsequent traffic is examined against this cached data. The traffic from the source must arrive on the correct interface to be processed further.

WEAKNESSES OF MOSPF

Because the Dijkstra algorithm must be run every time a new (source, group) pair is seen, it would be easy to overwhelm the routers in an area by spraying in multicast packets with randomly chosen (source, group) pairs. If any of the randomized groups actually existed, the resulting cache entries would quickly erode all the MOSPF memory in that area. In addition, this could consume valuable CPU cycles that OSPF might normally use to process unicast routing changes, or that the router might use in the course of forwarding other, legitimate, traffic. Even if there are no Group-Membership LSAs present in an area's link-state database, the router still must verify that this packet to a random (source, group) pair cannot be forwarded.

The above issue, while perhaps a component of a malicious denial-of-service attack, is not likely to happen in real networks. In an intranet setting, the right management tools applied carefully should allow an offending node to be identified; perhaps not by its source IP address (which may vary), but by its source MAC address (not as likely to vary).

DEPLOYING MOSPF

As multicast routing protocols become more widely implemented, it would seem likely that vendors who already support OSPF might be inclined to also support MOSPF. Intranets that are based on OSPF routing, then, would have a natural choice of multicast routing protocol. Another option for intranet managers, even if their network is 100% OSPF, is to deploy a new multicast routing protocol such as one or both of the PIM protocols, or CBT. These multicast routing protocols may be attractive because they are (unicast) protocol-independent and can seamlessly work across an OSPF AS boundary. Certainly, if an intranet is not 100% OSPF, one of these unicast-protocol-independent multicast routing protocols may be a better choice.

MOSPF's attractiveness lies primarily in its leverage of an existing, well-understood, popular, IETF-sanctioned protocol: OSPF. MOSPF is probably the most natural choice for OSPF shops when deciding how to deploy multicast IP, provided OSPF is relatively ubiquitous within these intranets.

Initially, a challenging issue will be finding implementations. As the IETF's recommended interior gateway protocol, OSPF has achieved broad implementation and widespread deployment. MOSPF, however, has not—yet—been widely implemented. One implementor was heard to say: "it's a lot simpler (to implement) than it looks." Presumably, the market will decide if MOSPF is important or not. Certainly, if users ask for it, vendors will eventually provide it.

In an intranet with mixed OSPF and non-OSPF domains, obviously MOSPF can only run in the OSPF regions. Another routing protocol would have to run between the regions (in MOSPF terms, to facilitate inter-AS forwarding). Such an intranet may find it more effective to use one of the PIM protocols or CBT instead (even over the OSPF regions) so that their intranet has a common multicast routing protocol. Another choice would be to knit together the MOSPF regions with another multicast routing protocol.

Mixing MOSPF and OSPF Routers within an OSPF Routing Domain

MOSPF routers can be combined with non-multicast OSPF routers. This permits the gradual deployment of MOSPF and allows experimentation with multicast routing on a limited scale. Selected interfaces may be multicast-enabled before all-out deployment happens.

It is important to note that an MOSPF router must eliminate all non-multicast OSPF routers when it builds its source-based shortest path delivery tree. An MOSPF router can determine the multicast capability of any other router. Each MOSPF router must set the multicast-capable bit (MC-bit) in the Options field of its link-state advertisements.

The omission of non-multicast routers may create a number of potential problems when forwarding multicast traffic:

- The designated router for a multi-access network must be an MOSPF router. If a plain (non-multicast-capable) OSPF router is elected the DR, the subnetwork will not be able to join any multicast groups. This happens because a non-MOSPF DR cannot generate Group-Membership LSAs for its subnetwork, simply because it is not running IGMP; thus, it won't process IGMP Host Membership Reports, or generate Group-Membership LSAs to distribute within its area.

- Even though there may be unicast connectivity to a destination, there may not be multicast connectivity. For example, the only possible path between two points might require traversal of a non-multicast-capable OSPF router.
- The forwarding of multicast and unicast datagrams between two points may follow different paths, making some routing problems a bit more challenging to solve. To help eliminate this problem, it is wise to have your multicast topology closely match your unicast topology; perhaps at the end of your MOSPF deployment you'd have every OSPF router configured as multicast-capable.

PART IV

INTRANET MULTICAST ROUTING TOMORROW

The most recent additions to the set of multicast routing protocols are classified as "sparse mode" protocols, which are designed from a different perspective than the "dense mode" protocols that we have already examined. Sparse-mode protocols are not data-driven, in the sense that forwarding state *must* be set up in advance—before any multicast data can flow. Also, they trade off using bandwidth liberally, which is a valid thing to do in a densely populated intranet/LAN environment, for techniques that are much better suited to application over large WANs, where bandwidth is scarce and considerably more expensive. Certainly, if your "intranet" has a large WAN component, these protocols are quite likely to be attractive for use within your intranet.

These emerging routing protocols include Core-Based Trees (CBT) and Protocol-Independent Multicast—Sparse Mode (PIM-SM).

While these routing protocols are designed to operate efficiently over a wide area network where bandwidth is scarce and subnetworks containing group members may be widely scattered, this is not to imply that they are only suitable for small groups. Sparse doesn't necessarily imply small; rather, it is meant to convey the concept that subnetworks with group members are widely dispersed, and thus it is wasteful to flood their groups' data periodically across the entire internetwork.

Interestingly, despite the fact that PIM-SM is clearly designed for use over large WANs, many initial deployments of PIM-SM have been in campus LAN environments or over metropolitan-scale IP backbones. This is not meant to imply that it is not suited to its original purpose, just to point out that it is not restricted to use on WANs.

CBT has not been widely implemented yet, so deployment experience relative to PIM-SM is virtually nonexistent. However, PIM-SM evolved from the basic ideas in CBT, so it is instructive to compare the protocols to see how they are similar and how they differ.

CHAPTER 11

CORE-BASED TREES (CBT)

Core-Based Trees is a multicast architecture that is based on a shared delivery tree. It is specifically intended to address the important issue of scaleability when supporting multicast applications across the public Internet, and is also suitable for use within private intranetworks.

Similar to PIM-SM, CBT is protocol-independent. CBT employs the information contained in the unicast routing table to build its shared delivery tree. It does not care how the unicast routing table is derived, only that a unicast routing table is present. This feature allows CBT to be deployed without requiring the presence of any specific unicast routing protocol.

"Protocol-independence" doesn't necessarily have to mean that multicast paths are the same set of routers and links used by unicast routing, although it is easy to make this assumption; in fact, it may hold true in some cases. An underlying routing protocol could collect both unicast- and multicast-related information, so unicast routes could be calculated based on the unicast information, and multicast routes on the multicast information. If the path (set of intervening routers and links) used between any two network nodes is the same for multicast and unicast, then it can be said that the unicast and multicast topologies overlap (for that set of paths).

Where multicast and unicast topologies do happen to overlap, multicast and unicast paths could be calculated from one set of information (i.e., unicast). However, if the set of routers and links between two network nodes differs for multicast and unicast traffic, the unicast and multicast topologies are incongruent for that

*network path. It's a matter of policy whether unicast and multicast topologies are
aligned for any set of network links.*

INTRA-DOMAIN BOOTSTRAPPING

This process of discovering which core serves which group(s) is referred to as "bootstrapping." The current version of the CBT specification has adopted a bootstrap mechanism
similar to that defined in the PIM-SM specification, which will be discussed in the next
chapter. It is an implementation choice whether a dynamic or static mechanism is used for
discovering how groups map to cores. Use of the dynamic bootstrap mechanism is only
applicable within a multicast region, not between regions. Each group has exactly one
core, but a given core might serve multiple groups (see Figure 11–1).

The advantage of dynamically discovering core/group mappings is that a region's
CBT routers need less configuration. The disadvantage is that core placement could be
particularly suboptimal for some set of receivers. Manual placement means that each
group's core can be "better" positioned relative to a group's members. CBT's modular design allows other core discovery mechanisms to be used if such mechanisms are considered more beneficial to CBT's requirements.

Efforts are underway to separately specify, and perhaps even standardize, a common mechanism for inter-domain RP/core discovery, with the intent that any shared tree
protocol could implement this common inter-domain discovery mechanism (using its own
protocol message types).

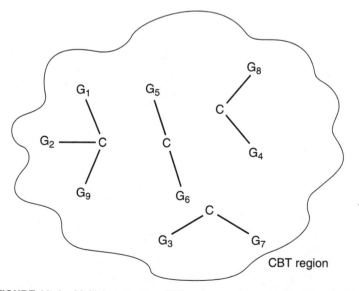

FIGURE 11–1   Multiple cores in a CBT region, each serving its own set of groups

Joining a Group's Shared Tree

As usual, a host that wants to join a multicast group issues an IGMP Host Membership Report. This message informs its local CBT-aware router(s) that it wishes to receive traffic addressed to this multicast group. Upon receipt of an IGMP Host Membership Report for a new group, the local CBT router issues a JOIN_REQUEST hop by hop toward the group's core (see Figure 11–2).

If the JOIN_REQUEST encounters a router which is already on the group's shared tree before it reaches the core router, that router issues a JOIN_ACK hop by hop back toward the sending router. The core router is ultimately responsible for responding with a JOIN_ACK if the JOIN_REQUEST does not encounter an on-tree CBT router along its path toward the core (see Figure 11–3).

As each router forwards the JOIN_REQUEST toward the core they are required to create transient "join state." This transient "join state" includes the multicast group, and the JOIN_REQUEST's incoming and outgoing interfaces. This transient state information allows an intermediate router to forward returning JOIN_ACKs along the exact path back to the CBT router which originated the JOIN_REQUEST.

As the JOIN_ACK returns toward the original CBT router, each intermediate router creates new "active state" for this group. New branches are established by having the intermediate routers remember which interface(s) is (are) downstream (away from the core).

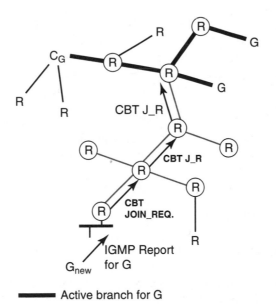

━━━━━ Active branch for G

FIGURE 11–2 IGMP report for G causes CBT JOIN_REQUEST toward G's core

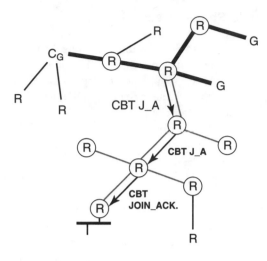

—— Active branch for G

FIGURE 11–3   A JOIN_ACK retraces the steps of the JOIN_REQUEST

CBT TREE MAINTENANCE

Once a new branch is created, each child router monitors the status of its parent router with a keepalive mechanism, the CBT "Echo" protocol. A child router periodically unicasts an ECHO_REQUEST to its parent router, which is then required to respond with a unicast ECHO_REPLY message. If, for any reason, the link between an on-tree router and its upstream neighbor should fail, or the upstream neighbor is otherwise unreachable, the on-tree router transmits a FLUSH_TREE message on its downstream interface(s). This tears down all the downstream branches for this group. Figure 11–4 illustrates both procedures.

After receiving a FLUSH_TREE message, each formerly downstream router is responsible for attempting to reattach itself to the group's core, thus rebuilding the shared delivery tree. Leaf routers only rejoin the shared tree if they have at least one directly attached group member.

CBT'S DESIGNATED ROUTER

CBT's designated router (DR) for a given broadcast-capable subnetwork is elected by CBT's "Hello" protocol. The DR functions as the only upstream router for all groups using that link. Note that in shared trees, "upstream" is the direction toward the center of the group's tree, as opposed to source-based trees, in which "upstream" is the direction toward the source.

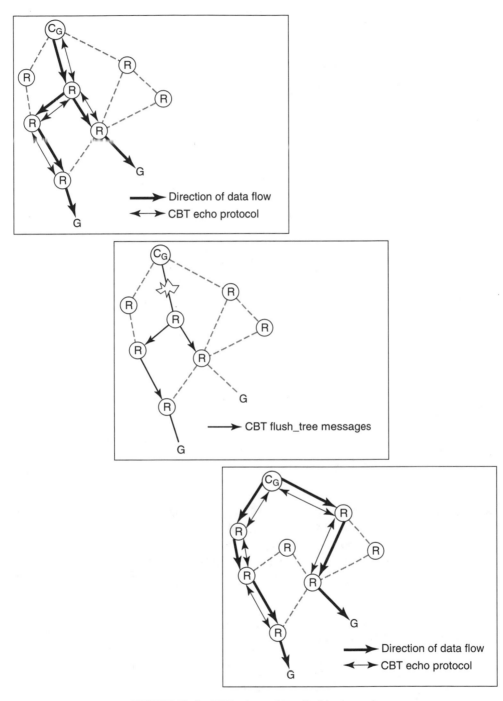

FIGURE 11–4   CBT echo and tree-flushing procedures

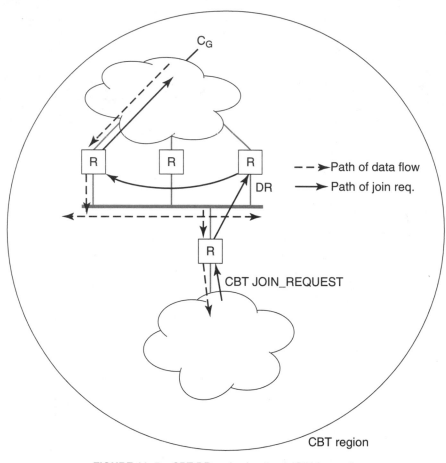

C_G

R   R   R

DR

- - ► Path of data flow
—— ► Path of join req.

CBT JOIN_REQUEST

R

CBT region

FIGURE 11–5   CBT DR and suboptimal JOIN forwarding

As depicted in Figure 11–5, the DR is not necessarily the best next-hop router to every core for every multicast group. The implication is that it is possible for the DR to receive a JOIN_REQUEST over a LAN, but the DR may need to redirect the JOIN_RE-QUEST back across the same link to the best next-hop router toward a given group's core. Data traffic is never duplicated across a link, only JOIN_REQUESTs, which should be an inconsequential volume of traffic.

DATA PACKET FORWARDING

When a JOIN_ACK is received by an intermediate router, it either adds the interface over which the JOIN_REQUEST was received to an existing group's forwarding cache entry, or creates a new entry for the multicast group if one does not already exist. The new entry would simply consist of the group plus one outgoing interface: the interface on which the JOIN_REQUEST was received (this is the interface that leads toward a group member).

CBT's Forwarding Cache

CBT's forwarding cache consists of entries of the following form:

```
(group, {outgoing interface list})
```

Forwarding decisions are made by using the destination group address as the search key into the forwarding cache. A packet is forwarded onto all interfaces in the outgoing interface list. The only exception is that a packet is never forwarded onto the interface on which it arrived, whether or not the incoming interface is listed among this group's outgoing interface list.

CBT's designers believe that its scaling characteristics are enhanced by not allowing source-specific forwarding state. The designers of CBT believe that this is a critical decision: When multicasting becomes widely deployed, they believe that routing protocols should maintain the least amount of state information possible.

Interestingly, CBT's state is bidirectional. This feature is unique among all existing multicast routing protocols. Data may flow in either direction along a branch. Thus, data from a source which is directly attached to an existing tree branch need not be encapsulated. (In CBT, non-member sources' traffic is encapsulated as IP-in-IP to get from the source's subnetwork to a group's core.) Another benefit of bidirectional state is that there is no waiting period while new forwarding state is created.

The fact that CBT's state is not source-based means that the amount of state information is invariant with the number of sources. In one group, every subnetwork with group members could have at least one source; in another, there may only be one source (which may not even be a group member!). In either case, the CBT routers still keep the exact same amount of state:

```
(group, {outgoing interface list})
```

The only differences in the state recorded in the various routers would depend on their degrees of "fan-out" for each group. The routers in a group may have different numbers of outgoing interfaces for a particular group; in a certain router, a group may have just a single outgoing interface, while at another router it may have eight outgoing interfaces, and yet another may have three, or seventeen. Depending on the implementation, this might mean that the state information in each of these cases will consume variable amounts of memory.

One can envision an implementation that uses a bit mask to encode its outgoing interfaces. So a router with a maximum of 512 total interfaces (physical + logical) could use a 512-bit-wide mask (64 octets) to enumerate its potential outgoing inter-

faces. Then, regardless of its fan-out, a group's outgoing interface "list" at any of its routers would be a fixed-size bit mask, with those bits corresponding to the group's active outgoing interfaces set to 1 and the other bits in the mask set to 0.

For example, if the outgoing interface list for a group at a given router was {1, 3}, the 64-octet bit mask would have all zero bits except for bits number 0 and 2, which would be set to 1. Another router may have an outgoing interface list {18, 33, 58}, so those corresponding bits could be set, indicating that those interfaces are used to reach active members of this group.

Note: The author is not aware of any implementation that actually works this way.

NON-MEMBER SENDING

Similar to other multicast routing protocols, CBT does not require that the source of a multicast packet be a member of the multicast group. This is a basic requirement of the IP multicast host group model. However, for a multicast data packet to reach the active core for the group, at least one CBT-capable router must be present on the non-member sender's subnetwork (Figure 11–6). This router knows the location of this group's core. In order for the source's packets to reach the group's member, that source's traffic must be delivered to the core. The source's local CBT router employs IP-in-IP encapsulation and unicasts the data packet to the group's core for delivery to the rest of the multicast group.

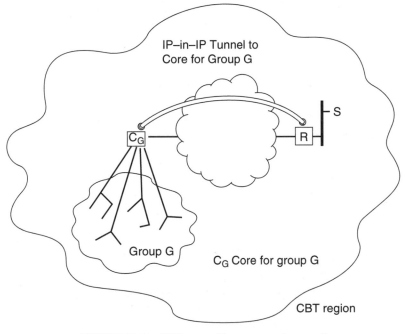

FIGURE 11–6   CBT support for non-member sending

CBT Tree Building and Forwarding Summary

CBT trees are constructed based on forward paths from the receiver(s) to the core. Any group only has exactly one active core, as you recall. As CBT is an explicit-join protocol, no routers forward traffic to a group unless there are pre-established active receivers for that group within the CBT domain.

Trees are built using each CBT router's unicast routing table, by forwarding JOIN_REQUESTs along the best unicast path toward a group's core. The resulting non-source-specific state is bidirectional, a feature unique to CBT. If any group member needs to send to the group, zero extra forwarding state needs to be established; every possible receiver is already also a potential sender, with no penalty of extra forwarding state (e.g., [source, group] state) in the routers. Note that once the tree is set up for the group, it is automatically set up for all other intragroup sources; future senders from within the group incur no setup delay.

Sources within the CBT domain that are not group members are connected to the core by IP-in-IP tunnels from a local CBT router to the core. Because no source-specific state needs to be created, non-member senders also experience no setup delay. Once their traffic reaches the core, it is forwarded to all currently active group members.

CHAPTER 12

PROTOCOL-INDEPENDENT MULTICAST—SPARSE MODE (PIM-SM)

As described previously, PIM also defines a source-based tree "dense-mode" variant. Again, PIM-SM and PIM-DM are separate protocols, other than sharing common control messages. The two PIM protocols use very different protocol machinery to accomplish their design goals. Note that while PIM integrates control message processing and data packet forwarding among PIM-Sparse and -Dense modes, PIM-SM and PIM-DM must run in separate regions: A multicast routing region may be either sparse or dense, but sparse and dense regions may never overlap.

PIM—Sparse Mode (PIM-SM) has been developed to provide a multicast routing protocol that provides efficient communication between members of sparsely distributed groups, the type of groups likely to be common in wide-area internetworks. PIM's designers observed that several hosts wishing to participate in a multicast conference do not justify having their group's multicast traffic periodically broadcast across the entire internetwork.

Noting today's existing MBone scaling problems, and extrapolating to a future of ubiquitous multicast (overlaid with perhaps thousands of small, widely dispersed groups), it is not hard to imagine that existing multicast routing protocols will experience scaling problems. To eliminate these potential scaling issues, PIM-SM is designed to limit multicast traffic so that only those routers interested in receiving traffic for a particular group will "see" it.

PIM-SM differs from existing multicast protocols in two key ways:

- PIM-SM builds shared trees which must be explicitly joined by downstream routers.

    Routers with adjacent group members are required to explicitly join a sparse-mode delivery tree by transmitting join messages toward a group's "Rendezvous

Point." If a router does not join the shared delivery tree before data begins flowing, it cannot receive any multicast traffic addressed to the group.

The default forwarding action of implicit-join routing protocols is to broadcast all traffic away from the source, while the default action of a sparse-mode protocol is to send traffic only where it has been explicitly requested. Dense-mode protocols assume downstream group member presence and broadcast multicast traffic downstream until explicit prune messages are received. The DVMRP and PIM-DM are both implicit-join protocols.

MOSPF is an explicit-join protocol that does not use broadcast-and-prune; however, MOSPF does spread Group-Membership information across the entire OSPF autonomous system, which is excessive because not all routers should need to know about all groups. Ideally, a router should only have to know about those groups' tree(s) of which it is a component.

Note that despite their differences, the DVMRP, PIM-DM, and MOSPF all build source-based trees.

- PIM-SM evolved from the core-based trees (CBT) approach, in that it employs the concept of a "core" (or rendezvous point, RP, in PIM-SM terminology) where receivers "meet" sources.

When joining a group, each receiver uses IGMP to notify its directly attached router, which in turn joins the multicast delivery tree by sending an explicit PIM-Join message hop by hop toward the group's RP. A source uses the RP as a conduit to members that have joined the group. The source's PIM-SM router knows how to reach the RP (the exact mechanism will be described below) and forwards traffic from this source to the RP; once reaching the RP, the traffic is forwarded to all the group members (see Figure 12–1).

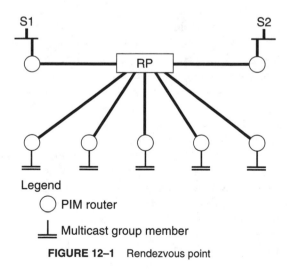

Legend

◯ PIM router

⊥ Multicast group member

FIGURE 12–1   Rendezvous point

This model requires sparse-mode routers to maintain a small amount of state (the RP-Set for the sparse-mode region) in addition to forwarding state. There is only one RP-Set per sparse-mode domain. By using a hash function, each PIM-SM router can uniquely map a group address to one of the members of the RP-Set. All routers within the PIM-SM region use this method to uniquely determine the group's RP.

In the event of an RP's failure, a new RP-Set is distributed which does not include the failed RP. If only a single RP were available for use by a multicast group, the group's communication would be vulnerable to disruption should the RP become unreachable. Employing a set of available RPs significantly increases the protocol's robustness. A small set of PIM-SM routers within a domain are configured to act as candidate RPs (C-RPs), and periodically send C-RP advertisements to the elected bootstrap router (BSR).

At any point in time any group has only a single active RP. If the BSR notices that an RP is no longer reachable, it deletes the unreachable RP from the RP-Set, omitting that RP from the RP-Set in the next bootstrap message. Upon receipt of the new RP-Set, all PIM-SM routers within this region must rehash all the groups that previously hashed to the now-unreachable RP.

PIM-SM BOOTSTRAP MECHANISMS

Each PIM domain has a dynamically elected BSR. The domain's BSR is responsible for constructing and distributing the RP-Set, and for originating bootstrap messages.

BSR election begins when selected PIM-SM routers within the sparse-mode region send bootstrap messages indicating that they are candidate BSRs (C-BSRs) for the region. All PIM-SM routers within a region are not necessarily C-BSRs; intranet managers must decide which PIM-SM routers may be C-BSRs and configure them accordingly. C-BSRs participate in the BSR election, and are capable of assuming the role of BSR if elected. For robustness, PIM-SM dynamically elects the BSRs from a pool of available C-BSRs. A robust network design should place C-BSRs in well-connected locations within the network topology, to facilitate the flooding-like RP-Set distribution to be discussed shortly.

The BSR election process employs a spanning-tree-like protocol. Candidate BSRs emit RP-Set messages hop by hop. These RP-Set messages include their IP addresses and a preference value, which is configurable by the intranet manager. The C-BSR with the highest preference value is elected BSR. If two or more C-BSRs share the highest preference value, the C-BSR with the numerically highest IP address is elected BSR.

Once the domain has successfully elected a BSR, it begins to collect C-RP advertisements sent by all PIM-SM routers which have been designated as potential RPs by the intranet manager. At the manager's discretion, C-RPs are configured to participate as RPs for all, or perhaps only some, groups. The C-RP advertisement binds each C-RP to its allowed group prefix(es). The RP-Set information is distributed to all PIM routers in a region via bootstrap messages.

Once the BSR has collected a list of C-RPs, it distributes the list as an RP-Set across the PIM-SM region. Each router in the region uniquely determines the RP for a group by using a hash function, which has the following independent variables as input:

1. G, the group whose RP is being sought
2. IP addresses, RP_n, of C-RPs whose group-prefix covers G
3. M, a hash mask which allows a small number of consecutive groups to resolve to the same RP

The hash function is the following:

$$\{1103515245 * ([1103515245 * (G\&M) + 12345] \text{ XOR } RP_n) + 12345 \} \bmod 2^{31}$$

Once determined, some unique RP is found to be the rendezvous point for the group G's shared tree, also known as G's RP-Tree.

A DIRECTLY ATTACHED HOST JOINS A GROUP

When more than one PIM router is connected to a multi-access LAN, the router with the highest IP address is selected to function as the designated router (DR) for the LAN. The DR sends Join/Prune messages toward the RP on behalf of the LAN.

Upon receiving an IGMP Host Membership Report message for a new group, the DR performs a deterministic hash function over the sparse-mode region's current RP-Set to uniquely determine the RP for this group.

After performing the lookup, the DR creates a multicast forwarding cache entry for the (*, group) pair and transmits a unicast PIM-Join message toward this group's RP. The (*, group) notation indicates an (any source, group) pair. The intermediate PIM-SM routers forward the unicast PIM-Join message, creating a forwarding entry for the (*, group) pair only if such a forwarding entry does not yet exist. Intermediate routers must create a forwarding entry so that they will be able to forward future traffic downstream toward the DR which originated the PIM-Join message. See Figure 12–2.

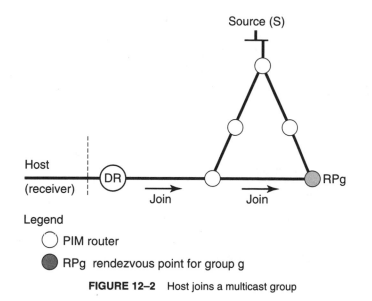

FIGURE 12–2   Host joins a multicast group

DIRECTLY ATTACHED SOURCE SENDS TO A GROUP

When a source transmits a multicast packet to a group, its DR must forward the datagram to the RP for subsequent distribution along the group's delivery tree. The DR encapsulates the source's initial multicast packets in PIM-SM-Register packets and unicasts them toward the group's RP. The PIM-SM-Register packets inform the RP of a new source. The RP may subsequently elect to transmit PIM-Join messages back toward the source's DR to join this source's shortest path tree (SPT), which will allow future unencapsulated packets to flow from this source's DR to the group's RP. *The RP never has to join the source's SPT;* it can keep receiving the source's packets encapsulated in unicast PIM-SM-Register packets for as long as the source has traffic to send.

Unless the RP decides to join the source's SPT, rooted at the source's DR, the (source, group) state is not created in any of the routers between the source's DR and the RP, and the DR must continue to send the source's multicast IP packets to the RP as unicast packets encapsulated within unicast PIM-SM-Register packets. The DR may stop forwarding multicast packets encapsulated in this manner once it has received a PIM-Register-Stop message from the group's RP. The RP may send PIM-Register-Stop messages if there are no downstream receivers for a group, or if the RP has successfully joined the source's SPT. See Figure 12–3.

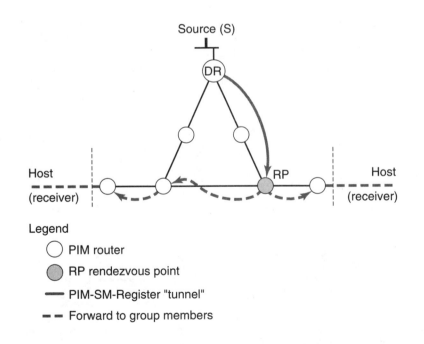

FIGURE 12–3   Source sends to a multicast group

SHARED TREE (RP-TREE) OR SHORTEST PATH TREE?

The RP-Tree provides connectivity for group members but does not optimize the delivery path through the internetwork. PIM-SM allows routers to either (a) continue to receive multicast traffic over the shared RP-Tree, or (b) subsequently join a source-based SPT on behalf of their attached receiver(s). Besides reducing the delay between this router and the source (beneficial to its attached receivers), the source-based SPT also reduces traffic concentration effects on the RP-Tree.

A PIM-SM router with local receivers has the option of switching to the source's SPT (i.e., source-based tree) once it starts receiving data packets from the source. The change-over may be triggered if the data rate from the source exceeds a predefined threshold. The local receiver's last-hop router does this by sending a PIM-Join message toward the active source. After the source-based SPT is active, protocol mechanisms allow a Prune message for that source to be transmitted to the group's RP, thus removing this router from this group's shared RP-Tree. On the other hand, the DR may be configured to never switch over to the source-based SPT, or some other metric might be used to control when to switch to a source-based SPT. See Figure 12–4.

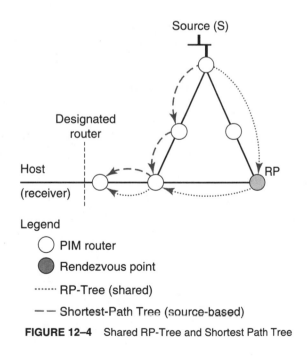

FIGURE 12–4   Shared RP-Tree and Shortest Path Tree

Besides a last-hop router being able to switch to a source-based tree, there is also the possibility that the group's RP could join the source's SPT. Similar controls (bandwidth threshold, administrative metrics, etc.) may be used at an RP to influence these decisions. The RP only joins the source's DR's SPT if the RP's local policy controls permit this.

While PIM-SM uses shared trees by default, it can selectively switch to source-based SPTs—on a per-source basis—if the routing policy permits. It is actually possible for a single group's PIM-SM tree to have both shared tree and source-based tree subtrees simultaneously, even if there is only one source, because PIM-SM routers that are downstream of the rendezvous point may choose to join the source's source-based tree, then leave the shared RP-Tree. It is also conceivable, though unlikely, that a sparse-mode group's receivers could all be joined to the source's SPT, with no receivers using the shared RP-Tree.

PIM-SM TREE BUILDING AND FORWARDING SUMMARY

PIM-SM can use either source-based or shared trees. By default, PIM-SM uses shared trees rooted at a group's RP. Regardless of which tree type is in use, there is no broadcasting of any data traffic. Once interested receivers have used IGMP to join a group, the subnetwork's PIM-SM DR then issues PIM-Join messages on their behalf toward the group's RP. These join messages establish forwarding state in the intermediate routers which is cached to support future forwarding decisions. If the rendezvous point receives a packet for which there is no pre-established forwarding state, the packet is dropped.

As each packet is received, a reverse-path check is performed. This is consistent with the forwarding technique used by PIM-DM, and also DVMRP. Once it passes the reverse-path check, it must match a preexisting forwarding cache entry. The unicast routing table provides the necessary information to determine the best route toward the group's RP; the packet must have arrived on the interface this router would use to send traffic toward the group's RP. Note that the forwarding state created by PIM-SM is unidirectional in that it only allows traffic to flow away from the RP, not toward it.

PART V

INTERNET MULTICAST ROUTING

Today, multicast routing in the Internet is a strictly experimental service. No Internet Service Provider (ISP) charges for MBone access, and no provider really supports it. The IETF has created an "MBone Deployment," or "MBoneD" working group, to identify and hopefully resolve the operational issues required to move beyond today's MBone to a future "multicast-enabled Internet." Everyone's goal seems to be the same, but no one seems to know how to get there. Unfortunately, no existing multicast routing protocol is suited to operation over the worldwide Internet.

There are many lessons to be learned from today's MBone, however, so we will briefly describe the history and scaling problems of today's MBone. In light of this history, we will discuss various prerequisites for a future in which the MBone is perhaps nothing more than a fond (?) memory.

CHAPTER 13

TODAY: "MBONE"

MBONE DEFINED

The Internet Multicast Backbone (MBone) is an interconnected set of subnetworks and routers that support the delivery of IP multicast traffic. The goal of the MBone was to construct a semi-permanent IP multicast testbed to enable the deployment of multicast applications without waiting for the ubiquitous deployment of multicast-capable routers in the Internet.

The MBone has grown from 40 subnets in four different countries in 1992 to many thousands of subnets worldwide by July 1997. With new multicast applications and multicast-based services appearing, it seems likely that the use of multicast technology in the Internet will keep growing at an ever increasing rate.

The MBone is a virtual network that is layered on top of sections of the physical Internet. It is composed of islands of multicast routing capability connected to other islands, or "regions," by virtual point-to-point links called "tunnels." The tunnels allow multicast traffic to pass through the non-multicast-capable parts of the Internet. Tunneled IP multicast packets are encapsulated as IP-over-IP (i.e., the protocol number is set to 4) so that the intervening routers see only their wrappers, regular unicast IP packets. The encapsulating IP header is added on entry to a tunnel and stripped off on exit. This set of multicast routers, their directly connected subnetworks, and the interconnecting tunnels constitutes the MBone (see Figure 13–1).

Since the MBone and the Internet have different topologies, multicast routers execute a separate routing protocol to decide how to forward multicast packets. In some cases, this means that they use a multicast routing protocol that includes its own internal unicast routing protocol, but in other cases the multicast routing protocol relies on the routing table provided by the underlying unicast routing protocols.

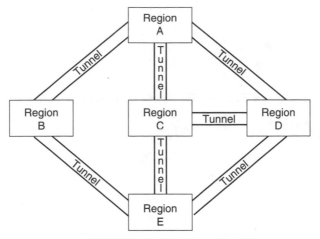

FIGURE 13–1   Structure of the MBone

The majority of MBone regions are currently interconnected by the Distance Vector Multicast Routing Protocol (DVMRP). Internally, the regions may execute any routing protocol they choose: multicast extensions to OSPF (MOSPF), the Protocol-Independent Multicast (PIM) routing protocol(s), or the DVMRP.

As multicast routing software features become more widely available on the routers of the Internet, providers may gradually decide to use "native" multicast as an alternative to using lots of tunnels. "Native" multicast exists when a region of routers (or set of regions) operates without tunnels. All subnetworks are connected by at least one router which is capable of forwarding their multicast packets. In this case, tunnels are not required: multicast packets just flow where they need to, based on the relative locations of the source(s) and the receiver(s).

EXPERIMENTAL OVERLAY

Because any new feature, such as multicasting or IPv6, cannot be simultaneously enabled across the whole core of the Internet, it is sometimes useful to tunnel these new packets across the Internet. The Internet's MBone is a set of tunnels between various organizations that have been experimenting with "live" multicasting.

Many scaling problems with multicast routing protocols have been identified as a result of this large-scale testbed. It is much more useful to experiment with a realistic-sized network which interconnects many different organizations than to have many isolated experiments going on. Building a large network, optimizing implementations for scalability and robustness, has taught lessons that all these researchers could probably not have discovered by working independently.

Tunneling allows the "old" Internet routers to see these packets as unicast IPv4 packets. The tunnel endpoints are responsible for wrapping the newfangled packet in a IPv4 header, destined for the IP address of the other end of the tunnel, and also for receiv-

```
+-+-+-+-+-+-+-+-+-+-+-+-+-+-+-+-+-+-+-+-+-+-+-+-+-+-+-+-+-+-+    \  Protocol = 4
|Version|  IHL  |Type of Service|         Total Length         |  |  (0000 0100)
+-+-+-+-+-+-+-+-+-+-+-+-+-+-+-+-+-+-+-+-+-+-+-+-+-+-+-+-+-+-+    |  means IP-in-IP
|          Identification        |Flags|    Fragment Offset    |  |
+-+-+-+-+-+-+-+-+-+-+-+-+-+-+-+-+-+-+-+-+-+-+-+-+-+-+-+-+-+-+    |   +----------+
| Time to Live |0 0 0 0 0 1 0 0|      Header Checksum           |  \  | Outer IP |
+-+-+-+-+-+-+-+-+-+-+-+-+-+-+-+-+-+-+-+-+-+-+-+-+-+-+-+-+-+-+   =>| (Tunnel) |
|        Source Address (Local Tunnel Endpoint Address)         |  /  | Header   |
+-+-+-+-+-+-+-+-+-+-+-+-+-+-+-+-+-+-+-+-+-+-+-+-+-+-+-+-+-+-+    |   +----------+
|     Destination Address (Remote Tunnel Endpoint Address)      |  |
+-+-+-+-+-+-+-+-+-+-+-+-+-+-+-+-+-+-+-+-+-+-+-+-+-+-+-+-+-+-+    |
|                    Options                    |    Padding    |  |
+-+-+-+-+-+-+-+-+-+-+-+-+-+-+-+-+-+-+-+-+-+-+-+-+-+-+-+-+-+-+    /


+-+-+-+-+-+-+-+-+-+-+-+-+-+-+-+-+-+-+-+-+-+-+-+-+-+-+-+-+-+-+    \
|Version|  IHL  |Type of Service|         Total Length         |  |
+-+-+-+-+-+-+-+-+-+-+-+-+-+-+-+-+-+-+-+-+-+-+-+-+-+-+-+-+-+-+    |
|          Identification        |Flags|    Fragment Offset    |  |
+-+-+-+-+-+-+-+-+-+-+-+-+-+-+-+-+-+-+-+-+-+-+-+-+-+-+-+-+-+-+    |   +----------+
| Time to Live |    Protocol   |      Header Checksum           |  \  | Inner IP |
+-+-+-+-+-+-+-+-+-+-+-+-+-+-+-+-+-+-+-+-+-+-+-+-+-+-+-+-+-+-+   =>| (Native) |
|        Source Address (Source Address of this Multicast)      |  /  | Header   |
+-+-+-+-+-+-+-+-+-+-+-+-+-+-+-+-+-+-+-+-+-+-+-+-+-+-+-+-+-+-+    |   +----------+
|       Multicast Destination Address (Class D Address)        |  |
+-+-+-+-+-+-+-+-+-+-+-+-+-+-+-+-+-+-+-+-+-+-+-+-+-+-+-+-+-+-+    |
|                    Options                    |    Padding    |  |
+-+-+-+-+-+-+-+-+-+-+-+-+-+-+-+-+-+-+-+-+-+-+-+-+-+-+-+-+-+-+    /


+-+-+-+-+-+-+-+-+-+-+-+-+-+-+-+-+-+-+-+-+-+-+-+-+-+-+-+-+-+-+    \
|                                              |  |  |
/                                              /  |  |
:                                              :  \  +----------+
|                                              |   =>| Packet's |
:                                              :  /  | Data     |
\                                              \  |  | Payload  |
|                                              |  |  +----------+
+-+-+-+-+-+-+-+-+-+-+-+-+-+-+-+-+-+-+-+-+-+-+-+-+-+-+-+-+-+-+    /
```

FIGURE 13–2   IP headers of a tunneled multicast packet

ing packets from the other tunnel endpoint, then extracting the newfangled packet from the IPv4 header and forwarding it as appropriate. See Figure 13–2.

Another similar testbed is the 6Bone, a live IPv6 network interconnecting sites around the world which are doing early IPv6 testing and prototyping.

WHICH ROUTING PROTOCOL IS USED?

The MBone was initially composed of multicast routers (a.k.a. "mrouters") using only DVMRP. Early adopters of multicast routing technology consisted of government and industry research labs, as well as university computer science and other departments. The

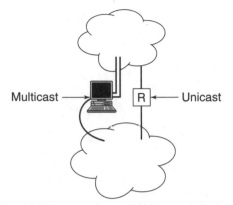

FIGURE 13–3   UNIX mrouters in parallel with stand-alone unicast routers

dawn of the MBone era, in 1992, was well before any router vendor had implemented any form of multicast routing; the initial implementation of DVMRP was done under UNIX™, in a program called `mrouted` (pronounced em-route-dee).

MBone-attached organizations used these UNIX-based mrouters to provide local multicast routing among their attached interfaces (it is possible to put multiple network interfaces into a UNIX™ workstation, such as Ethernet and FDDI). These mrouters could be deployed in parallel with unicast routers to enable the native multicast forwarding the stand-alone routers could not yet provide (see Figure 13–3).

Besides their physical interfaces, the UNIX-based mrouters had one or more virtual interfaces. Virtual interfaces, or `vifs`, are used either to interconnect multicast islands within an organization's network (as in Figure 13–4) or to provide MBone connectivity for an organization via a tunnel to another mrouter in another organization's multicast island elsewhere on the Internet. In choosing appropriate nodes on the MBone with which to tunnel, it was—and still is—best to choose a tunnel neighbor that is "nearby" in the unicast sense.

As router vendors have implemented multicast routing protocols, more choices of routing protocols have emerged. Cisco, undeniably the prominent vendor in today's Internet router market, has implemented PIM and the DVMRP. Cisco uses PIM's RPF engine as their core forwarding engine, which means that their fundamental forwarding decisions are driven by the unicast routing table. There are provisions for interoperating with the DVMRP routers via tunnels. Proteon implemented MOSPF before anyone else, and provided for interoperability of MOSPF with DVMRP as well as an innovative technique to run the DVMRP "over" an MOSPF domain (treating the router-based MOSPF internetwork "cloud" as a multicast-capable extended LAN). Of course, at the time there were no other multicast routing protocols. Other vendors, including 3Com, Bay Networks, and Alantec/Fore have implemented multicast routing in routers and switches. As multicast routing becomes more widespread over time, it is likely that more protocols will become available from each router vendor.

The conclusion is that the MBone is no longer the homogeneous, DVMRP-only internetwork it once was. Today, most edge domains are probably not running the DVMRP,

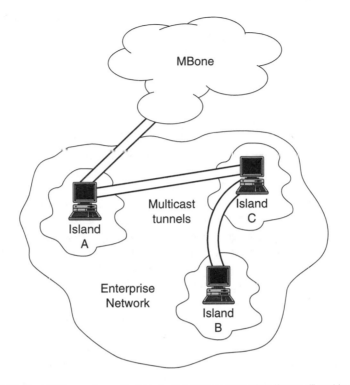

FIGURE 13–4   UNIX mrouters attaching to the MBone and other "internal" multicast islands

except to attach to the MBone. PIM is probably the most popular intradomain multicast routing protocol at this time, mostly due to Cisco's market dominance. CBT is not yet available commercially, but its simplicity may make it attractive to users wanting a shared tree protocol that is not quite as complicated as PIM-SM. Also, CBT seems to be quite well suited to operation in intranets due to its bidirectional forwarding state.

MBONE APPLICATIONS

As a testbed for multicast routing protocols, the MBone has been quite successful. It has also demonstrated what sorts of applications work well over large DVMRP networks, and which do not.

The MBone carries audio and video multicasts of Internet Engineering Task Force (IETF) meetings, NASA Space Shuttle Missions, U.S. House and Senate sessions, and other content (occasional rock concerts, lectures, sporting events, etc.). Public and private sessions coexist on the MBone. Sessions that are meant for public consumption are announced to the world via the session directory (sdr) tool, itself a multicast-based application. sdr allows users to see a list of current and future public sessions for which they are within the sender's "scope." Also, from within the `sdr` tool they can launch those multi-media applications necessary to observe a session in progress. Some of the most popular tools include `vat` (the visual audio tool), `vic` (videoconferencing tool), and `wb` ([shared] whiteboard tool). These public-domain applications are available for many flavors of UNIX and Windows 95/NT.

MBone Application Traits

One lesson learned is that large DVMRP-based networks are not suited to serving many small groups, or a few large groups with multiple senders. The problem with having many small groups is that most DVMRP routers in the MBone are not on most of the (source, group) distribution trees, and therefore must keep prune state. As the number of sources and groups increases, this becomes a noticeable drain on the memory in mrouters. Also, the broadcast-and-prune design of the DVMRP means that all the traffic from all the active groups are broadcast across the entire MBone whenever their prune state expires. All of these small sessions can collectively waste substantial amounts of bandwidth. Typically, therefore, the MBone has limited itself to a small number of simultaneous sessions, with few senders per session (usually one).

The DVMRP also does not lend itself to a great degree of interactivity among group members. Large numbers of active sources means large numbers of distribution trees and collectively large amounts of off-tree prune state. If a source is inactive for long enough, its forwarding state will timeout and be removed. Once it sends data to the group again, the forwarding state and prune state will be recreated, after the traffic is rebroadcast across the entire internetwork. This constant state maintenance is a drain on the CPU of all the mrouters in the MBone.

Because the MBone is one large, flat routing domain (with a DVMRP backbone), it is subject to these scaling problems in the extreme. With thousands of mrouters, it would appear that the limits of the current generation of DVMRP are being approached. The imminent release of `mrouted` 3.9 promises to add some useful enhancements. Hopefully, the MBone can be maintained in a useful state until a true interdomain routing protocol can be designed, implemented, and deployed. It is also possible that the MBone will be maintained in its tunnel-based state for a while, with a newer core multicast routing protocol, as we await the arrival of the aforementioned interdomain multicast routing protocol.

MBONE MYTH—NOT LIMITED TO 512 KBPS

As stated earlier, `mrouted` was the original multicast router implementation for the MBone. Through version 3.8, it has had a default rate limit of 512 kbps on each tunnel interface. MBone developers thought that multicast traffic might be perceived as being able to consume all available bandwidth on some links of the Internet, so a rate limit was warranted. For reference, common customer links to the Internet run at a speed of 1.544 Mbps today, called a T-1 or DS-1 circuit. T-1 links have 1.536 Mbps of available payload capacity, so 512 kbps is exactly one-third of a T-1.

Many people deduced from `mrouted`'s default tunnel rate limit of 512 kbps that the MBone had a total backbone capacity of 512 kbps! When the MBone rate limits were conceived, most ISP backbones were based on T-1 circuits. Since that time, typical ISP backbone circuits have moved from T-1 (1.544 Mbps) to T-3 (44.736 Mbps), OC-3 (155.52 Mbps), and even faster in some cases: OC-12 (622.08 Mbps) has seen limited deployment, and OC-48 (2488.320 Mbps) is just around the corner. . . .

Originally, `mrouted`/DVMRP did not support pruning, causing multicast traffic to be periodically broadcast across the entire MBone. However, DVMRP pruning is now commonplace. As ISP backbone bandwidth has steadily increased, and pruning-capable multicast routers have replaced old non-pruning mrouters, the rate limit has become increasingly irrelevant in the core of the MBone.

CHAPTER **14**

TOMORROW: WHO KNOWS?

One clear lesson learned from the MBone is that ISPs need more ways to implement effective multicast routing policies. No existing multicast routing protocol provides policy controls that are even a pale shadow of those available in unicast routing, especially inter-domain routing. The MBone today is a science-fair project, not a production-level service. Try to imagine running RIP on a network on almost the scale of the Internet and you see the problem. The MBone is within one order of magnitude of the size of the Internet. (There are about 45,000 routes in today's Internet, and about 5500 routes in today's MBone.)

In the unicast world, the clear distinction between "interior" and "exterior" routing protocols has facilitated the effective scaling of the routing infrastructure. The "hard stuff" of routing policies is in the exterior domain. No true two-layer hierarchy yet exists for multicast, nor is a credible model yet on the drawing board, although work has begun toward solving these problems. You may say that the MBone has a two-layer hierarchy today, but logically it is still one flat routing domain. While individual organizations may run PIM or MOSPF internally, they still must seamlessly integrate with the DVMRP backbone, making it appear as if they were running DVMRP internally. There is little aggregation, which could help reduce the backbone routing tables.

Once ISPs have products which implement exterior multicast routing policies, and routing protocols that can incorporate these policies, they will be far more willing to consider the global deployment of native multicast. Again, none of today's protocols (DVMRP, MOSPF, PIM-DM, PIM-SM, or CBT) are suitable for use as an exterior routing protocol that could enable ISPs to deploy native multicast. They are all applicable to use within intranets as interior routing protocols, but they don't address the deployment and management issues that ISPs really care about.

WHAT'S THE GOAL?

Multicast-Enabled Internet!!

Everyone seems to think that multicast in the Internet is on a track toward "native" operation (*sans* tunnels), but no routing protocol exists yet to support such a service.

One possibility of adding policy controls to multicast routing is being pursued in the proposed multicast extensions to BGP (M-BGP). At the BGP level, policy controls can be applied to enforce routing requirements and business arrangements between multicast providers, analogous to the way routing policies are used today between unicast providers. ISPs should be able to select preferred paths over which to receive multicasts from certain sources.

A tree-building protocol would take the routing table produced by BGP, which embodies the local organization's policies, and use it to build distribution trees. Any of today's tree-building protocols could use the data gathered by M-BGP, or a new protocol could be specifically designed for this purpose.

Another proposal was called "global unified multicast" (GUM), now known as "border gateway multicast protocol" (BGMP), which is based on a "shared tree of domains" design.

Implication: Eliminate the MBone

Once one or more true exterior multicast routing protocols exist, it will be possible to eliminate the MBone. "The MBone is dead! Long live the MBone!" Perhaps the MBone would still serve a purpose as a nonproduction large-scale testbed of new multicast technologies and applications, but it will not be a quasi-production network as it is today.

M-BGP?

An explicit goal of M-BGP is to separate the routing-data-gathering and tree-building components of multicast routing. The big feature lacking from any of today's multicast routing protocols is policy control, an essential feature if providers are to adopt multicast as a production service. Separating policy from tree building seems like a requirement to the designers of M-BGP.

At the routing-data-gathering layer, it is natural to want to reuse BGP's well-understood policy mechanisms. ISP operations are already built on BGP, and this would be a very natural extension of their existing policy enforcement mechanisms. As noted earlier, a new tree-building protocol could be designed to work with M-BGP, or one of the existing protocols could build trees based on topology data derived from M-BGP.

Perhaps BGMP will assume both roles, or another protocol will be designed to work "over" M-BGP. We are still very early in the design phase of true interdomain multicast routing, and it will be some time before designs are finalized, implementations are built and productized, and the resulting products are deployed in the Internet.

At the Memphis IETF meeting in the Spring of 1997, M-BGP was initially described as a unique modification to BGP-4. However, since that time, several other enhanced-BGP-4 proposals have been extended to support multicast IP, in addition to other "multiprotocol" features (such as the ability to support IPv6 routing and IPv4 routing within the same routing protocol). At this point it seems more likely that a unified next-generation BGP-4 supporting IPv4 (unicast and multicast) and IPv6 (unicast and multicast) will be standardized and deployed, rather than a special-purpose protocol that only integrates multicast IPv4 alongside BGP-4's unicast IPv4 support.

One requirement for any true interdomain routing protocol is that it should allow graceful migration from the MBone to the new "native" multicast infrastructure. The initial M-BGP draft goes into some detail on how this can be accomplished. These transition ideas would work as well with a complete next-generation BGP-4 as they would with a special-purpose set of multicast extensions for today's BGP-4. The transition from the MBone will not be trivial, since it is one very large, flat DVMRP routing domain. Any workable interdomain routing protocol will need to facilitate the subdivision of the MBone while still providing connectivity to the remainder of the MBone, until no MBone remains. . . .

BGMP/GUM?

Building on concepts from CBT and PIM-SM, BGMP (formerly known as GUM) requires that a "root domain" be associated with every global multicast group. BGMP can build two kinds of trees, similar to PIM-SM. Active groups can use shared trees, but BGMP also allows receivers to join interdomain source-specific trees. In a departure from other multicast routing protocols, trees in BGMP are trees of domains, not trees of routers.

BGMP presumes that groups of class D addresses have been assigned to each domain. For all groups in its range, each domain is the root of all its shared "domain trees." An address allocator that takes group addresses from within its own domain's address block will be more effective: In such cases, the root domain is identical to the local domain. Figure 14–1 illustrates this.

As we have seen, the design choices made by CBT and PIM-SM are better suited to the intradomain case (even if wide area). BGMP and other shared-tree protocols have the following two main differences:

1. Unidirectional vs. bidirectional trees (*vis-à-vis* third-party dependencies):
   Bidirectional trees help reduce third-party dependencies. One reason PIM-SM is unacceptable to ISPs is that the RP for a group could be inside another ISP's infrastructure. That is a third-party dependency. (Also, for PIM-SM to operate over the Internet, it would need to be one large PIM-SM region. This is not much better than the situation with DVMRP today.)
   This potential dependence on a third party prevents the ISP from having full operational control. Also, this could limit performance (the RP may be far away from a group's receivers), or problems may be difficult to resolve due to lack of

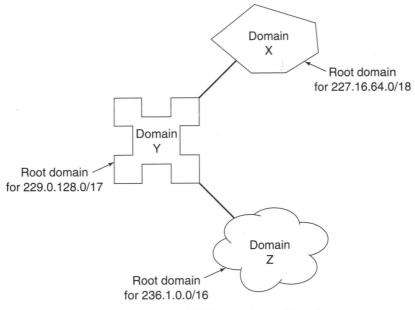

FIGURE 14–1   BGMP shared tree of domains

management access to remote routers owned by other ISPs. It would appear that any interdomain routing protocol needs to operate in a manner which minimizes third-party dependencies, implying use of bidirectional trees.

BGMP's designers claim that an advantage of unidirectional trees is that they have better loop prevention, due to simpler forwarding rules. One could argue that CBT's forwarding rules are about the simplest we have seen thus far. CBT is a bidirectional-state protocol that simply forwards on all non-incoming interfaces that are known to lead to group members.

BGMP supports bidirectional trees because it has to: It is designed for the interdomain case, where third-party dependencies must be kept to a minimum. However, BGMP also supports unidirectional branches, thereby (allegedly) allowing more efficient pruning than is possible with a strictly bidirectional-tree protocol.

2. Method of choosing a group's shared tree root (domain):

For intra-domain protocols, the choice of a core or RP is largely driven by the desire to share the load among a set of essentially equivalent cores/RPs. In contrast, the inter-domain world has many more opportunities for cores/RPs to be placed in suboptimal localities, relative to the source(s) and receiver(s). At a minimum, this is because a future inter-domain ubiquitous-multicast Internet is so much bigger than any intranet!

Policy and performance drive the choice of an inter-domain group's shared tree root. In the inter-domain case, all roots are not equivalent. BGMP is taking an approach which chooses a group's root domain primarily based on administrative and performance inputs.

BGMP is the product of some very talented researchers in the multicast routing community, but it is still quite early in its development. As with any new idea, this protocol could disappear into the dim mists of history, or it could survive its design and development phase, eventually being placed on the standards track. Assuming it will survive beyond its current infancy, many changes to the proposal should be expected as it is refined by the community and, later, by operational experience.

PART VI

RELATED TOPICS

Multicast IP routing does not exist in a vacuum. There are other relevant dimensions to any discussion of multicast:

1. Routing protocol interoperability schemes
2. Fundamental multicast-enabled applications, especially for intranets, such as the Service Location Protocol
3. Transport protocols over multicast IP: reliable multicast

CHAPTER 15

MULTICAST ROUTING INTEROPERABILITY FRAMEWORKS

Two major frameworks exist which can facilitate interoperability between various multicast routing protocols. A more formal scheme is being promulgated by the IETF, while a less formal scheme (proxy IGMP hack) has been implemented by some vendors already and looks like it could be useful in some scenarios.

REQUIREMENTS FOR MULTICAST BORDER ROUTERS

In late 1996, the IETF IDMR working group began discussing a possible formal structure for a multicast border router (MBR). The working group wants to generically describe the way different multicast routing protocols should interact inside an MBR. This work-in-progress can be found in the internet draft `draft-thaler-interop-00.ps` or its successor.

The draft covers explicit rules for the major multicast routing protocols that existed at the end of 1996: DVMRP, MOSPF, PIM-DM, PIM-SM, and CBT. The draft aims to be generic so that it may be applied to any future multicast routing protocol(s) as well. The framework is in its earliest stages of development, so substantial changes could occur prior to its eventual standardization. As with any new idea, it is also possible that this is a dead end, and will go no further. Time will tell.

For practical reasons, it is preferable to focus on a generic interprotocol MBR scheme, rather than having to write 25 documents (20 detailing how each of those five protocols must interwork with the four others, plus five detailing how two disjoint regions running the same protocol must interwork inside a border router).

Thaler's scheme imposes some topological constraints in order to limit the scope of the problem space; if the problem is made simpler, the solution(s) can be simpler. The goal is to enable effective multicast delivery across an internetwork with an arbitrary mixture of multicast routing protocols. It is not clear at this time if this proposal could be objectively classified as "simple." It is, however, the only proposal currently on the table, so it bears investigation. At a minimum, this should illuminate the problem by showing one possible, but not necessarily optimal, solution.

Each multicast routing domain, or region, must be connected within a "tree of regions" topology. If more arbitrary interregional topologies are desired, a hierarchical multicast routing protocol would need to be invented; such a protocol could carry topological information describing how the regions are interconnected. Given that no such protocol currently exists, Thaler restricts his proposal to the case of a tree of regions (see Figure 15–1) having one centrally placed "backbone" region. Each pair of regions is interconnected by one or more MBR(s).

An MBR is responsible for injecting a default route into its "child regions," and also injecting subnetwork reachability information from the child regions into its "parent region," optionally using aggregation techniques to reduce the volume of information while preserving its meaning. Figure 15–2 illustrates this.

Note that every parent region is also a child region, forwarding its own and its collective children's subnetwork reachability information toward the backbone region. Each parent region also accepts a default from a higher-level router, which it forwards on to its children. The only region that is not a child region is the backbone region. It collects subnetwork reachability information from all of its children, and advertises a master default route to all of its children. The only regions that are not both parents and children are leaf regions, which only accept a default route, and only advertise their local subnetwork reachability information upward. MBRs that comply with `draft-thaler-interop-00.ps` have other characteristics and duties, including:

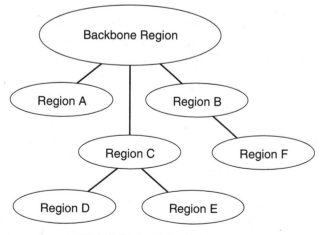

FIGURE 15–1   Tree of regions

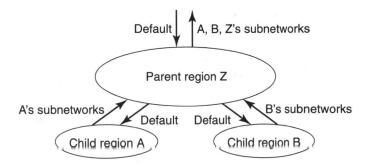

FIGURE 15–2 Parent and child regions

- Almost by definition, the MBR must consist of at least two active routing components, each an instance of some multicast routing protocol. No assumption is made about the type of routing protocol (e.g., broadcast and prune or shared tree; distance vector or link state) any component runs, or the nature of a "component." Multiple components running different copies of the same protocol are allowed.
- An MBR forwards packets between two or more independent regions, with one or more active interfaces per region, but only one component per region.
- Each interface for which multicast is enabled is "owned" by exactly one of the components at a time.
- All components share a common forwarding cache of (source, group) entries, which are created when data packets are received and can be deleted at any time. The component owning an interface is the only component which may change forwarding cache entries pertaining to that interface. Each forwarding cache entry has a single incoming interface (iif) and a list of outgoing interfaces (oiflist).

AN INTEROPERABILITY HACK: "PROXY IGMP"

One way to glue one multicast routing domain to another is to use IGMP as the glue protocol (see Figure 15–3). For instance, if an ASBR for an MOSPF domain does not support PIM, but the other routers on a common exchange LAN do support PIM, the MOSPF border router could be made to imitate a very busy host.

The MOSPF border router knows all the group memberships for the entire MOSPF AS, because all areas within the AS flood their Group-Membership LSAs into the backbone area. Therefore, any ASBR within the backbone area can make a list of active groups within its AS. If the ASBR is in a transit area, it will have incomplete knowledge of which groups are present within the OSPF AS. If it does know about all the existing groups, it can simply act like a host that is a member of all these groups. To do this, IGMP Host Membership Reports must be sent out by this ASBR onto the intermediate LAN, joining every group that is active within the MOSPF domain.

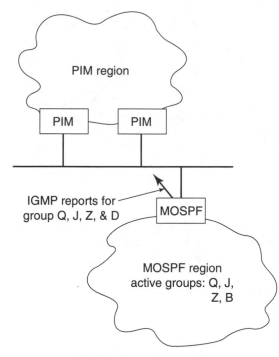

FIGURE 15–3   Proxy IGMP scenario

MOSPF is a perfect example for this scenario, because it has global knowledge (at the backbone area level) of all active groups within the AS. So as long as the ASBR in question is within the backbone area, it has complete knowledge of all group members present within the whole AS. This functionality is generically known as "domain-wide reports." Not all multicast routing protocols have this capability, so the IETF IDMR Working Group plans to specify a domain-wide report function that can be used with any multicast routing protocol.

Another scenario in which IGMP is used this way is with dial-up communications servers which support multicast. All groups that have been joined by the dial-up users must be joined by the communications server on their behalf. A domain-wide report scheme would allow any multicast routing domain to be attached to any other across a common exchange LAN, as described above.

CHAPTER 16

EXPANDING-RING SEARCHES AND SERVICE LOCATION

ISSUES WITH EXPANDING-RING SEARCHES

Expanding-ring searches may be used when an end station wishes to find the closest example of a certain kind of server. One key assumption is that each of these servers is equivalent in the service provided. Ask any of them a question pertinent to that service and you should get the same answer. Another assumption is that the servers are capable of responding to requests received via multicast, know to join the appropriate groups, and so on. In the sense of all servers being equivalent, such a service is the DNS (though no standards yet exist for DNS discovery via expanding searches).

The searching client sends a query packet with the IP header's TTL field set to 1. This packet will only reach its local subnetwork. If a response is not heard in a certain timeout interval, a second query is issued, this time with the TTL increased to 2. This process of sending and waiting for a response, while incrementing the TTL after each cycle, is an expanding-ring search. Expanding-ring searches can facilitate auto-configuration or resource-discovery protocols. See Figure 16–1.

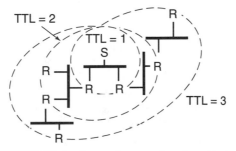

FIGURE 16–1   A generic expanding-ring search

Another key assumption is that the multicast infrastructure provides the ability to radiate equally well in all directions from any source. This usually implies that all routers in an internetwork support a multicast routing protocol; however, it turns out that not all multicast routing protocols support this requirement equally well.

There are two classes of routing protocols to consider when discussing expanding-ring searches: DVMRP and PIM-DM make up one class, with CBT, MOSPF, and PIM-SM constituting the other. The first two protocols are implicit-join, while the last three are explicit-join protocols.

Expanding-Ring Searches over Implicit-Join Protocol Regions

Expanding-Ring Searches over DVMRP Regions

DVMRP supports expanding-ring searches fairly well for a reasonable number of sources. The downside of using DVMRP is that there is source-specific state kept across the entire DVMRP region. As the number of sources increases, the amount of state increases linearly. Due to DVMRP's broadcast-and-prune nature, the tree for each source will quickly converge to reach all receivers for a given group (within a packet's TTL).

Note that for a resource to be found by an expanding-ring search, even in the context of a broadcast-and-prune protocol, the receiver should join the required group. If we assume that all routers in your internetwork speak the DVMRP, these TTL-based searches will have the desired result: As the TTL is incremented, the packets will cross successively further routers, radiating away from the source's subnetwork.

Expanding-Ring Searches over PIM-DM Regions

PIM-DM is very similar to DVMRP in the context of expanding-ring searches. We must continue to assume that all routers in a given internetwork support the same multicast routing protocol, and that the resources wishing to be discovered have already joined the necessary group. Since both PIM-DM and the DVMRP are based on the reverse-path multicasting (RPM) algorithm, it will ensure that any source's traffic is broadcast to the edges of the entire internetwork, within the limits of each packet's TTL.

Expanding-Ring Searches over Explicit-Join Protocol Regions

You might wonder why an explicit-join protocol is any different than an implicit-join protocol for expanding-ring searches. The difference is subtle. Even in a broadcast-and-prune protocol, the services being found still must announce their group membership to their edge routers. This is because the truncated reverse-path broadcasting technique (TRPB), a foundation for RPM, will not forward traffic onto a LAN unless a group member is known to be present. Again, how is this different than an explicit-join protocol? Well, the difference is that under RPM, the traffic is broadcast from the source, whether or not any group members are known to exist.

Under an explicit-join protocol, traffic will not get past the center of the tree (or, in the case of MOSPF, no tree will be built at all if no Group-Membership LSAs are present in the link-state database), unless the group members' local routers have already joined the group on their behalf. In a broadcast-and-prune environment, any LANs that must be crossed to reach routers further downstream will see the packets—even if no servers on that LAN have joined the group yet.

The only LANs that will never see traffic—unless there is at least one group member present—are the subnetworks at the very edge of the internetwork. The truncation procedure will ensure that no traffic will be forwarded onto the LAN unless there is a group member present.

Explicit-join protocols do not necessarily lend themselves to supporting expanding-ring searches. The one property PIM-SM and CBT share in this regard is that their trees must be set up in advance or no packets are forwarded away from the rendezvous point (RP) or Core, respectively. These are not only "explicit-join" protocols, but also "shared-tree" protocols. As we will see below, MOSPF also has this explicit-join characteristic, although it is not a shared-tree protocol.

In the case of PIM-SM, no packets are forwarded by the RP unless at least one group member has joined the group somewhere within the PIM-SM region. The RP cannot deliver any packets unless interested receivers (i.e., the servers we're searching for) have already joined this group.

CBT shares this "weakness" of PIM-SM, in that any servers wanting to be found by expanding-ring searches must join a group's core-based tree before they will get any packets from end stations conducting expanding-ring searches.

Otherwise, PIM-SM and CBT have excellent scaling properties for multicast routing and forwarding in support of "normal" multicast applications. Do not judge them based only on their lack of suitability to this one, rather contrived, application.

Expanding-Ring Searches over PIM-SM Regions

PIM-SM, by default, does not build source-based trees. Consider the case of a sender in a PIM-SM region: Multicast packets sent with TTL = 1 will only reach end stations on the local subnetwork, but TTL = 2 packets will be tunneled by the source's designated router (DR) inside PIM-SM-Register packets destined for the RP. Since PIM-SM's forwarding state is unidirectional, the source's traffic must be tunneled to the RP even if the source happens to be on a LAN that is part of the group's distribution tree. See Figure 16–2.

Once at the RP, the PIM-SM-Register wrapper is removed, exposing the original multicast packet. That packet should now have its TTL = 1, because the source's DR should have decremented the TTL by one before forwarding the packet through the PIM-SM-Register "tunnel." The RP can now forward the original packet over its attached outgoing interfaces for this group.

Since the first packet to reach the RP has its TTL = 1, the RP will not be able to forward it further. Future packets, with incrementally higher TTLs, will then radiate outward from the RP over any active outgoing interfaces for this group, as shown in Figure 16–3. Thus, the search will locate resources that are closest to the RP, not the source (unless the RP and the source happen to be very close together). The behavior of the search will be

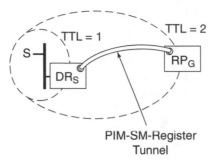

FIGURE 16–2   Beginning of an expanding-ring search in a PIM-SM region

perfectly radial around the source only if the source is on a subnetwork that is directly
connected to the RP for this group.

Expanding-Ring Searches over CBT Regions

The latest specification of CBT version 2 does not have this core-centric problem. CBT
does not need to encapsulate packets to get them to the group's core, provided the end station doing the expanding-ring search is present on the tree between the core and the group
members. (Non-member senders' traffic still must be sent to the core by IP-in-IP encapsulation.)

Despite being a little better than PIM-SM in this regard, CBT is not perfect for these
searches. The effectiveness of a CBT search depends on the density of branch points for
the group's shared tree in the immediate vicinity of the source. If we assume that all
routers are also CBT routers, the search can be quite effective.

Finally, because CBT's state is bidirectional, any receiver can also be a sender with
no tree-setup penalty. This feature may be attractive for highly interactive multicast applications, but it may not be beneficial in an expanding-ring search. It will only be beneficial
if the searching clients share the tree with the servers being sought. If the searching client
is not on the tree, CBT is the same as PIM-SM insofar as the expanding-ring search "application."

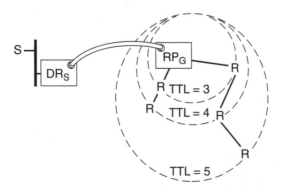

FIGURE 16–3   Packets radiating from the RP

Expanding-Ring Searches over MOSPF Regions

MOSPF supports expanding-ring searches particularly well as long as some servers have joined the group in advance. It keeps source-specific state, and thus has the same scaling issues as DVMRP with respect to state (forwarding cache) increasing linearly with the number of searching sources.

MOSPF doesn't forward any multicast traffic unless some member servers have already joined the group when the expanding-ring search begins. The servers' IGMP Reports result in Group-Membership LSAs being injected into the OSPF link-state database. These Group-Membership LSAs enable any MOSPF router to compute a tree from the source, through itself, to those receiver(s) downstream from it. If there are no Group-Membership LSAs in the link-state database for this group, no tree can be built, so no packets can be forwarded.

Each MOSPF router has the unique capability of knowing the topology of its local OSPF area via the unicast components of the OSPF link-state database. An important by-product of this knowledge is that for a given (source, group) pair, each MOSPF router knows the minimum TTL needed to reach the closest group member, in terms of number of hops from itself. If a packet's TTL is not at least this large, the MOSPF router can silently discard it rather than wasting the downstream routers' time with a packet it knows can't reach any part of this destination group within the local OSPF area. This conserves bandwidth that would otherwise be wasted by the intermediate iterations of successively larger TTLs. This behavior is depicted in Figure 16–4.

SERVICE LOCATION PROTOCOL

Expanding-ring searches may be fine for certain kinds of searches, but they are rather informal and achieve mixed results depending on which multicast routing protocol is in use. A more formalized search service has been under development in the IETF for some time, and IP multicast is one of the key elements of its bootstrap mechanism.

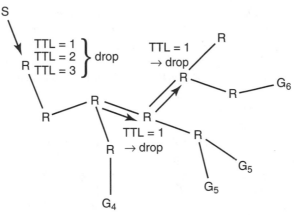

FIGURE 16–4 MOSPF can preemptively drop packets

The Service Location Protocol (RFC-2165) has recently been published as a standards-track RFC with Proposed Standard status. Under the IETF standards process, "Proposed Standard" is the first of three levels of standardization, followed by "Draft Standard," then full "Standard" status.

As indicated by its name, this protocol is designed to help clients locate desired services matching their requirements. The SLP is meant to bring more ease of use to IP-based networks, somewhat comparable to the user experience of Novell IPX-based or Apple's AppleTalk-based networks.

AppleTalk clients have a service (and server) selection program called the "Chooser," which can query the internetwork to see if servers matching user-selected services are available. Servers do not periodically advertise their offered services. There is simply a process at initialization time to ensure that each server's name is unique within its "zone."

AppleTalk networks may be subdivided into logical groupings called "zones," and the lookups for services will return a list of the servers that are currently offering the desired service within the chosen zone. In the case where the entire network is one zone, the Chooser allows users to select a service icon, and then displays matching servers—in this case from across the entire AppleTalk internetwork. The AppleTalk routers must maintain a mapping table showing which zones are defined on which network segments so that they can forward Chooser lookups to all parts of the desired zone.

Novell IPX clients constantly receive "RIP and SAP" broadcasts that flow across the entire IPX internetwork. RIP is a distance-vector routing protocol that is very similar to the RIP of the IP suite of protocols. SAP is the "Service Advertising Protocol," which servers use to advertise their presence across the network. IPX SAP is very similar to a distance-vector routing protocol; clients can directly determine which servers offering a desired service are "closer" (in terms of hop count) than others.

Even though most clients do not cache the entire SAP routing table, the routers must. Clients can broadcast requests on their local LAN to "Get [the] nearest server" offering a particular service. The router then determines which of the servers matching the request is closest, and informs the client.

The advantage of IPX SAP's broadcast technique is that if everything is working properly, every router on the IPX internetwork knows the address of every server, and every service. However, the more servers you have, offering multiple services per server, the more the resulting broadcast background traffic on every LAN in your IPX internetwork increases. In addition to consuming increasing quantities of your bandwidth as your network grows to offer more services, the SAP "routing table" entries also consume increasing amounts of router memory.

Both AppleTalk and IPX make it easy for users to find servers matching selected criteria. However, they both require their routers to "help" in the service selection, and both service-location schemes can consume non-negligible amounts of router resources and bandwidth in larger networks. Despite their user friendliness, AppleTalk and IPX have given more than one network manager a few grey hairs.

The goal of the SLP is to preserve the user-friendly aspects of these service-location designs while trying to improve on them. Hopefully, the SLP will have much better scaling qualities while also improving the ease of use of IP-based applications.

SLP can operate in two possible modes. First, at smaller sites, clients could contact servers directly. At larger sites, special SLP "directory agents" (DAs) may be set up, with which servers could register their services' existence. Clients would then contact the DA and be directed to the appropriate server offering the desired service.

How Are Directory Agents Discovered?

Non-multicast Methods

The natural question to ask now is "How do the clients discover the address(es) of the DAs?!" There are several possibilities. The most obvious but least desirable way is to manually configure each SLP user agent with the DA's address(es). While this would suffice, it is not in the spirit of having this protocol improve ease of use, hopefully with little or no static preconfiguration.

A less static method is also specified, using DHCP to return the DA address(es) with other configuration information such as the client's IP address, its subnet mask, its default router's address, the intranet's DNS server addresses, and so on. One problem with using DHCP is that it is only a good choice if your intranet primarily uses DHCP for IP address assignment.

Before an intranet's DHCP infrastructure can be used to support SLP, the DHCP client and server software will need to be upgraded to support the SLP's new data elements. This update cycle is likely to take some time. First, vendors of DHCP clients and servers must modify their existing DHCP code to support the SLP. These changes must be designed, implemented, and debugged. Since DHCP clients are usually bundled inside IP stacks, some users may need to upgrade their operating system to get an SLP-savvy DHCP client in their IP stack. At a minimum, a new IP stack or patches to an installed IP stack will have to be installed. Planning to update the IP stacks and update the DHCP servers will take time; then actually upgrading the entire intranet will take still more time. Because the SLP specification was first published in mid-1997, there will probably be some lag before SLP-enhanced DHCP software appears on the market.

Directory Agent Discovery via Multicast

The last option, which we will focus on here, is that of using a well-known "directory agent discovery" multicast address. If multicast is employed, SLP could be downloaded as a separate piece of code that augments the IP stack in the client. The advantage of using multicast is that all installations of the SLP can use the same well-known multicast address for this purpose. This eliminates any requirement for static configuration, since every implementation is built to recognize this address.

Multicast is the most natural bootstrap mechanism since the clients can discover the DA without needing any configuration. Note that this "natural" technique only works if your intranet supports multicast.

Once the DA has been discovered (via multicast), future communications between the client's user agent and the DA occur via unicast.

Details of SLP

Ideally, the user agent (UA) needs no configuration to begin its operation. The UA collects information to build queries representing the user's desired services. Responses to earlier queries, if cached, may be used to locally answer requests if sufficient information is available.

SLP UAs have two basic modes of operation.

1. The first mode is used in the case when the UA already knows the address of a DA. In this case, the UA transmits its requests to it via unicast. Likewise, the DA will unicast its reply to the UA. If no reply is received in a reasonable amount of time, a UA simply reissues its request until a reply is received. To prevent UAs from bombarding "live" DAs forever, the DA will either return an error code or a null response. At least the UA will know that the DA is up, but cannot answer this request.

2. The other case is when the UA hasn't yet discovered the existence of a DA. This case also corresponds to the situation in which there *is no* DA on this intranet. The SLP has a second discovery mechanism for this situation.

   Each service is being assigned a "service-specific" multicast address, to which the UA multicasts a request. The IANA has been requested to assign a block of 1024 *contiguous* multicast addresses for use as service-specific multicast addresses. In the meantime, there is a generic multicast address, called the "service location general multicast address," 224.0.1.22, which may be used in lieu of a service-specific multicast address. If known, the service-specific address should be the UA's preferred choice.

   If a matching service exists on this intranet, then the server's service agent (SA) will hear this request and make an appropriate response. In fact, all matching SAs will respond, provided that (a) they are "tuned in" to the appropriate service-specific multicast address, and (b) their offered service can satisfy the UA's request. Figure 16–5 shows a UA's service location decision tree.

   Directory agent discovery uses a similar mechanism, albeit with a different multicast address. After all, DAs are offering a service of their own, the "SLP Directory Agent service." In order to find servers offering the DA service, the following service-specific multicast address has been defined: 224.0.1.35.

The previous algorithms describe how a UA may find a particular matching service. However, it is possible that a user may want to find all services that match certain selec-

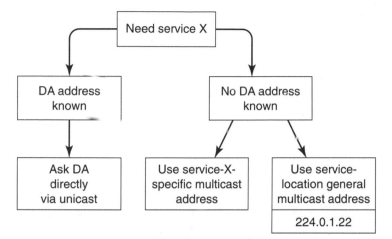

FIGURE 16–5 A user agent's service location decision tree

tion criteria. In this case, SLP has a retransmission algorithm that allows convergence on the final set of all the servers. To accomplish this, the UA must retransmit requests repeatedly, but the UA includes a list of previously heard responders in each request. If a service agent sees this type of request and finds itself in the list of previous responders, it knows that it need not answer again. However, service agents that are not listed in the request and *do* offer the required service should reply. This process continues until no further responses are seen. Now, the process is considered to have converged on the complete set of servers offering this service.

Due to the finite length of the SLP's packets and the variable lengths of the service-selection criteria, only around 60 "previous responders" may fit into a single packet. If there are more servers than this, the SLP has procedures to discover them as well. This multicast/convergence process is useful for discovering services, but it is not expected to be commonly used. Before networks grow large enough to challenge the limits of this multicast/convergence procedure, they have become good candidates for DA deployment.

Again, UAs will use a unicast request/response transaction in their communications with DAs. In these transactions, the SLP can communicate with either TCP or UDP. Whether using TCP or UDP, the port number that the IANA has assigned to the SLP is 427. UAs communicating with DAs via unicast may use either TCP or UDP, but *only* use UDP over multicast.

Not all implementations of SAs are required to support receiving multicast requests. These "lightweight" SAs are not useful unless DAs are present in the network. While listening to multicast requests is optional, it is highly desirable that SAs not only accept multicast queries (including using the IGMP to join their service-specific multicast group and the service-location general multicast group), but also register with a DA so that this server can be discovered by either method. The key to the SLP's scalability is that the DA must be discovered by both the UAs, to facilitate service lookups, and the SAs, to facilitate service registration.

Service registrations are not "forever," but include a lifetime. Once that lifetime expires, the DA will forget that this service was ever provided by this server. It is possible that the server may need to be rebooted, or otherwise become unavailable before the expiration of the service's registered lifetime. SAs that know their services are being disabled are expected to withdraw their service registrations, by notifying the DA of their earlier-than-expected unavailability. Every SA must also keep track of its registrations so that it can refresh its registrations before they expire, thus ensuring continuous service reachability.

SLP Scalability

The SLP was designed with environments supporting either DHCP or multicast in mind. The SLP builds on these foundations to provide solutions for service location at many different intranet size regimes.

We will present how the SLP is used in several network scenarios, showing the SLP's scalability from very small to very large intranets. This scalability is powered by IP multicast.

Tiny Networks

The smallest internetworks do not require DAs. UAs simply use multicast to contact the services they desire. Other than the initial installation of the SLP software, this is a zero-administration scenario. This is fine for one LAN, or an intranet with only a handful of LANs. Eventually, the proliferation of servers will overwhelm a client's request with many responses. An enhanced solution is required for medium-sized networks.

Medium-Sized Networks

Upon reaching a certain size, intranets will eventually require a DA. The DA enhances scalability because it reduces the number of messages the SLP uses. The DA handles the requests from all UAs (once they have discovered the DA), and it collects registrations from all SAs. DAs shield SAs from seeing every UA query. From the UA perspective, DAs filter all the SA registrations, only returning matching services to each UA's queries.

Typically, networks in the medium-sized regime need only one DA. However, a single DA is likely to become an increasingly critical single point of failure eventually, especially in networks with many services. A desire to have DAs back each other up or to serve different regions of very large networks characterizes the next level. However, an intranet need not be truly large before it may beome convenient to use multiple DAs.

Large Networks with Multiple DAs

This next larger network regime is characterized by needing to break up your intranet so that each DA, or set of DAs, serves subsets of the entire intranet. The SLP allows SAs and the services they represent to be collected into logical groupings known as "scopes." Each scope will contain at least one DA. It is possible to use multiple DAs but still not use scopes. Scopes are added to improve scalability for very large intranets, where it is a given that multiple DAs will be needed.

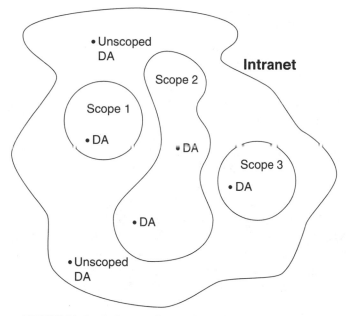

FIGURE 16–6   Reference diagram for understanding scopes

Rules about Scopes   There are several rules about scopes that must be followed; Figure 16–6 provides a diagram.

1. SAs making scoped registrations must register with all DAs within the scope's multicast radius.
   a. Even if SAs are configured to register with DAs having some scope (perhaps even a set of scopes), they must also register with any unscoped DAs.
2. Unscoped service registrations may only register with unscoped DAs.
3. DAs may only be queried by UAs that are within the same scope. UAs must be configured to know what their scope is.
   a. UAs may query unscoped DAs despite being configured to use a specific scope. This may be useful since any unscoped DAs will know about all service registrations (scoped and unscoped).
4. Since all SAs must register with unscoped DAs, and since UAs can query unscoped DAs if they so choose (although they will only find unscoped services), the unscoped DAs may find themselves overwhelmed. Therefore, if a UA has been configured with a scope, it should only use DAs within that scope. Otherwise, the unscoped DAs could become overloaded, presenting a scaling problem. A DA within the UA's scope should always be preferred over an unscoped DA.

   If scoped DAs are used, they will not accept unscoped registrations or requests. UAs that issue unscoped requests will discover only unscoped services. They *should* use a scope in their requests if possible and *should* use a DA with their scope in preference to an unscoped DA.

5. For administrative reasons, SAs may be configured to register only with some list of DAs. If the intranet manager has configured them in this manner, it may be the case that some services may not be available to all UAs, and this may be exactly what was intended. Take care so that mis-configurations do not lead to unintentional service-unreachability.

Scalability Summary for the SLP

The SLP has three basic operational states.

1. The first is a "zero-administration" state, suitable for a single LAN or a small number of LANs, including SAs and UAs but no DAs.

2. The second state requires that the intranet manager set up a DA. SAs and UAs will automatically discover a DA, if it exists (provided suitable multicast or DHCP mechanisms exist within the intranet). This state is suited to a limited number of interconnected LANs with a reasonable number of end stations.

3. The third state is suited to larger networks, up to and possibly exceeding the scale of campus-sized intranets, and requires that all DAs have scopes configured. Also, the use of scopes implies some planning and execution on the part of the intranet manager. Once scopes are in place and functioning properly, users must be informed about which scopes are suitable for their use. The use of scopes involves some up-front administrative overhead and configuration. However, it should result in an environment wherein users may discover nearby services with no further assistance. One final caution is that unscoped DAs should be avoided in large environments. All service registrations are sent to unscoped DAs, which could lead to scalability problems.

CHAPTER 17

INTRODUCTION TO "RELIABLE" MULTICAST TRANSPORT PROTOCOLS

At the network layer, multicast packet delivery is a datagram service, as is unicast packet delivery. This means that multicast packet delivery is also connectionless, provides no guarantee of reliability, and does not promise sequential delivery. The only difference is that unicast packets only go to at most one place, whereas multicasts go where the receivers are. Multicast packets are not treated specially by the network; a datagram is a datagram is a datagram.

Until about 1994, most proposals for reliable multicast were not scalable to large groups, or were slow and/or inefficient. Error recovery tended to collapse the transport protocol back to the replicated-unicast scenario, in which the sender ends up sending multiple copies of the same data. But then, in 1994 and 1995, various researchers began discussing some potential ideas for truly scalable reliable multicast based on ideas first published in 1990. As we will see later, these protocols all have mechanisms to keep a lid on their control traffic, and most attempt to handle "repairs" (i.e., retransmissions) by asking the source for help only as a last resort.

Before delving into the actual mechanics of reliable multicast, we should understand the high-level functionality the researchers are trying to achieve. Then we can dive deeper into a set of proposals and examine specific reliability mechanisms that have emerged so far.

WHAT IS RELIABILITY?

Over multicast, reliability is many-faceted. Multicast reliability means different things to different reliable multicast application designers. With unicast, reliable means "get all the data there, ordered as it was sent, however long it takes." One reason multicast reliability is much more challenging is due to the variations that are possible across a distribution tree.

A distribution tree cannot be assumed to be homogeneous. It will have links of many different speeds (from 128 kbps and below, to 155.52 Mbps and above), connected by routers with different CPU and memory resources, with time-varying levels of buffer utilization and congestion, each with different levels of fan-out. Also, the receivers will have different capabilities, such as the type and speed of CPU, their internal bus speed, operating system architecture, speed of disk subsystem, amount of RAM, speed of RAM, type of RAM, system activity level, and so on.

To one degree or another, all these differences are likely to be present across any group's members. Also challenging for any multicast reliable transport protocol is the fact that the links which make up the delivery tree will probably have different path MTUs. Not only that, but multicast (or unicast) routing changes are likely to dynamically alter the shape of a tree during the transmission. This could result in a change to the set of path MTUs across which the group is reached, even though the actual group membership may not have changed.

To avoid fragmentation in routers it is best to send data packets with lengths up to the smallest of the set of path MTUs, so no packet is large enough to require fragmentation across any path within the distribution tree. Routers generally cannot fragment and forward IP packets as quickly as ones needing no fragmentation. Efficient transport protocols, such as the Transmission Control Protocol (TCP), often try to find the "just large enough" MTU so that they get the most data transferred per packet, without incurring the forwarding performance penalties associated with router-based fragmentation.

This packet size will easily traverse links with MTUs larger than the packet's MTU, but will not need to be fragmented across links that have exactly this MTU. Unfortunately, there is not yet a multicast version of path MTU discovery (RFC-1191). It might be nice if it were easy to determine the "group MTU," which would be the smallest MTU of any link in the current distribution tree for this group.

Different multicast applications have disparate requirements for reliability. Each of these requirements has different design implications for a reliable multicast protocol.

- Some applications require only that all the data be received by each group member, regardless of what order it arrives in, and regardless of how long it takes (within reason).
- Some applications require reliable reception, plus total ordering of data across the group.
- Some applications require many or all the members to send data, in contrast to other applications with only one sender, or perhaps only one sender at a time.
- Small, "closed" groups may be a requirement for some apps; others might need to support thousands (millions?) of receivers.
- Controlling delay within certain bounds across the group may be critical for some applications, but others may be more tolerant of delay, or completely tolerant of

delay. The application's delay tolerance will determine which retransmission strategy is most suitable.

- Some applications may want to move bulk data, and have steady and efficient delivery to the group.
- The burstiness of the senders in some applications may be extreme.

In the few cases where the application's requirements for reliable multicast are well understood, it is not at all clear which is the most appropriate of the (many) underlying mechanisms for providing reliable multicast. Also, as has already been observed, it is generally agreed that a single reliable multicast framework is not likely to meet the needs of all applications over groups of any size. In general, it is difficult to know how to map between application-specific requirements and the many potential reliable multicast transport mechanisms.

The IETF, in standardizing reliable multicast applications and transport protocols, needs these reliability mechanisms to be robust, especially as the number of receivers grows. If these mechanisms do not scale well for large-scale use (i.e., large numbers of groups, with large numbers of users distributed across the Internet), they are less likely to receive the endorsement of the IETF.

Other (nonreliability) application requirements might fall outside the domain of a transport protocol. Perhaps the delay or time-limit constraints would fall into the domain of the Resource Reservation Setup Protocol (RSVP). RSVP could, conceivably, establish network paths with the required timing or bandwidth constraints, over which the reliable multicast protocol(s) could operate. RSVP, along with quality-of-service routing techniques, could help ensure that delay bounds are maintained across certain branches of the delivery tree.

POINTS OF REFERENCE

Reliable Unicast Transport (Transmission Control Protocol)

The Transmission Control Protocol (TCP) is an elegant protocol that operates end to end between two communicating entities, identified by "sockets": On each end, a socket is the end station's IP address concatenated with the TCP port number, a different port for each connection. Each connection is identified by a unique *pair* of sockets.

TCP provides an end-to-end reliable byte-oriented delivery service over an unreliable datagram service that does not necessarily preserve packet ordering or timing, or even guarantee delivery. IP's datagram service is often called "best-effort." Some also half-jokingly refer to it as "fire and forget."

TCP does not achieve its reliability for free. There is a trade-off between delay and reliability (and throughput and money . . .). If a packet is lost, the sender's TCP notices this (after a timeout period which has been dynamically determined for this connection) and a retransmission occurs. The entire TCP-based data transfer is interrupted while the receiver "catches up" with the sender. After the error is corrected, the transfer resumes.

In order to maximize throughput, TCP gradually increases the offered load to the network until congestion is detected. Paradoxically, packet loss is crucial to the process whereby TCP maximizes its throughput. TCP's loss detection mechanism is founded on noticing lost packets. Each side of the connection is constantly acknowledging the sequence number of the last byte received from the other side by indicating the sequence number of the next byte it expects to receive. Any missing sequence numbers (missing ACKs) will trigger the error-correcting retransmission phase.

TCP is very robust. As long as there is some path available through the network, TCP will maximize its transfer rate to the size of the smallest unused resource in the end-to-end network path (slowest link, router with most congested buffers, etc.). Given time, TCP almost always succeeds in delivering all the packets necessary to complete a requested data transfer. TCP is extremely tenacious, but it is not *necessarily* speedy. This is not to imply that TCP can't go fast—it has been clocked at over 800 Mbps—but it works over 9.6 kbps dialup lines, too. For given network conditions, TCP is probably the fastest way to *reliably* get data between two points.

What enables TCP to go fast? It is essential to use the largest packets that can be supported by the end-to-end path without fragmentation. Path MTU discovery allows TCP to send the most data at once, thus maximizing the value of each interrupt in the sending and receiving CPUs. Also, TCP gradually tests the network, using its "slow start" algorithm, so it can dynamically find the fastest rate at which it can send. TCP steadily increases its transmission rate until it detects congestion, the source can't send any faster, or the receiver can't receive any faster.

Unicast applications requiring reliable transport have two choices: Use TCP, a well-designed and ubiquitously available protocol (although not necessarily uniformly well-implemented), or invent an application-specific reliable transport protocol. Certainly there is nothing keeping developers from the latter choice (in fact, it may be a requirement of their application), but using TCP is less work, and it is debatable whether a developer could do better than TCP.

Multicast Option for TFTP

Probably one of the simplest reliable multicast applications is TFTP, extended as specified in RFC-2090. A client negotiates the multicast option with the TFTP server. Assuming the server accepts this option with an Option ACK, or OACK, it will begin multicasting a requested file to the group. The first client in the group to have successfully negotiated this option is the "master client." The master client acknowledges each packet it receives from the TFTP server by sending ACKs. It operates as a proxy for the other group members so that they need not all send ACKs for every packet. The master client does not know or care whether or not the other group members have received any of the same segments it has.

Each data segment is numbered, and once the master client has received all the data it wants, it relinquishes control to another client, which must also negotiate the multicast option with the sender and receive an OACK. This client now becomes the new master client for the remaining group members. Any missing data segments that the new master client needs may be requested at this time. At any time, any nonmaster client which has received all the data segments can drop out of the group, leaving only those clients who joined late or missed some segment(s).

Each new master client may request missing data segments (all the other group members will see these retransmissions), or it can request retransmissions of segments that were sent before it joined the group. Other group members may see multiple copies of segments during this process. Gradually, the group will have only one member remaining, and this member will receive its OACK and request unseen segments as well.

While RFC-2090 specifies an experimental protocol, it is a reliable protocol in the sense that all the clients eventually get all the segments. However, the sender may have to resend some of the data multiple times, and some receivers may have to hear many retransmitted segments. However, this "transport protocol" is tightly linked to the application, and it is not directly usable for other apps.

TFTP's multicast option serves to illustrate one way in which a reliability mechanism can be built over multicast. Note that this is a somewhat trivial example: Since TFTP uses fixed-size segments (512-octet), there are no meaningful MTU differences across the group, and IP's minimum path MTU is 576 so fragmentation is not an issue. Besides using a small MTU, TFTP is strictly a lock-step protocol. Lock-step means that no new packet may be sent until the previous packet has been acknowledged. At any given time there is only one packet "in flight" between the server and client(s). In other words, TFTP does not use sliding windows as TCP does to improve throughput. (Sliding windows allow multiple packets to be outstanding at one time, in order to attempt to "keep the pipe full.")

RELIABLE MULTICAST—EXPECTATIONS

A reliable multicast transport protocol should not devolve into "just send the data n times" if the internetwork is experiencing problems. Had we wanted this solution, we could have just used replicated unicast in the first place; however, replicated unicast is the most inefficient choice, consuming the most bandwidth. The search for efficient reliable multicast transport protocols centers around techniques that can use the group to back itself up, or other mechanisms to offload the work of retransmission from the sender, hopefully without inundating the sender with control traffic in the process! Some proposals call for some receivers, or even multicast routers, to locally cache data until the receivers all acknowledge that they have the data. The various techniques are only limited by the researchers' imaginations.

As mentioned earlier, it is likely that there will be at least one, likely many, reliable multicast transport protocols, each suited to a certain class of applications requiring reliable multicast transport.

Here is a scorecard of good features that researchers want reliable multicast protocols to have:

1. Easy on the source:

    In other words, try to avoid overburdening the sender with control traffic and retransmission duties. Who handles retransmission, and how retransmissions are handled, is a key distinguishing factor among reliable multicast transport protocols. The source is ultimately responsible for retransmissions, but that doesn't necessarily mean it has to be directly involved in each of them.

2. Able to handle delivery to heterogeneous groups fairly and efficiently:

    It should be able to deliver the data to a group in a timely manner, without underloading fast receivers or overloading slow ones. Does the protocol cater to slow receivers, leaving fast receivers waiting? Does it cater to fast receivers, leaving slow receivers in the dust to catch up later? Does it try to strike a fair balance between these extremes?

3. Good performance:

    For a given amount of data needing reliable transfer, deliver it to the group in the shortest possible time.

4. Capable of handling "large" groups:

    How big is "large?" That's open for debate: On paper, many protocols scale to arbitrarily large groups. In reality, it is difficult to test such assertions. Reliable multicast transport protocols purporting to support applications over huge groups must pass the strictest scalability and robustness tests in order to protect the network infrastructure from possible ill effects.

5. Minimal control traffic:

    The control technique used by each reliable multicast transport protocol is one of its most strongly differentiating features. This is the mechanism whereby retransmissions (repairs) are requested and fulfilled, plus how successful delivery is indicated. Not all protocols positively acknowledge each packet; some protocols use ACKs, while others use negative acknowledgements, or NAKs (some people call these "NACKs"). Some reliable multicast transport protocols use a hierarchical retransmission scheme based on either ACKs or NAKs at each level. Whatever mechanisms are in use, their operation should interfere as little as possible with unicast traffic, especially TCP traffic.

6. Mixed-mode:

    Can a protocol combine reliable and unreliable transport to the same group?

7. Late joiners welcome?

    Some protocols do not support receivers that join the session after it has started. This behavior may be appropriate for some applications, but not others.

REQUIREMENTS FOR MULTICAST RELIABLE TRANSPORT PROTOCOL(S)

Contrary to the unicast world, it is unlikely that there will be a universal "one-size-fits-all" multicast reliable transport protocol. Each multicast application has vastly different requirements. It is more likely that several classes of multicast reliable transport protocols will be developed to match common multicast applications which desire reliability. Also, some multicast applications with truly unique requirements may come bundled with their own transport protocol.

It is clear that not all applications require reliability. Interactive multimedia conferencing is a very delay-constrained environment. If we trade off extra delay variability for reliability with these applications, there could be noticeable delays in the conferencing application, which may not be acceptable to users. Also, note that in a so-called multimedia conference, different apps may have different requirements. For instance, a shared whiteboard or workspace will definitely need reliable transport, but audio and video streams require completely different transport designs. If reliability for these streams is desired, it would have to be an extremely efficient protocol that does not introduce much delay variation (i.e., jitter).

It is possible to structure an application's data such that the application appears reliable, when in fact it tolerates a small amount of loss. Some applications naturally have this characteristic (self-refreshing), as we shall see in Example 1. Other applications (specifically certain video encoding techniques) can "layer" their data so that the largest percentage of the traffic is the least important. Any loss experienced will be statistically more likely to affect data of little consequence. Both of these techniques are not reliable transport protocols, but they appear to be from a user's perspective. Finally, another techniqe to achieve reliability without using a reliable multicast transport protocol is to do forward error correction. Up to the limits of the algorithm employed, some loss will be tolerable. Here are some examples where the data is transient (but self-refreshing), or uses data coded to survive packet loss reasonably well.

Example 1: Non-Mission-Critical Multicast Stock Ticker

This is not a stock ticker delivery service that might be employed in a stockbroker's office. In that case, reliability is of the utmost importance, and a lost price quote could prevent a trading program from executing properly, possibly costing the broker and their customers dearly. This application scenario is more appropriate for people who like to casually keep up with stocks of interest during the day. Granted, the stockbrokers are an important market, but there are a lot more casual stock watchers than there are stockbrokers.

Stock quote data is self-refreshing. If you want to keep up with the latest market prices, getting a stock quote feed by multicast is a smart way to go. Your feed could list all quotes for all stocks, allowing the end stations to filter only the stocks of interest to that user, or different group addresses could be used for different groupings of stocks.

- One way to segment stocks might be by their sectors, such as tech stocks, agriculture, transportation, and energy. Each sector could have its own group address.
- Another possible segmentation could use three group addresses, one for the American Exchange (AMEX), one for the New York Stock Exchange (NYSE), and one for the NASDAQ exchange.
- A straightforward segmentation might use 26 group addresses, one for securities whose symbols start with "A," on up to one for symbols starting with "Z." A user could join a set of groups corresponding to the starting letters of their securities of interest.

Whatever the details of the stock ticker delivery service, the loss of a quote is not fatal to the casual stock observer. The next time a quote for that stock comes by, it will refresh the current price. The display program can time-stamp the quotes, so it is obvious that an infrequently traded security's quote is outdated. Perhaps if you were considering buying or selling that security, you would use a web browser to contact your online stockbroker to get a current quote and initiate buy or sell requests. You might even use a telephone for this.

The bottom line is that lost packets are not mission-threatening for this application. Frequently traded securities will recover from a lost packet by generating a new ticker update the next time there is a sale.

Example 2: Video with Layered (Hierarchical) Coding

It is possible to encode data for transmission over a potentially lossy channel. In the case of video, there are a very large number of "high-frequency" changes in the frame per second, such as slight movements (blinking eyes, birds flying outside a window, flickering candles, etc.). There are much fewer "medium-frequency" events, which are considerably more important to your perception of the events (arm and head motion, mouth motion, closing/opening doors, dogs jumping, etc.). Finally, there are rare low-frequency events such as scene changes, and fade-ins and fade-outs to and from commercials.

The curious thing is that the high-frequency items are generally low-bandwidth (taken individually). Also, the loss of a few packets won't materially alter your perception of a scene. A bird flitting around in a tree outside a window is not part of the script! As one moves down the scale from higher-frequency to lower-frequency events, we find that the number of these decreases, while individually increasing the bandwidth required to convey the change.

The data could be encoded such that most of the packets sent correspond to the higher-frequency, low-bandwidth (and low content) minor changes. Relatively fewer packets would be sent in the other categories. If a packet is lost, it will more likely be one of the virtually irrelevant ones describing some high-frequency event. Upon reconstructing the video signal on the other end, the receiver could "smooth over" or omit any missing packet easily if it corresponded to a high-frequency event. This should not significantly alter the user's perception of the scene. This technique depends on the law of averages: If you send mostly irrelevant packets, hopefully those will be proportionately more likely to be lost. Of course, there is always Murphy's law to deal with, so this technique isn't perfect, but might be very usable over internetworks where you have control over the loading, and therefore the likelihood of packet loss.

One Other Technique

Something that could be viewed as "giving in" to packet loss is using a forward error correcting scheme. As long as the packet loss rate was low enough (not necessarily zero), the data could be completely reconstructed at each receiver.

None of these techniques are "reliable transport" protocols; they are simply ways of structuring the data to improve its resistance to packet loss. For true reliability, we need a protocol that allows each receiver to ensure it has received all the data which the sender has multicast to the group.

WHY NOT JUST RUN TCP OVER MULTICAST?

This is a natural question. What would happen? Well, first we'd need to hack our sender's TCP so it could use a multicast address as a valid destination address. Then it could send TCP segments out in a succession of multicast datagrams. Group members would receive the segments. That's not too bad so far.

In TCP, how does the sender know how to pace itself, to share the network? It uses a dynamic sliding window protocol, initialized by a "slow start" procedure that gradually increases the load from the sender until it detects congestion by losing a packet. In the case of multicast, each of the paths to the receivers will have different congestion characteristics, line speeds, and so on, and will require windows of different sizes. A block of three packets, each 512 octets long, might be fine for a T-1 span on the way to a set of receivers, but it might overwhelm a V.34 dialup link to another receiver. This hacked TCP could only use one window at a time—as far as it can tell, the multicast group address is a single logical destination. Therefore, different branches of the delivery tree would experience different losses, depending on how inappropriate the sender's data window was relative to their branch of the delivery tree.

Assuming that all the branches could carry the source's TCP windows equally well (or equally poorly), the next problem will severely confuse the TCP of the sender: ACK implosion. If the group has 24 receivers, and they all get their copy of the data, they will all send an ACK back to the sender. First problem: 24 ACKs, from 24 unknown IP addresses for which the sender has no valid sockets, but all these ACKs will be destined for its IP address and the proper TCP port. Second problem: If only 22 of the receivers get the data, how can the other two tell the source to retransmit? This source's hacked TCP assumes that a packet of data must either succeed or fail to reach its destination (partial success is not possible over unicast IP). With multicast, a segment can partially succeed in reaching the "destination." How can the source retransmit if 22 out of 24 receivers got the data? Must they all see the data again, so that the two who did not receive it will get it? That isn't very efficient. The source isn't even congizant of the individual receivers, and has no way to attempt a partial retransmission.

A Partial Fix: Single Connection Emulation

There is an approach by some researchers at Georgia Tech, called "single connection emulation." SCE is a "shim" layer, under TCP and over IP, allowing TCP to operate—essentially unmodified—over multicast. The shim layer establishes per-receiver TCP state, and only sends ACKs up to the sender's TCP once all receivers have acknowledged each segment. The shim handles retransmission to each receiver. This is not perfect, but for small groups SCE may be a clever "poor man's" reliable multicast transport protocol. It certainly has the advantage of compatibility with the most unmodified applications.

One unfortunate aspect of SCE is that the burden is on the sending machine's shim layer to handle all retransmissions to the group. If the group is experiencing high loss due to temporary network undercapacity, the sender may have to effectively send multiple copies of the data to each individual receiver. This unnecessary duplication of traffic was what multicast was invented to avoid! One other disadvantage of SCE is that because delivery is synchronized across the group, late joiners cannot be supported.

One benefit of SCE is that the receivers need not run SCE, only have their TCP implementations altered in three small ways. Also, SCE not only provides reliability, but also supports per-source ordering because it leverages TCP.

CHAPTER 18

SOME RELIABLE MULTICAST TRANSPORT PROTOCOLS

Reliable multicast transport protocols and applications are currently an extremely active area of research and development. Despite the fact that several current proposals are developed enough to be described here, it is very important to note that they are each in a very early stage of development. Perhaps in a year or two these will only be a faint memory, or they may be wild successes. Although the specifics of these protocols may change over time, these fundamental mechanisms are likely to remain important. At a minimum, they should be instructive examples of how multicast reliability may be achieved.

SOME CURRENT RESEARCH PROJECTS IN RELIABLE MULTICAST

In the sections that follow, we will outline characteristics of several protocols which are in various stages of development. The reason SRM is being covered first (i.e., not in alphabetical order) is that it was the first reliable multicast protocol of which the author became aware, several years ago. Its position in this list is not meant to imply that it is better than any of the others.

Scalable Reliable Multicast

SRM is being developed by a group of individuals who have already made significant contributions to the Internet: Sally Floyd, Van Jacobson, Cricket Liu, Steve McCanne, and Lixia Zhang.

SRM is targeted at operation over a future Internet in which multicast is nearly ubiquitous. It has been demonstrated over today's MBone, which is far from being ubiquitous but is large enough to be interesting. SRM's goal, shared with the other reliable multicast protocols, is scalability. Also, there is a strong desire to ensure that multicast reliability mechanisms do not interfere with the operation of TCP, the primary unicast reliability mechanism. SRM has the design goals of being able to work over very large networks with groups that are potentially very large. Another goal is to not require special support from the IP layer. Finally, SRM aspires to operate efficiently, even in the face of dynamic group membership. Note that these design goals are not necessarily unique to SRM, but we will see that various proposed reliable multicast protocols have invented very different techniques to achieve these, and other, goals.

Multicast has turned the rules (or expectations) for reliability upside down. In the unicast world, the sender is responsible for error detection and recovery. The sender adapts to changing network conditions throughout the duration of the TCP connection. The finely honed congestion window size adjustment algorithms, which adapt by using the data to measure the path as it is traversed, do not generalize to the case of a multicast distribution tree. The fact is that the senders do not know who their receivers are; they are blindly sending to a group address, and are not necessarily aware of whether or not anyone is listening. Also, group membership is dynamic. While a transmission is in progress, the size of a group could vary considerably.

In 1990, Clark and Tennenhouse described an extension to the familiar unicast end-to-end approach, called "application level framing" (ALF), in which the applications have more control over their communication. All data is exchanged as "application data units," with data expressed in an application-specific name space, and the application's data is encoded to suit its reliability needs. SRM is an example of an ALF-derived protocol. Note that SRM is not a purely theoretical exercise: The MBone's whiteboard (wb) tool currently uses the SRM machinery.

In terms of ALF, reliability consists of the following rather minimalist definition: "All members get all the data that has been sent to the multicast group." Interestingly, there is no expectation that the data should arrive at the receivers in any particular order (e.g., the order sent). ALF acknowledges the extreme variation of application requirements and does not impose unnecessary reliability semantics on applications that do not need them. Each application has different expectations of a reliable transport service, so it makes sense to design for only the narrowest definition of reliability. Once this general-purpose infrastructure is in place, each application can meet its requirements by using this minimalist reliability in conjunction with whatever other mechanisms the application requires.

SRM depends on the receivers to take an active role in the reception of the sender's data. This receiver-oriented approach is designed, as is multicast IP, to scale to large groups. In SRM, group members actually collaborate to help each other recover in case a local subgroup misses part of a transmission. Because group members aid in retransmission (the term in multicast reliable protocols is often "repair"), SRM avoids implosion of control messages at the source, or at any node of the distribution tree.

SRM only uses multicast transmission, and each session has a bandwidth limit. Some reliable transport protocols, as we will see, handle repairs via unicast, but SRM multicasts its repairs. As long as the session's traffic is below its limit, multiple senders can be active. Repairs from other group members that did get the data can be multicast simultaneously alongside fresh data transmission from the sender. See Figure 18–1.

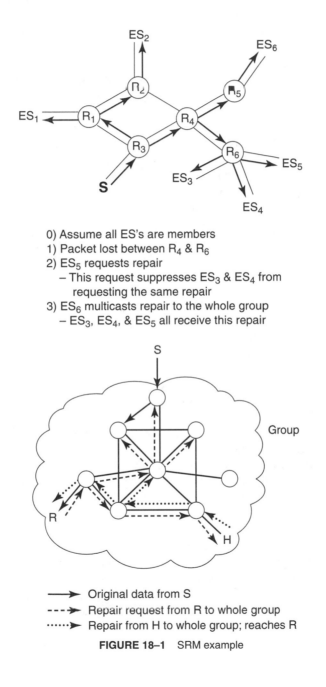

0) Assume all ES's are members
1) Packet lost between R_4 & R_6
2) ES_5 requests repair
   – This request suppresses ES_3 & ES_4 from requesting the same repair
3) ES_6 multicasts repair to the whole group
   – ES_3, ES_4, & ES_5 all receive this repair

⟶ Original data from S
---➤ Repair request from R to whole group
······➤ Repair from H to whole group; reaches R

FIGURE 18–1 SRM example

Similar to the Realtime Transport Protocol (RTP), which is discussed in Chapter 19, group members send low-frequency status messages so their neighbors can learn their status. These messages are quasi-periodic, unlike the Realtime Transport Control Protocol's (RTCP's) messages, which are sent at a variable rate inversely proportional to the group's size.

SRM's status messages (known as "session messages") allow group members to measure the delay among themselves and report their current reception state. If a receiver detects a lost or corrupted packet, it requests assistance via multicast. Any other receiver with the data can help repair the outage. To avoid a flood of repair requests, each receiver seeking repair waits a random time before requesting repair. During that time, another nearby receiver may also have missed (or received a corrupted) packet, and may have already asked for a fresh copy. In that case, the other receivers that are also waiting for it will have heard the repair request and know they should suppress their request for the same repair. The repair request is not suspended indefinitely because the other request for repair may not propagate far enough to reach a receiver which is capable of helping out, or perhaps the repair may not make it all the way back.

Another way a pending request for repair can be suppressed (or canceled in this case) is for a previously requested repair to be received. This situation could arise in a part of the tree that is near a relatively faster part of the tree: On the faster portion, a receiver could already have noticed a missing or corrupted packet, and initiated a request for repair. A nearby part of the tree could be still waiting to notice that it needs a repair when the repair for the faster part of the tree is received. All receivers are required to cache previously received data and supply the requested repair(s) when necessary. Since the repair is multicast, the expectation is that all the receivers needing repair will be fixed at essentially the same time. Those that do not receive a repair "in time" will issue their own repair requests until every one of the receivers has all the data.

As we have seen, receivers wait for a random time before issuing repair requests, in case another node issues a repair request for the same data. This is done to prevent an explosion of repair requests. Similarly, while many receivers can reply to a repair request, it would be bad if they all did, so as they hear repair requests for which they can provide assistance, they also wait a random time. If they hear another receiver provide a repair, they suppress their own repair transmission.

The fact that all these messages are multicast enables the group to work together in a loosely coupled manner, with a minimum of excess traffic. Also, despite not explicitly using an expanding-ring search, repair requests do take time to emanate from the locality of the requester, so nearby nodes are more likely to provide a repair response than distant group members.

Random variables squelch duplicates in cases where several nodes at similar distances could all help with a repair. The choice of random timing variables controls how responsive the protocol is to given loss scenarios in certain topologies. A fixed choice of variables will only work well in certain topologies with certain patterns of lost or corrupted packets, so SRM adapts the random (timing) control variables depending on the shape of the group (inferred from Session Messages) and from the previous patterns of duplicate requests or repairs seen.

The repair request and repair response procedures do differ slightly. A requester persists with its request until it hears a repair which allows it to cancel its request. However, in the ideal case, repair responses are sent at most once per request by any given node.

SRM is not perfect. If there are multiple links in the topology with high packet loss, it is possible for a node behind a lossy link to notice a missing packet and request a repair. A nearby neighbor could then multicast a repair (these go to the whole group), which is hopefully seen by the original node on the far side of the lossy link. However, the repair may not cross other lossy links in the group, which will enable future repairs for the same lost packet to be multicast across the group again.

In networking, it is rare that a device or link fails completely. Often, failures are partial (as above with the lossy link). Such a situation affects SRM in way that has been dubbed the "crying baby" problem, in which a bad link affects the whole group. Group members downstream of the flaky link will be sending higher than normal numbers of repair requests. These repair requests or responses could be lost at the link in question, causing even more repair traffic. (Remember that the repairs and requests are sent to the entire group.)

Future work on the SRM framework seeks to develop techniques to limit the scope of the repair requests and responses, tuning them so that they need not cross the entire group. Such techniques would greatly reduce the extra overhead due to lost requests or responses. The extra overhead would still be present—locally—but at least the rest of the group would not be bothered by this local difficulty.

One mechanism to help localize the scope of requests and repairs is the "local recovery group" concept. Under this scheme, a receiver proposes a multicast address to use for local recovery when it first sends a repair request. Other local receivers that suffered the same losses would then join that group, and future requests and repairs are sent to this group rather than the entire session. As new members join the group, they are obviously unaware of the local recovery group. Once they experience their first loss event, they can follow the normal procedure of initiating a repair request to the entire group, but then local members would inform them of the proper local recovery group, and the new member would switch recovery groups at that point.

It is clear that SRM is not a solution to all reliability problems. Other areas of future research, development, and testing include improving multicast congestion control by adjusting traffic load in response to the observed performance. Another idea is to distribute session messages hierarchically to improve scalability. Now we will examine some other promising reliable multicast transport protocols to see what other reliability mechanisms are possible.

Reliable Multicast Transport Protocol

RMTP is being developed by researchers at AT&T's Bell Laboratories, a division of Lucent Technologies. As you might guess from its name, RMTP provides for reliable delivery over multicast distribution trees. The reliability service it provides is ordered and lossless. Besides the reliable mode of operation, it has a quasi-reliable mode as well. RMTP may be layered either on top of UDP/IP, or above IP alone.

RMTP achieves reliability via an n-level hierarchy of regions, in which each region's receivers back each other up. Each region elects a designated receiver (DR), which is also a member of the next higher region in the hierarchy. The DR collects status messages from the region, indicating which packets have been successfully received (see Figure 18–2).

In RMTP, the sender sets the maximum data rate "speed limit" before the transmission begins. The actual rate will depend on the capabilities of the receivers and may never approach the absolute maximum specified by the sender. RMTP uses a TCP-like slow-start algorithm (linear increase in window size with multiplicative backoff). Late join is supported in RMTP via a two-level cache (at the DRs and sender), but it is up to the sender to determine if a join is too late.

The RMTP status message consists of a bit mask indicating which packets were received or not, relative to the lower end of the current window of data. Simplistically, if the current window of data is 16 packets, and a status message includes at least 16 status bits, then each bit may indicate successful reception or a missed packet. The status message must also indicate to which window of data the bit mask applies.

If the DR has a copy of a missing packet, it transmits repairs to the local region. Repair messages are either unicast or multicast depending on a threshold. If more than a certain number of receivers in a local region needs the same repair, it makes more sense to multicast the repair than to send a number of unicast repairs.

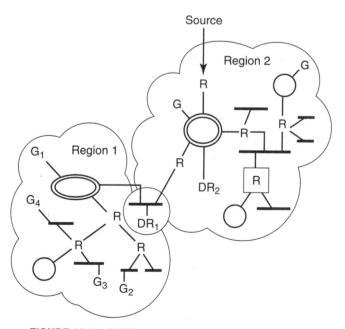

FIGURE 18–2   RMTP regions and designated receivers

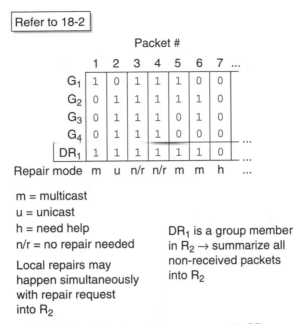

Refer to 18-2

Packet #

	1	2	3	4	5	6	7 ...
G_1	1	0	1	1	1	0	0
G_2	0	1	1	1	1	1	0
G_3	0	1	1	1	0	1	0
G_4	0	1	1	1	0	0	0
DR_1	1	1	1	1	1	1	0

Repair mode   m   u   n/r   n/r   m   m   h   ...

m = multicast
u = unicast
h = need help
n/r = no repair needed

Local repairs may
happen simultaneously
with repair request
into R_2

DR_1 is a group member
in $R_2 \rightarrow$ summarize all
non-received packets
into R_2

FIGURE 18–3   Collection of status messages by DRs

As the repairs are completed at each level of the hierarchy, it is always possible that a given region's DR will not have a local copy of a packet, and thus will not be able to complete a repair locally. In such a case, the DR summarizes this window's received and missing packets for its region (via the mask in the status message) into the next higher layer of the hierarchy. The status messages at that level are collected (see Figure 18–3), and that level's DR again makes all local repairs for which it has data. At any layer, the DR makes all possible local repairs.

As the status messages flow upward in the hierarchy, they may encounter a layer whose DR can repair a missing packet. At an intermediate layer, a DR's repair may need to cascade down several layers before the repair is completed. This depends on how far down the original outage extended. As the status messages flow upward, hopefully the missing packets can be repaired before the repair request reaches the source. If a lower region's DR gets a repair for a packet which was missing from within its region, it uses that packet to repair itself* and forwards the repair to other receivers at its local level.

Each region's DR, at each layer of the hierarchy, implements a similar procedure until the top layer of the hierarchy (the one that includes the sender) is reached. At that layer, repairs are requested for any missing packets (which could be from any lower sublayer). These repairs are then carried back downstream, using the unicast/multicast threshold rules inside each region, until all the receivers have all the packets of a given window.

*Clearly, if the DR had had the packet, it could have repaired its region's outage without needing to forward the repair request into the next higher region. Therefore, in this situation, this layer's DR must have needed the repair, too.

The unique feature of RMTP is its hierarchical organization, with regional aggregation of status messages. This prevents the sender from being inundated with status messages, and minimizes the number of group-wide repair messages. RMTP has been tested over the tunneled infrastructure of the MBone with encouraging results. It has also been tested on a private, switched "native multicast" (i.e., nontunneled) network within AT&T, over which it also performed well.

Reliable Multicast Protocol (RMP)

In the words of the designers of RMP, it was designed to be a high-performance myth buster, showing that a reliable multicast protocol could be not only reliable, and provide totally ordered delivery service, but also be *fast*. RMP is being developed at West Virginia University in conjunction with NASA, and is being commercialized by GlobalCast (who is also planning to ship an implementation of SRM).

RMP senders can encode each packet they transmit with a different delivery mode. Possible per-packet modes are "unreliable," "reliable," "reliable+ordered," and "reliable+totally ordered." For the reliable modes, a TCP-like flow control procedure is used, with sliding windows, slow start, and so on. RMP is tailored for real-time collarborative applications such as distributed simulations, shared environments, and whiteboards.

The design of RMP is based on negative acknowledgments (NAKs). It uses a rotating token scheme to ensure reliability, ordering, and stability. The token scheme is called "post ordering rotating token." In this scheme, a token is passed between "sites," or groups of receivers. The site with the token is the designated control-traffic producer for recent packets.

NAKs are multicast to the whole group to avoid an explosion of control traffic (i.e., to avoid an implosion of control traffic at the source). Once missing packets have been identified, the source remulticasts them to the group. Any receivers that have already received this packet must simply discard the duplicate copy. RMP uses the repair/request policies of the scalable reliable multicast (SRM) framework.

Reliable Adaptive Multicast Protocol (RAMP)

RAMP has been developed by TASC, a division of Primark. RAMP was originally designed to distribute large image files for collaborative applications, and was therefore designed to provide both high performance and low latency. RAMP was initially described as part of an informational RFC entitled "Requirements for Multicast Protocols" (RFC-1458). It has evolved considerably since being published as an RFC in May 1993.

RAMP is unique in that it is both sender- and receiver-reliable, unlike most other reliable multicast protocols. This capability should be well suited to applications involving collaboration, because end stations act as both senders and receivers over the course of a session.

RAMP guarantees reliable and orderly delivery using a NAK-based scheme. Repairs may be either unicast or multicast. RAMP's designers claim that NAKs minimize

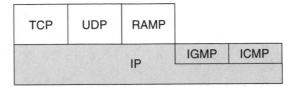

FIGURE 18–4   RAMP's place in the IP protocol stack

return (i.e., control) traffic. They must be assuming that missing or corrupted packets are an unusual occurrence. Surely if many packets are lost or corrupted, the flow of NAKs could be quite large. In terms of the IP protocol stack, RAMP is just another transport protocol over IP, alongside TCP and UDP. RAMP's position in these terms is illustrated in Figure 18–4.

One unusual characteristic of RAMP is that the sender must know the unicast addresses of all the receivers, as well as the group address which collectively represents them. RAMP's designers claim that this allows the transmission to be stopped immediately if there are no receivers. Beyond knowing who the receivers are, RAMP maintains no per-receiver session state. That amount of state would present too much of a burden to the sender(s), and would become especially limiting over large groups.

RAMP, like several other reliable multicast protocols, supports late join and leave; interestingly, the receivers control their own QoS. The flow control is rate-based, with a sender's rate scaled linearly by the NAK rate. As with many other reliable multicast protocols, RAMP uses a modified slow-start algorithm, allowing a sender to "test the waters" to see how fast it can go. Once the first NAK is received, the NAK rate will equalize the sending rate until a loose equilibrium is reached. For example, if the number of NAKs per minute increases by 10%, the number of packets per second could be reduced by approximately 10%. Likewise, if the number of NAKs per minute decreased slightly, the packet rate could be increased proportionately.

COMMERCIAL RELIABLE MULTICAST OFFERINGS

Certain vendors have been shipping proprietary reliable multicast solutions to customers for several years now, with some installations active for as long as a decade.

GlobalCast's Offerings

GlobalCast is a recent startup that is implementing a number of reliable multicast protocols under a common API. The founders of GlobalCast were intimately involved with the development of the Reliable Multicast Protocol (RMP), so it is not surprising that RMP is one of their initial products. They are also implementing SRM within their architecture, and a home-grown reliable protocol called Asymmetrical Reliable Multicast (ARM), among others. GlobalCast claims that their suite of reliable protocols can enable push-oriented applications to reliably reach *millions* of users. GlobalCast is actively involved in the standardization of reliable multicast, but—like other companies in this space—is not waiting for standards.

It is clear that GlobalCast's business is based on the proposition that customers exist today who need these solutions. Their customers will likely be commercial push software developers and corporate intranet push application developers. Similar to TIBCO (see the next section), they are mainly providing "middleware," not applications.

TIB from TIBCO

GlobalCast's middleware is not as comprehensive as TIBCO's, since it is "limited" to an API and several reliable transport protocols. TIBCO's main product is also middleware, called The Information Bus, which provides not only reliable multicast services, but also connectivity to legacy data, relational database access, and other functions. The original concept for TIB came from the observation that a hardware bus ties together the components of a computer, but there was no analogous software "bus" over which applications could share data.

TIBCO (in case you hadn't already guessed: The Information Bus Company) aims to be the leader in "event-driven" networking, based on a publish-and-subscribe paradigm. An event can be almost anything, but using their information delivery protocols (partially based on IP multicast), users can be informed in essentially real time. Users must subscribe to information sources, and as new information becomes available it is instantly delivered to the receivers. The big advantage of IP multicast-based push is that the data goes out from the source; receivers don't have to manually retrieve it. One of the problems with manual retrieval is that while a user checks for new data many times, s/he will rarely actually find any changes! If the data is sent to presubscribed receivers, the minimum traffic will have crossed the network, and everyone will be completely up to date at all times.

TIBCO's TIB middleware is their software which enables these so-called event-driven applications to be written and deployed. In their model, users (receivers) subscribe to the groups representing classes of information in which they have interest. Information "publishers" anonymously send data to these groups, and currently active receivers anonymously receive it. Their publish-and-subscribe technique is aided by subject-based addressing, in which applications' data from different sources is mapped from the group address to a human-readable text-based subject name.

StarBurst's MFTP

StarBurst has invented and patented (U.S Patent 5,553,083) the Multicast File Transfer Protocol (MFTP), which they are in the process of publishing as an informational RFC. MFTP operates above UDP/IP, supporting the reliable transfer of files to thousands of receivers. StarBurst claims that by using "aggregators," their name for MFTP relay points, it is potentially possible to "simultaneously" reach millions of receivers.

MFTP in fact comprises two protocols. An administrative protocol is used to manage the sessions, consisting of setting up and tearing down groups. MFTP's actual work is accomplished via a separate data transfer protocol, which reliably transmits files to the group, though not in real time. MFTP is targeted at non-real-time data transfer operations and is optimized for that case. Real-time "streaming" reliable multicast protocols are a different case entirely, having very different interactivity and delay characteristics. MFTP is not intended to be a general reliable multicast protocol.

While MFTP is being published as an informational RFC, it will not be a standards-track protocol. Therefore, it will not necessarily interoperate with other reliable-multicast-enabled applications, unless they specifically support MFTP's transport + application package. By the same token, there is something to be said for being first and establishing de facto standards. It is still far too early to pick the winners in this horse race. StarBurst has been selling this solution to customers for some time now, so it is clear that there is a demand for it.

CHAPTER 19

THE REALTIME TRANSPORT PROTOCOL AND RELIABILITY

While not a reliable multicast protocol, RTP does provide end-to-end transport layer services to support real-time applications over multicast (or unicast). Real-time applications include those such as audio- and videoconferences. Also, shared environments (e.g., shared "whiteboards") could possibly operate over RTP. However, this sort of application generally needs some form of reliable transport, which RTP does not directly support.

The RTP architecture includes a control protocol, the Realtime Transport Control Protocol (RTCP). RTCP is designed to scale to very large multicast groups. One function of RTCP is to enable receivers to send multicast status messages to the group, permitting senders to monitor the quality of reception across the group. See Figure 19–1.

RTP together with RTCP enables the following functionality to be provided over best-effort datagram networks:

- Identification of group members
- Other elementary control messages
- Identification of the data's source and payload type
- Data sequence numbering
  - which enables lost packets to be detected by receivers
- Timing marks for synchronization
- Delivery status monitoring
  - enables tools for fault diagnosis, such as `rtpmon`
  - gives sender feedback on how well its packets are being received by the group

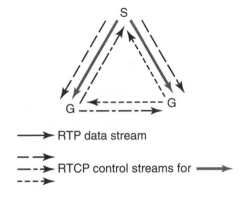

RTP data stream

RTCP control streams for ────▸

FIGURE 19–1   RTP vs. RTCP: logical flows

RTP does not guarantee quality of service (QoS) to applications, nor does it provide for resource reservations. Of course, protocols such as the resource reservation setup protocol (RSVP) and Integrated Services over Specific Link Layers (ISSLL) standards could be used in conjunction with RTP and QoS-based routing to give certain traffic special handling. These extra features are outside the scope of RTP.

While RTP and RTCP are specified independently of the underlying transport and network layers, many implementations so far have been over UDP/IP.

OVERVIEW OF RTP

RTP, like the Scalable Reliable Multicast (SRM) framework, is not a protocol unto itself. It is extensible, designed to support common application requirements. Its functionality is designed to be a least common denominator, which applications extend to meet their needs. RTP provides common functions that many real-time applications will need.

RTP is designed to operate over packet-switched networks such as the Internet. Packet-switched networks may not deliver packets in the order in which they were transmitted, or may add variable amounts of delay to them while in transit. Packet-switched networks also sometimes fail to deliver a packet to its destination. To help overcome these obstacles, the RTP's header contains a sequence number alongside timing information. Given this information, the receivers may reconstruct the original packet stream's timing.

For example, if a source were emitting consecutive bursts of audio traffic, each of a 50-millisecond duration, the receiver would be able to play back the audio bursts at the same rate (and in the same order) as the source transmitted them. Each source's timing is independent of the others, so receivers must keep a separate "playback buffer" for each source. One nice side-effect of having sequence-numbered packets is that the receiver can tell how many packets it is missing.

Playback Buffers

Playback buffers are a way to trade off time for accuracy. The basic idea is that if you wait 10 to 100 packet times, you can accumulate a lot of the data stream in a receiver's memory. If some of those packets were delayed in transit, they could still arrive before you need to deliver the stream to the user. Also, if some of the packets were lost, and your sample time is small enough, you may be able to interpolate, or mathematically "smooth over" the missing pieces, using the samples before and after the missing packet to approximate its contents.

The RTP and SRM frameworks are both embodiments of the Application Layer Framing paradigm which was initially presented by Clark and Tennenhouse in 1990. Because RTP is generic and application-independent, it does not exist as an autonomous layer, but will usually be integrated into an application's processing. The RTP specification is intentionally incomplete: It is expected to be extended to support the differing requirements of various real-time applications (see Figure 19–2).

To completely specify a given application operating over RTP, one would require the RTP specification (RFC-1889) plus at least one additional specification. One kind of additional specification is called a profile specification. It would define how the application's different payload types are identified (defining the necessary RTP payload type codes), plus describe how these types map to payload formats. The RTP is quite unique, in that its own header may be altered to suit an application's needs (or the needs of a class of applications). In other words, one application may use a different RTP header format than another! Another companion document is the payload format specification. A number of these exist already as RFCs (see the references). These documents specify how the RTP carries a given payload.

The actual mechanics of RTP do not involve a fixed UDP port, as you might expect from other UDP-based protocols. We will use a multicast session as an example. The type of data flowing is irrelevant, but it could be video, audio, or any other time-sensitive data. When a session is created, the session creator defines the multicast group that will be used for the session. A program like `sdr` may be used to claim a unique multicast address.

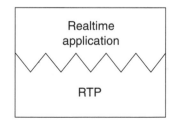

FIGURE 19–2   RTP's relationship with real-time applications

When the session is created, the creator also must pick a UDP port over which the data will be carried. RTP's rules specify that the session's data must use an even-numbered UDP port, and the corresponding RTCP session shall use the next higher odd-numbered UDP port. As a brief example, an RTP data stream may use UDP port 22222, while the corresponding RTCP control packets for that session would use UDP port 22223.

All senders to the session encode their data the same way. The RTP header indicates the data encoding method (e.g., if it were audio, the indicated encoding method might be PCM, or pulse code modulation) and encapsulates the data. Again, the RTP header also includes sequence numbers and timing information. The UDP header then encapsulates the RTP header plus data on an even-numbered UDP port.

Some sessions might have only one sort of "medium," such as audio or video. Other sessions may be "multimedia," distributing synchronized audio and video streams in one logical program. RTP allows all of a session's streams to be transmitted independently. Thus, the audio program is one RTP stream with its own RTCP stream. The video would be another RTP stream, with a different corresponding RTCP stream. If a receiver only wished to receive one of these subchannels (e.g., video only), it would not be a problem. If a sender is originating multiple data types to the same related session, it should identify itself consistently in each session. This allows the receivers to synchronize the sender's streams.

Since we are imagining this application over multicast, note that the group address for video will carry that traffic only to interested receivers; likewise for the audio and any other related channels. Perhaps a training video is offered in eight languages; then any given user will only listen to one of the languages. The multicast tree for any given audio group will only span those listeners who understand that group's language. Presumably, the video might be of interest to all, though receivers have the flexibility to receive audio only (at the user's discretion). Had the data been integrated into one stream, this decoupling would not have been possible except at the receiver: the video stream plus the multiple language tracks would all be received on a common distribution tree, then the receiver could throw away the languages the user did not understand. This would be a waste of network bandwidth and require more processing at the receiver.

RTP packets may be carried within a wide variety of network and transport protocols. In general, the RTP abides by these four rules unless some application overrides them:

1. Usually, RTP expects the lower-layer protocol (e.g., UDP) to support demultiplexing of an RTP data stream and its corresponding RTCP control stream. As we have seen already, over protocols like UDP, RTP uses an even-numbered port for data and the next higher odd-numbered port for RTCP control information.

2. Because RTP headers do not indicate the payload length, it falls to the lower layer to delineate the packet's length. RTP has no maximum packet length; that is a limit of the underlying transport protocol.

3. RTP operates well over packet-oriented transport layers such as UDP. However, it may also operate over octet-stream-oriented transports. In such cases, RTP's encap-

sulation over this transport must specificy a framing mechanism. The framing method depends on the transport, and is not defined in the RTP's specification.

4. Even over packet-oriented transports, some applications may find that RTP-level framing is a desirable feature. This could allow several RTP packets to be carried together in one transport-layer packet (e.g., a UDP packet). This technique may be very useful for easing synchronization between related streams, and also for reducing the RTP+transport overhead on a per-packet basis.

OVERVIEW OF RTCP

The Realtime Transport Control Protocol (RTCP) will now be briefly discussed. RTCP provides feedback to senders on the quality of their transmission. It provides RTP sources with a persistent transport-level identifier, and conveys minimal session information. RTCP also has the ability to automatically adjust its control traffic rate as the size of the group increases.

RTCP periodically transmits control packets to all the session participants. RTCP uses the same transport as the data; therefore, the underlying transport protocol must support (de)multiplexing of the data and control packets. Such an underlying protocol is UDP, which allows unique port numbers to be used for data and control packets.

The main reason RTCP exists is to provide the sender(s) with feedback regarding the quality of their data distribution. This feedback is essential for RTP to succeed in its role as a transport protocol; RTCP's feedback mechanism is analogous to the flow and congestion control functions of other transport protocols. In the case of IP multicast-based sessions, this reception feedback enables an observer—perhaps even a third party to the session, such as an intranet manager—to monitor a session's status. Any problems may be detected and corrected while the session continues. RTCP's Sender and Receiver Reports (SRs and RRs) constitute its feedback mechanism. RRs and SRs are just "recommended" for RTP sessions in general, but they are mandatory for multicast sessions.

The RRs can enable the senders to adapt their RTP data encodings to better accommodate the observed session loss characteristics. For instance, if a session started out with a high-fidelity audio coding that used a relatively large amount of bandwidth, and then an end station joined the group over a lower-bandwidth connection, it may receive the session poorly. Based on this feedback, the sources could choose to modify their audio coding to a more bandwidth-efficient scheme, which may allow much better reception over lower-bandwidth links. The RRs can also allow the session to adapt to variable congestion in its midst. As the congestion increases, the senders may begin to see the reception quality decrease, which may cause the senders to use a more efficient encoding which would be easier on the network.

Another critical component of RTCP is that all RTP sources are identified by persistent transport-level identifiers called CNAMEs (no relation to "CNAME" resource records in the Domain Name Service). The CNAME enables receivers to properly associate multiple data streams from a given participant across a set of related RTP sessions (e.g., to synchronize audio and video streams from the same source). CNAME usage is mandatory for multicast sessions, but only "recommended" for unicast RTP sessions.

The feedback (SR and RR) and CNAME mechanisms are only effective if every session participant sends RTCP packets, but as the number of session members increases there is a chance of excessive control packets. The relationship between the number of group members and their RTCP traffic could be linear. A group with 20 members that grew to 200 members would experience exactly ten times as much RTCP traffic. In some sessions, the RTCP traffic could exceed the data traffic, unless some mechanism was in place to keep the RTCP control traffic from increasing without bound. It is clear that the control packet rate must be throttled in order for RTP to safely scale up to an arbitrarily large number of participants.

The rule that has been adopted to control RTCP is that a bandwidth limit is imposed on a session when it is created. The participants, especially the sender, know this limit when their applications are launched. The RTCP rate is limited to, on average, 5% of the session's defined bandwidth (see Figure 19–3). As the number of receivers increases, the RTCP has mechanisms to ensure that all necessary RRs are heard without swamping the session with control traffic. These mechanisms scale to work over sessions with only a few receivers to sessions with very large numbers of receivers.

The adaptive algorithms that control how fast RTCP transmits control traffic, especially RRs, depend on each group member knowing how many other group members are present. The RTCP transmission interval is dynamically determined, and if a group member has not been heard from in more than five of these intervals, it is assumed to have dropped out of, or been cut off from, the session. Normally, when a user decides to leave a session, their application will transmit an RTCP "BYE" packet on their behalf. This explicit mechanism signals to the group that it has been reduced in size, so the remaining members can quickly recalculate their RTCP transmission parameters.

A benefit of having each participant send its control packets to the whole group is that each member can independently observe the number of participants and their identi-

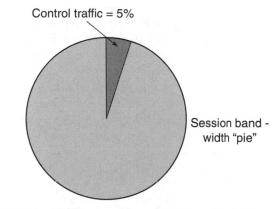

FIGURE 19–3   RTCP's slice of the session bandwidth "pie"

ties. Such information may be used in RTP-based software to create a display of all current session members. Recent versions of the public-domain (MBone-heritage) audio-conferencing tool known as "vat" are based on RTP; the display of the session's participants in the main vat window is derived from this session control information. In so-called "loosely controlled" sessions, where members may join and leave as they wish, RTCP serves as a convenient channel to reach all the participants; however, RTCP alone is not expected to serve all of an application's control communications.

RTP-BASED RELIABLE MULTICAST TRANSPORT PROTOCOLS

RTP has been increasingly accepted in the commercial sector, and it has even been adopted by the ITU for some conference control and transport services. Due to its popularity and ubiquity, certain researchers are considering it as a platform upon which reliability may be layered. We will examine two research projects that aim to enhance RTP to support applications needing reliable transport. One of these proposals is the Lightweight Reliable Multicast Protocol (LRMP) out of INRIA, the French networking research powerhouse. Another is the SRM enhancements to RTP (SRM/RTP) from Peter Parnes of Sweden.

Some researchers believe that RTP is a poor foundation for reliable multicast, presumably because its fundamental design is not centered on providing reliability. We should all remember that the proof is in the pudding: The market will often adopt good enough solutions if they are first to market in lieu of architecturally pure or allegedly technically superior solutions that may take longer to perfect. Also remember that these proposals are not meant to be universal reliable multicast transport protocols. Their existence certainly does not hinder the development of other such protocols.

Lightweight Reliable Multicast Protocol

Researchers at INRIA in France began to develop a suite of applications and protocols in May 1996, called WebCanal. This suite is written entirely in Java™, and is a multicast-enabled set of "push" applications. Multicast delivery is ideally suited to the needs of push applications.

As noted earlier in the book, replicated unicast is very inefficient. Real-world proof of this comes from a survey by Optimal Networks. The survey has quantified just how inefficient replicated unicast can be: It turns out that today's unicast-based push applications are the largest consumer of Internet bandwidth. The World Wide Web is the single largest category of traffic carried across the Internet, and within that class "push" applications account for 17% of the Web's traffic, despite being used by only 12% of the Web's users (see Figure 19–4).

These unicast-based push applications often use the Web's HyperText Transport Protocol as their transport method. HTTP operates on TCP port 80. This is why these

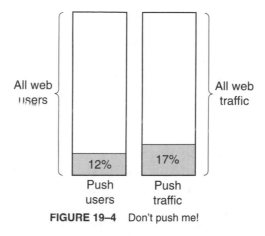

FIGURE 19–4   Don't push me!

push applications, of which PointCast™ is perhaps the most familiar example, are counted as a subclassification of Web traffic.

This survey expresses in very clear terms why a better solution is called for. It is certainly not possible to continue using unicast technology for push applications. Push technology is becoming increasingly popular, and if the number of users of these applications increases at the current rate, the load on the network will become extreme. Push is just not scalable over unicast.

WebCanal is designed to operate over multicast to distribute push-oriented content as efficiently as possible. The WebCanal suite (Figure 19–5) includes the following applications today: WebConf, WebCaster, WebTuner, MTalk, and two diagnostic tools, LRMPmon and RTPdump.

The LRMP was designed to be a low-overhead protocol that would demand little of its clients. The applications of WebCanal require reliable multicast delivery, but in 1996 there were few "off-the-shelf" reliable multicast transport protocol specifications that WebCanal's designers could implement. One of the few reliable multicast protocols available at that time was the SRM framework; however, SRM was not exactly a perfect match for WebCanal's requirements.

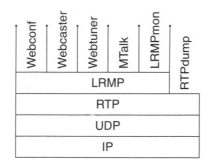

FIGURE 19–5   The WebCanal suite of applications

SRM had three main drawbacks in the eyes of the implementors of WebCanal:

1. SRM involves the whole group in any needed repairs; LRMP's designers felt this would limit scalability over very large groups.
   a. SRM's researchers are addressing this issue; however, a solution is still not available.
   b. A local recovery mechanism is slated for a future version of the LRMP, although at the time of this writing no such mechanism exists within the LRMP.
2. SRM does not provide for ordered delivery, a requirement of the WebCanal applications.
   a. To be fair, SRM was only designed to provide reliable delivery, leaving ordering and other issues to higher-layer protocols.
3. SRM did not specify a means of flow control, which WebCanal also required.
   a. Again, SRM was only designed to provide reliable delivery.

LRMP's Design Goals

The LRMP was intended to be suitable for reliable applications running over MBone-based groups. LRMP would be suited to applications with loose real-time constraints that need ordered delivery. Of course, these applications also implicitly require reliable delivery; otherwise, existing unreliable transmissions would have been sufficient. As with all reliable multicast protocols, scalability is a primary design goal. The LRMP's designers want it to be able to scale to operate over large, geograpically dispersed groups whose delivery trees include WAN components.

Another goal was for the LRMP to be lightweight (hence the name). It was designed to have low overhead and low amounts of control traffic, to allow the receivers to be simple. LRMP has minimal CPU requirements and minimal memory buffering requirements at the receiver. A related design goal is that the LRMP should have reasonable performance.

Finally, for the WebCanal designers, the LRMP needed to be general-purpose so that it could support a variety of applications. To meet this goal, the LRMP does not cater to any specific application; it is a generic transport protocol.

LRMP's Architecture

The LRMP is designed as an extension of the RTP. SRM and non-SRM techniques are built on the RTP framework. RTP supports application data typing (providing for the identification of the data being transmitted) and framing (delimiting data transmissions), two things that the LRMP required. LRMP's control packets are defined as new types of RTCP packets. Under SRM, nodes must specifically request repair if required; thus, SRM is considered to be "NAK-based," and LRMP is also NAK-based.

ACKs vs. NAKs

ACKs or NAKs are control traffic. If a sender needs to multicast 1000 data packets to a 1000-member group, it would be a drag if each of the 1000 members had to say "got it" once for each of the 1000 packets. That would be a total of 1 million

ACKs!! To review: In this scenario the sender has sent 1000 packets, and in order to know that they all got through successfully, it needs to receive 1,000,000 packets. This effect is known as control traffic "implosion." If the data is flowing smoothly and without errors, it might be possible to simply have each receiver say "got all 1000 packets" when the sender is done (only 1000 control packets in this case, instead of 1,000,000).

Now consider a pure NAK-based system. In this case, if all the packets were received completely, there would be no control traffic at all. If, during a given time interval, 1% of the receivers missed a packet, there would be 10 NAKs during that time interval. If the error rate increased to 5% per time interval, the NAK rate would be 50. As you can see, the more errors there are, the more control traffic there is. This is why real NAK-based systems aggregate their control traffic, or attempt to do local recovery as close as possible to the outage. As with the "million ACKs" case above, one strategy for the NAK case might be for each receiver to say something like "got all but 17, 753, and 990." There would be a maximum of 1000 such messages.

Both of these cases illustrate how easily the sender can become the focus of the group's control traffic, and why successful reliable multicast transport protocols will find creative ways to share the repair duties among the group members. The sender should only be involved as a last resort.

A minor debate surrounds whether ACK- or NAK-based reliable protocols are better. No single protocol design will work well in all topologies and loss scenarios. It is likely that the most adaptable protocols will be the most successful. Also note that some protocol designs will favor simplicity and sacrifice some scalability or performance. For instance, a more complex protocol may be able to work over 50,000-member groups, but a simpler protocol may not be able to work over groups of that size, but perhaps only 5000–10,000-member groups.

The data carried by LRMP is simply carried within RTP. RTP in turn, within Web-Canal as with many other applications, runs over UDP/IP. This means that the overhead related to LRMP data (in this case, the same as RTP data) comprises the RTP header (12 octets for the LRMP), the UDP header (8 octets), and the IP header (20 octets), for a total of 40 octets of overhead per LRMP packet (see Figure 19–6).

As with SRM, repairs are multicast to the group with the same TTL as the data. However, *the sender in LRMP must transmit all repairs*. This is different than SRM, in which any of a group's receivers may repair an outage, and this change is made to help simplify the protocol design for the receivers. In LRMP, receivers need not cache packets as long as they are received in order, compared to SRM in which all group members must

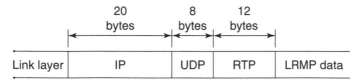

FIGURE 19–6 LRMP packet format

cache data in case it hears a repair request. This change reduces the system requirements on the receiver, at the expense of making the sender's work a bit harder. This design trade-off was made to better accomodate low-end receivers.

A planned extension to the LRMP is to enable limiting the TTL scope of the repair requests to create a "local recovery" mechanism. This has not been implemented yet, but is on the drawing board.

Flow Control and Ordered Delivery Techniques within LRMP

LRMP uses a rate-based flow control scheme, in which the sender defines the maximum rate at which data, including both original data and repairs, may be sent to this session. The rate is adapted based on observed network conditions; the RTP RRs are used to determine whether there is any loss to any group members. If there is, the sender's rate is reduced. The higher the reported loss, the more the sender will slow itself down. If the sender detects little or no loss to the group, it may increase its rate up to the predetermined limit.

The LRMP implements a straightforward technique to ensure that packets arrive in order at the receivers. In the default case, packets arrive in the same order in which they were sent. RTP sequence numbers allow receivers to be sure that they have not missed a packet, and moreover to be sure that all the packets have arrived in order. If packets arrive out of order, a receiver must cache this discontiguous group of packets and issue a repair request. Once the repair is received, the whole group of packets may then be delivered to the application all at once.

The LRMP allows applications to configure their sessions along three dimensions: (1) reliable or not, (2) ordered delivery or not, and (3) maximum bandwidth to be used by the application for this session.

The WebCanal suite has been publicly demonstrated, and is currently undergoing public testing. In one set of preliminary tests, the resilience of LRMP to high rates of packet loss was tested. Loss rates of 50% were introduced near the clients, and LRMP was still able to work well. However, losses of greater than 80% caused problems. Of course, if parts of your intranet are experiencing loss rates of this order, most of your applications will have problems! More testing is needed, especially with more recipients and more senders per group.

The WebCanal suite of applications, including the LRMP, is available for download and testing from INRIA, via the WebCanal home page at `http://webcanal.inria.fr/`. At the time of this writing, versions for Windows NT and UNIX™ were available, with Windows 95 support imminent.

Parnes' RTP Extensions to Support SRM

Peter Parnes, a networking researcher from Sweden, has independently developed a set of RTP extensions to support the SRM framework. Target applications include shared whiteboards, semi-reliable audio and video, and perhaps group-oriented message or other data transfers within so-called groupware applications.

To see why Parnes chose RTP as a basis for SRM extensions, it is useful to analyze the similarities and differences between SRM and RTP, and then decide how to augment RTP to support SRM.

- SRM and RTP both have a unique sender identifier.
- SRM and RTP both assign a unique sequence number to each packet.
- SRM-oriented timer calculations don't require changes to RTP or RTCP.

However, several enhancements must be made in order that RTP and RTCP may fully support the SRM framework:

- NAK (i.e., repair request) support must be added to RTCP. Parnes's proposal adds an RTCP packet type 205 to be used for NAKs.
- Repair response support must also be added to RTCP.
- Support for heartbeats (i.e., SRM's "session messages") must be incorporated into RTCP.

Parnes has chosen to implement these three extensions as a separate "SRM channel" which, because it uses a different group address, can benefit from having a tree that serves only interested recipients. In short, this means that a session could have a mixture of regular RTP receivers and SRM-enhanced RTP receivers. The fact that the normal RTCP channel is separate from the RTCP/SRM control channel means that non-SRM-aware clients will never see this SRM control traffic. Such nodes can still participate in the data portion of these RTP sessions, albeit without SRM's reliability service. The source only needs to send the data once; it is the extra RTCP "SRM channel" that adds the ability to request and receive repairs. See Figure 19–7.

Parnes has implemented two applications using his RTP extensions for SRM: File-Casting and WebCasting. Due to the similarity of this approach to LRMP, it seems that there could be some convergence of the two approaches. Of the two, LRMP appears to be more well defined, and certainly has more applications at the time of this writing.

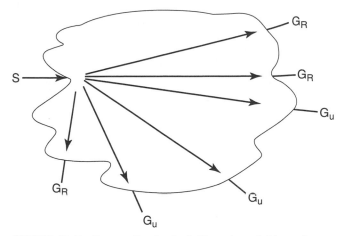

FIGURE 19–7 Group with mixed reliable and unreliable receivers

PART **VII**

CASE STUDIES

The following two case studies illustrate real networks in which multicast IP has been or is being deployed.

The first case study covers the InteropNet. While the InteropNet is a temporary network for the Networld+Interop trade show, it is a highly compressed microcosm of many of the issues encountered in production enterprise internetworks.

The second case study covers NASA's Jet Propulsion Laboratory, which is in the midst of deploying multicast IP. The case study will cover their design goals and objectives, and examine the rationale for the decisions they have made so far.

CHAPTER 20

NETWORLD+INTEROP'S "INTEROPNET"

WHAT IS THE INTEROPNET?

The InteropNet is a major component of the Networld+Interop trade show. Since the earliest days of the Interop trade show, a network has been present to interconnect the booths of the exhibitors at the show. In fact, in the very early days of Interop, it was not really a trade show, but an interoperability event. It gradually grew to include exhibits, becoming the premier industry tradeshow it is today. The interoperability testing heritage co-exists with the marketing aspects of the tradeshow today. Some examples of current technologies that are being tested on the InteropNet are ATM PNNI (Asynchronous Transfer Mode's Private Network-to-Network Interface) "routing," and Gigabit Ethernet switching.

In the very early days of the Interop show, the network was in place specifically to facilitate interoperability testing of Internet-based network technologies among the attending engineers, not to interconnect "exhibitors." Networld+Interop's show network, today called the InteropNet, has become one of the industry's largest technology showcases and interoperability demonstrations.

HOW IS THE INTEROPNET USED?

In its role as an interoperability testbed, new technologies are integrated into the Interop-Net as soon as they are stable enough to use in a production network, or perhaps a bit before. As an important emerging technology, IP multicast has been supported in the In-teropNet since 1994, shortly after the MBone had been created in 1992. From this beginning through 1997, the DVMRP has been the InteropNet's primary multicast routing protocol (it is true that MOSPF was used in the first full deployment in 1994, on Proteon routers, but future deployments have exclusively employed DVMRP). In 1994, multicast routing was experimental, but it has been one of the InteropNet's core suite of services since 1995.

The DVMRP's usage has changed over the years, accommodating evolving network designs and exhibitors' changing expectations of how they should receive MBone— or on-site "intra-InteropNet" multicast—connectivity. As you will see, far more multicast traffic is now sourced on-site for InteropNet-based receivers compared to externally-sourced MBone traffic. This pattern is likely to apply to most enterprise network scenarios, in which local intra-enterprise multicast traffic will dominate externally-sourced multicast traffic volumes.

OVERVIEW OF THE INTEROPNET'S DESIGN
THROUGH THE YEARS

Ribs connect all the exhibitors on or near an aisle, as depicted in Figure 20–1. The ribs have at least two routers attaching to them, to back each other up. The original design had a native Ethernet interface (e.g., a 10BaseT port) on a router connected to a rib's hub, but today the "connection" is a virtual one, with the router being a member of the rib's emulated LAN. Logically, the two scenarios are identical, but the physical implementations are quite different!

As depicted in Figure 20–2, each of these routers connects a set of 6–10 ribs to the InteropNet's backbone(s).

Originally, there was only one backbone, a thick Ethernet (10Base5) segment. This scenario is shown in Figure 20–3.

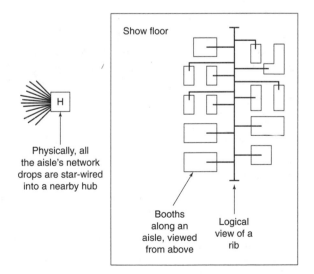

FIGURE 20–1 An InteropNet rib

Logical view of a single rib

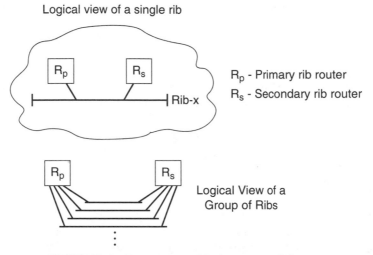

Rp - Primary rib router
Rs - Secondary rib router

Logical View of a
Group of Ribs

FIGURE 20–2   Router connectivity for a group of ribs

As the InteropNet has evolved, FDDI and other fiber-based technologies such as ATM OC-3, OC-12, and 100BaseFX, have been added to provide redundant backbones. An echo of the original Ethernet backbone still lives on today, as the "access Ethernet." It is no longer a backbone, nor is it based on thick Ethernet. It evolved into an extended LAN using bridges, then Ethernet switches with 10BaseFL* uplinks.

The "AccessEther" is a network which is in place for the convenience of managing the InteropNet. It spans the entire show floor, connecting terminal servers that attach to the consoles of each piece of network equipment. The AccessEther also provides connectivity for RMON probes, distributed packet analysis tools, and SNMP-controlled devices. The routing protocols are configured such that this network can never be used as a backbone over which traffic could be forwarded. It is strictly for out-of-band access between the Network Operations Center (NOC) networks and the devices on the show floor.

Through 1996, the ribs were built from 10BaseT hubs, with one collision/broadcast domain per rib. 10BaseT Ethernet is the standard network "drop" technology; other tech-

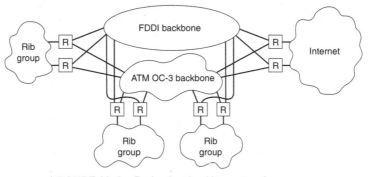

FIGURE 20–3   Redundant backbones topology

*10BaseFL was previously known as Fiber-Optic Inter-Repeater Link (FOIRL).

nologies such as 100BaseTX, Gigabit Ethernet over fiber (1000BaseSX or 1000BaseLX), or ATM may be ordered at an additional cost. Token Ring was an option through 1996, but is no longer available. One other technology that is no longer available for vendor drops is 100VG-AnyLAN, which was available in 1995 and 1996.

In 1997, for the first time, Asynchronous Transfer Mode (ATM) LAN Emulation (LANE) was used to provide switched 10 Mbps Ethernet to each exhibitor's booth (limited, partially successful, trial deployments were attempted in 1996). For the most part, the rib's local ATM LANE edge device contains its corresponding LAN Emulation Server (LES) and Broadcast and Unknown-destination Server (BUS). Each edge device has one local LES and one local BUS. The LAN Emulation Configuration Server (LECS) for all the ribs on the entire InteropNet is in the NOC.

Despite the skepticism of some NOC Team members regarding LANE's ability to support increasing amounts of multicast traffic, the 1997 design has worked very well through the Las Vegas and Tokyo shows in May and June, respectively. Conventional wisdom was that LANE couldn't handle lots of broadcasts or multicasts, but conventional wisdom was proven wrong. In fact, based on the trial deployments of LANE in 1996, the NOC Team provided feedback to vendors on necessary enhancements before their implementations would scale to networks that included increasing amounts of multicast traffic. Based on the NOC Team's input, from the real-world scenarios that were tested on the InteropNet, these vendors made changes that allowed successful deployment of ATM LANE as the primary rib connectivity technology in 1997. Now that their products have been improved and proven in the InteropNet, enterprise customers will have better success deploying LANE in their own intranets. This is a concrete example showing that the InteropNet is still a vital technology proving ground and interoperability testing environment to this day.

EVOLUTION OF MULTICAST USAGE ON THE INTEROPNET

Early

At first, when multicast was deployed on the InteropNet, the only multicast traffic was MBone traffic. In other words, the only multicast content that could be received was whatever was being transmitted over the MBone. The InteropNet was itself originating content to the MBone, typically two different video streams, "NOC-Cam" and "Floor-Cam."

The NOC-Cam stream allowed MBone users to peek over the collective shoulders of the NOC Team throughout the setup and operational periods of the show. Because the NOC Team tends to keep strange hours, sometimes people halfway around the world get to see live activities in the NOC. One year, a gent from Australia was able to enjoy watching the tired and punchy NOC Team members at 2:00 a.m. Eastern Time (during an Atlanta show).

The Floor-Cam stream would let people watch the amazing transformation from a large empty room to a large trade show. Occasionally, the NOC Team has been known to take a roving camera along during InteropNet tours, giving a tour to the MBone watchers as well as the physical tour attendees.

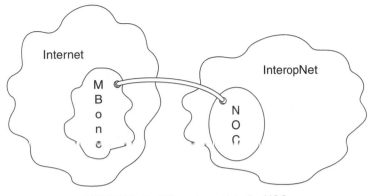

FIGURE 20–4 MBone tunnel into the NOC

During the pre-1994 experimental deployment, the only presence of multicast traffic was in the NOC, illustrated in Figure 20–4. Once full deployment happened at the Las Vegas show in early 1994, there were exhibitors on the floor that had tuned into the MBone. These exhibitors were seen to be watching a shuttle mission that happened to coincide with the show, as well as tuning in to the InteropNet's streams.

In the experimental-deployment phase of InteropNet multicast usage, MBone support was supplied via a tunnel from the NOC to those exhibitors who requested MBone connectivity, as illustrated in Figure 20–5. This was to prevent them from each getting their own tunnel to various points on the MBone. Multiple tunnels from the InteropNet to various points out on the MBone would have destabilized MBone routing, at least for the InteropNet. Also, multiple MBone tunnels would have overloaded the InteropNet's T-1 link to the Internet. Having one tunnel terminate in the NOC, feeding the interested exhibitors, kept multicast traffic to a bare minimum on the InteropNet's Internet link. Even today, there is still only one tunnel from the MBone to the NOC, but from there the multicasts are distributed natively into the fully multicast-enabled InteropNet.

In 1994, at the inaugural deployment of native multicast, MOSPF was used on Proteon routers that spanned the InteropNet. As a backup mechanism, BSDI UNIX-based

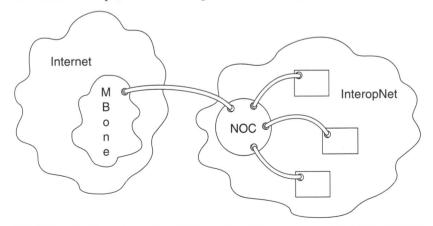

FIGURE 20–5 Tunnels from the NOC providing MBone access to interested exhibitors

PCs were deployed in parallel with the "native" MOSPF routers as a backup method. The PC-based multicast routers were not used later in 1994 or later, as the DVMRP was used to provide native multicast forwarding, and the NOC Team became gradually more confident in the stability of router-based DVMRP implementations.

Again, in this early time the awareness of multicast was very low, and thus there was no real demand from the exhibitor community for MBone tunnels. There were exceptions, including multicast-savvy companies such as Sun. As the awareness of multicast increased, interest in this service gradually picked up. Interest in and usage of multicast has exploded throughout 1996 and 1997, with multicast traffic now representing a sizable—and growing—fraction of the traffic on the InteropNet.

Later

As time passed, the usage of the DVMRP within the InteropNet evolved somewhat. Content was still limited to the MBone only, along with a small number of low-bit-rate video streams from the NOC to the MBone. At this point, there was still no real content on the MBone, unless a Networld+Interop show happened to coincide with a NASA Space Shuttle mission or some other MBone event. Other than the locally sourced NOC-Cam-like transmissions, very little (or no) content was sourced from the show. There was very little multicast traffic sourced from the exhibitors on the show floor throughout 1995, except possibly for some limited usage of `vat` and `nv` (the early network video tool that has since been eclipsed by `vic`).

The next phase was characterized not by an evolution in content, but by enhanced support by router vendors. As 1995 progressed, router vendors began to support the DVMRP in their products, so it became possible to enable all subnets on the show floor with native multicast routing. This reduced the management overhead related to multicast on the InteropNet, as tunnels to exhibitors were no longer needed. In this phase, the InteropNet "went native." It had become a non-tunneled multicast region as depicted in Figure 20–6.

One multicast tunnel remained, that which provided MBone access to the Interop-Net. At the beginning of this period, the MBone access tunnel still terminated in a UNIX

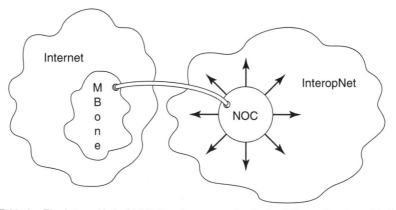

FIGURE 20–6   The InteropNet's DVMRP region connecting to the MBone via a tunnel in the NOC

workstation within the NOC. This quickly evolved to having the tunnel terminate in one of the contributed routers in the NOC.

The InteropNet's design is highly redundant to provide maximum uptime for exhibitors, which posed a challenge to early DVMRP implementations when it was enabled everywhere. The problem observed by the NOC Team was that pruning did not work in the InteropNet, despite the fact that the implementations in use purported to support this feature. In fact, these implementations had been observed to support pruning in other environments prior to their usage on the InteropNet.

The InteropNet's highly redundant design includes redundant backbones, and each rib is attached to the backbones with two routers. The DVMRP had been enabled on all of the routers in the InteropNet, so all these loops were visible to it. Technically, loops in the topology do not pose a fundamental challenge to the DVMRP's design. Even the version which was specified in Steve Deering's thesis, had it been fully and properly implemented, could have handled this case properly. However, the 1995-era donated implementations had not yet been deployed in these real-world situations. Their heritage was the code within `mrouted`, which had not typically been deployed in such topologies. Because of this, these limitations of the DVMRP's reference implementation had not yet been discovered in its years of use within the MBone experiment.

The loops in the InteropNet's topology reflect real-world network design practices (i.e., redundant backbones). Fulfilling one of its missions as a technology proving ground, the InteropNet was able to participate in the evolution of these implementations of the DVMRP.

MULTICAST ROUTING ALTERNATIVES
FOR THE FUTURE INTEROPNET

As we move into the late 1990s, the InteropNet still uses the DVMRP as its exclusive multicast routing protocol. As we saw earlier in the book, the DVMRP is perhaps not the best overall multicast routing protocol. Therefore, you may wonder why it continues to be used on the InteropNet. The NOC Team has considered using MOSPF, but there are a number of factors that make MOSPF an impractical choice in current and near-term future use (though as we have seen it was used in the initial native multicast deployment in Las Vegas during the late Winter of 1994).

Why not use PIM or CBT? These are not yet usable due to lack of availability on the InteropNet's contributed router products. In the future, these may become options. However, for the same reasons it would be difficult to deploy MOSPF (see below), it would likely also be difficult to deploy any non-DVMRP routing protocol in the InteropNet environment.

There are many reasons, some practical, some technical, that the DVMRP is still in use. From a backbone perspective, MOSPF could be a really good fit. The InteropNet's unicast core routing system is OSPF-based, and has been for years. The InteropNet's usage of OSPF and the Routing Information Protocol (RIP) is illustrated in Figure 20–7. In fact, the InteropNet was an early proving ground supporting OSPF interoperability testing between

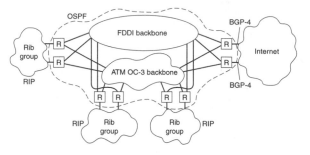

FIGURE 20–7   The InteropNet's usage of OSPF and RIP

3Com, Proteon, and Wellfleet (now part of Bay Networks). However, there is a practical problem in using MOSPF: It can only be used where OSPF is also in use.

While OSPF is exclusively used in the core of the InteropNet, RIP is used on the edge to support those exhibitors who attach to the InteropNet with routers.

Besides those exhibitors who attach their booth-internal subnetworks to the Interop-Net with a router, there are numerous booths that simply attach to the InteropNet with a small hub or switch. These exhibitors' booths are directly attached to their local rib, while the router-attached booth subnetworks are at least one hop away from the rib, "behind" their booth router(s). Figure 20–8 shows the choices available for booths to attach to one of the InteropNet's ribs.

Of those exhibitors who do choose to attach to the InteropNet with a router, very few are part of the OSPF routing system. Most use RIP to advertise their booth-internal subnetworks to the InteropNet core routers, and to receive a default route from them.

If an exhibitor wants to join the InteropNet's multicast routing system (and the MBone) with MOSPF, they would be required to use OSPF for unicast routing (at least on their router's interface that attaches to the InteropNet's rib . . .). As noted above, those

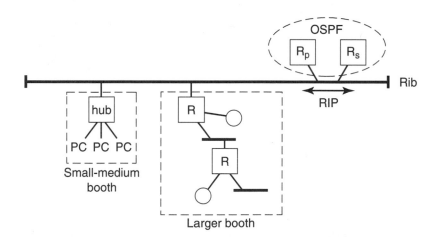

FIGURE 20–8   Different ways for exhibitors to attach their booths to the InteropNet

FIGURE 20–9   A possible way to use MOSPF and the DVMRP together

who attach to the InteropNet with routers mostly don't use OSPF*, so the DVMRP would still have to be supported on the ribs. If the DVMRP wasn't supported on the ribs, exhibitors would be unable to participate in the InteropNet's multicast routing system if their booth attaches to the InteropNet with a router and uses RIP. It is not simple to tell them to use OSPF, because requiring MOSPF would limit their choice of router vendors.** Not all router vendors currently support MOSPF in their products, but essentially all routers that support multicast routing do support the DVMRP, because it is required to join the MBone.

It is unlikely that MOSPF would be chosen for use on the edge, since that probably would require running two multicast routing protocols at the same time on each rib interface or establishing DVMRP tunnels into booths on request (an administrative nightmare). A decision to use MOSPF throughout the InteropNet would perhaps require that exhibitors change router vendors just to obtain multicast service from the InteropNet. It should be obvious that this is not a practical option, despite the theoretical suitability of MOSPF to the InteropNet's design.

One possible way to use MOSPF would be to imitate the unicast routing system, as depicted in Figure 20–9. The DVMRP would have to be used as an edge protocol (in those places where RIP is used now), while using MOSPF as the core multicast routing protocol. To make this work, we would need a reliable way to originate a DVMRP default route and to learn DVMRP routes from exhibitors. Also, we would have to allow for the fact that multiple DVMRP speakers on the rib would exchange routes with each other in addition to hearing the InteropNet-generated default route. Finally, multicast packets received from the rib would need to pass the DVMRP's RPF check before being accepted into the MOSPF "cloud."

For the foreseeable future, it would appear that DVMRP is well-suited to its current role within the InteropNet, though the NOC Team is always open to try new technologies as they become available.

---

*Why? Well, there is a lot of historical inertia in the collective experience of the InteropNet's exhibitors. They expect to be able to show up and use RIP to exchange routes with the InteropNet. OSPF has been supported for those vendors that request it, but RIP is the default. In enterprise networks, where the MIS department has more control, this is not likely to be a limitation.

**It would also require that exhibitor use recent software releases on their booth routers. Typically, these routers are two to three major releases out-of-date, because exhibitors know that if it worked before it is likely to work in the future.

GROWTH OF MULTICAST TRAFFIC

In 1996, for the first time in the author's memory, multicast was sourced from a rib and received on at least one other rib, thus demonstrating that exhibitors weren't just watching the MBone, but were sending and receiving local content. This new development is depicted in Figure 20–10. Precept was involved in demonstrations of inter-rib multicast connectivity at the first show of 1996, in Las Vegas, and more vendors generated multicast traffic as the year progressed. (In 1995, there may have been some very limited inter-rib multicast video transmissions.)

The spectacular growth in the volume of multicast traffic across the InteropNet has coincided with the presence of exhibitors such as Precept, White Pine, Intel, Microsoft, Xing Technologies, and many others*. These exhibitors, as a class, are software companies with (multimedia) applications that can work over multicast. Generally, these products are oriented toward audio- and videoconferencing.

Exhibitors are actually beginning to source local multicast content, and this trend seems likely to continue. Therefore, multicast must be a seamless, production-quality service working for all exhibitors, regardless of how their booth attaches to the InteropNet. The goal is to make it easy for exhibitors to plug in and have multicast "just work" (at least as well as unicast does!).

No matter which mix of multicast routing protocols is eventually chosen, IGMP must continue to be supported on each rib. Any machines that are directly connected to ribs shall be able to join a group simply by sending an IGMP Host Membership Report, as shown in Figure 20–11.

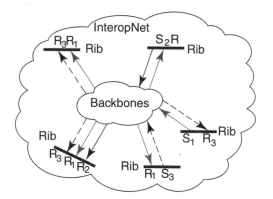

FIGURE 20–10   Internal multicast sources and receivers within the InteropNet

*Of the listed vendors, only Precept was shipping multicast-enabled software prior to 1997.

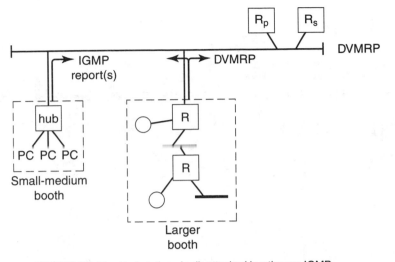

FIGURE 20–11   End stations in rib-attached booths use IGMP

CHAPTER 21

MULTICAST IP AT NASA's JET PROPULSION LABORATORY

One of the National Aeronautics and Space Administration's (NASA's) missions is to develop technology that may be transferred to and possibly commercialized by the public sector. NASA has participated in the research and development related to the Internet for quite some time. In fact, the network known as the NASA Science Internet (NSI) was once a peer backbone with the National Science Foundation Network (NSFnet) backbone and the United States Department of Energy's Energy Sciences Network (ESnet). As one of NASA's science centers, the Jet Propulsion Laboratory (JPL) has been closely involved with this networking research over the years.

Experimentaton with Multicast Technology

New things generally start small, and the MBone was no exception. The MBone's presence at JPL started with a few system administrators in the networking group who thought it was "cool." Later, NASA even funded some formal evaluation and testing of the technology under the aegis of networking research. JPL participated in this testing, as did other NASA science centers.

NASA has two kinds of centers: science and spaceflight. Science centers focus on science of all kinds related to the space program. Both science and spaceflight centers participate in unmanned missions, but manned spaceflight and related activities are generally the domain of the spaceflight centers.

Experimentation and Technology Evaluation

Early multicast experimentation may have been quite informal, but the technology was certainly compelling. The quality of the video was not great, but tolerable. The early users could see the potential of the technology and were excited about it. At this point, the MBone fell into the category of "cool toy." Of course, the Internet itself was in that category three to six+ years before.

Early on, it was important not only to expand the MBone network to get a feel for how well its routing protocol (the DVMRP) worked, but also to try out various applications to see how well they worked. The early users enjoyed watching events such as IETF meetings and other things on the MBone. JPL even originated one of the early MBone "channels," called "Radio Free vat." IETF meetings and the like are not the sort of content that will keep the kids up late on a school night. To a certain extent, today's MBone still lacks compelling mass market content (which is not surprising since it is well-understood that it is currently too immature to be a mass-market medium), but content providers are beginning to consider how they can take advantage of this new medium.

Radio Free vat

One of the eary MBone applications was called "vat," which stood for visual audio tool. The visual part of this was an interface that showed who was listening to the audio program, and also a loudness meter which showed a bar graph of the received signal strength.

In their process of early experimentation with the MBone and its applications, someone at JPL decided to start an audio session on the MBone that would transmit music. JPL effectively became the MBone's first radio station. The strange thing about this radio station is that anyone on the MBone could transmit to it. JPL created this MBone session, and transmitted its share of musical content, but anyone with MBone access and a UNIX workstation with a built-in CD-ROM drive could also join the fun. As long as only one sender was active at once, this worked great!

Another NASA MBone session that has been very popular since its introduction is the live multicasts of the space shuttle missions. There is something amazing about watching live events happening in orbit, in essentially real time—over the Internet/MBone! These MBone sessions emanate from NASA's Ames Research Center, and served to spark the interest of management at multiple NASA centers. The common interest concerned how best to deploy and utilize this exciting new multicast technology.

MAKING IT REAL

The management at JPL showed a two-faceted interest in multicast technology. First, they viewed it as another service that could be offered by JPL's network group. Second, it was viewed as a possible way to do video distribution at JPL.

A bit of background is in order: JPL, like many NASA centers, had a cable TV system in place for distributing video around the center. Typically, the video was viewable in public areas such as cafeterias, auditoriums, and so on. While this certainly worked, it was not a desktop technology (some offices were equipped with television sets, but the cost of equipping everyone's office with a television would be prohibitive). Rather than having a separate dedicated infrastructure for video, it would be nicer to have a way to get video onto most people's desktops. This goal is not unusual. In the future, many organizations both inside and outside of NASA hope to have a single integrated network that carries video and voice as well as computer data. Multicast is considered by many to be a critical enabling component of such a future "integrated services" network.

JPL's network group was formally tasked with investigating the implications of multicast deployment across the entire JPL user community, as well as determining what applications would be most useful.

Objectives of the Project

We have already seen two of the objectives of this deployment project: first, ubiquitous deployment of multicast across JPL; and second, determining what application(s) would be used over the new multicast infrastructure. One component of this investigation would be the cost of equipping thousands of users with multicast-capable IP stacks plus applications. A related objective was to determine how JPL's routing infrastructure could be modified to support multicast under reasonable cost constraints. It turns out that a software upgrade, to be introduced along with selected hardware upgrades that were already planned, would enable multicast to be deployed across JPL.

The network group had some requirements of its own to ensure the success and long-term viability of the project. The multicast routing architecture will need to be simple to configure, verify, and manage. While meeting those goals, it must be capable of scaling to reach the thousands of users on JPL's institutional network.

Finally, multicast must be integrated as tightly as possible with the existing network infrastructure. Not only does this objective help control costs, it also minimizes the total number of devices that must be managed as part of JPL's centerwide network infrastructure. The project could not be considered a success if the old cable-TV-based video system were replaced by yet another network in parallel with the "normal" data network.

Applications

Videoconferencing is one of the target applications of JPL's initial multicast project. JPL holds "Town Hall" meetings over their existing cable TV infrastructure, plus lectures by visting scientists and scientists-in-residence. Also, there is a scrolling videotext channel that updates people about coming events. These are the kinds of applications that JPL's management would like to migrate to a multicast-based infrastructure.

At least two forms of video content need to be available. One is live multicasts of real-time events, and the other is playback of stored content (also known as "streaming"). The live events could be lectures going out to dozens or hundreds of receivers, or small, interactive videoconferences with as few as three participants. Scientists at JPL could collaborate with each other locally, or participate in larger-scale online meetings.

Some applications that have been investigated are RealVideo from Progressive Networks, `vic` and `vat` (the free MBone tools), and Precept's suite of software, collectively called "IP/TV." The next section outlines IP/TV's features and intended applications, which should indicate why JPL is considering using it.

Spotlight on a Commercial Multicast Application: IP/TV

Precept was founded in 1995 to commercialize video over multicast IP. The IP/TV software runs on Microsoft's® Windows 95® and Windows NT® operating systems, and interoperates with the UNIX-based MBone tools `vic` and `vat`.

IP/TV is codec-independent, so it can accommodate future video coder/decoders (codecs). Codecs are implemented in software, so pure receivers need no special hardware. Some currently supported codecs are H.261, MPEG, and Intel's Indeo. Depending on the codec chosen for a video stream, its traffic could consume between 56 kbps and 3 Mbps.

Precept envisions that their software could be used for things like CEO broadcasts, or interactive collaboration within a distributed workgroup. It could support meetings, presentations, and related activities. Computer-based video training and distance learning are also considered to be likely applications. IP/TV is standards-based, implementing network- and transport-layer standards such as IGMP and RTP/RTCP.

IP/TV is one possible component of JPL's multicast application suite. They hope to enhance communications with and among employees. JPL's multicast infrastructure, when completed, will allow up-to-the-minute information about current events and projects at JPL to be conveyed almost instantly. Multicast will allow JPL to add value to their existing network infrastructure, making it an even more powerful information dissemination tool.

Prerequisites for Multicast Deployment

Unfortunately, enabling multicast on your network isn't as simple as flicking a switch. Not only must you get the routing infrastructure into a manageable condition, but it also helps to have users who are willing to learn about new things and help test your new infrastructure. One nice thing about these power users is that they understand what it means to be an early adopter. If you need to iron out a wrinkle in your plans, you want your users to support you by making any necessary changes on their end. You may just want to experiment with a different configuration and get feedback as to whether or not there was any improvement (or degradation).

At a minimum, these early adopters understand that they are not participating in a production service. Therefore, they will not complain during the brief periods when service may be unavailable due to network reconfigurations. Once you have a system that works pretty well, you'll have the experience and confidence to deploy a solution that has been proven in your own backyard.

If at all possible, you should try to do your pilot testing on a safe yet realistic part of your production intranet. If you build a special-purpose test network, it is very likely that you will be able to demonstrate these new applications successfully (almost anything works in a lab). However, you won't conclude your testing with the same level of confidence as if you had used part of your real network.

You may decide to start by adding a few multicast-enabled routers in parallel with unicast-only routers to test your desired routing topology. This will also test how well your new multicast applications get along with your existing unicast applications. Once you have confidence in the traffic mix, you could integrate the unicast and multicast routing functions in the same box, leaving the other router (in place in case of a temporary mishap).

Network Architecture

JPL's current multicast infrastructure in late 1997 is a patchwork of many UNIX-based mrouters. These have been operated for years by eager MBone users who couldn't wait for JPL to deploy its own native multicast service. One objective of the new multicast design is to make these mrouters unnecessary by providing a more stable and reliable production multicast service. For JPL-internal conferences, the performance should be even better than the old scheme. Also, if mrouter users abandon their local routers, it frees them from managing multicasting, transforming them into pure multicast users.

For all these reasons, it is hoped that the existing users will be motivated to migrate away from their UNIX-based mrouters to the new native infrastructure. Since these mrouter users are already familiar with multicast, they are a logical place to start the multicast routing deployment.

The JPL network architecture is fairly straightforward at the backbone level. Externally, there is an isolation FDDI subnetwork to which the WAN provider routers attach. Two routers connect between the isolation FDDI ring and the internal FDDI backbone ring. Multicast packets sourced from outside JPL arrive over one of the WAN routers, tunneled inside unicast IP packets to their tunnel endpoint.

The tunnel endpoint happens to be one of the two parallel isolation routers, as shown in Figure 21–1. The tunnel performs multicast routing by running PIM over Cisco's implementation of Generic Routing Encapsulation tunneling over IPv4 (see RFCs 1701 and 1702). The PIM-over-GRE-tunnel must pass DVMRP routing information between the DVMRP speakers at JPL (the `mrouted` machines) and—ultimately—the MBone, so the routers are configured to pass DVMRP routing information through the PIM cloud. Effectively, this means that the tunnel is emulating the functionality of a DVMRP tunnel, though strictly speaking it is *not* a DVMRP tunnel.

MBone connectivity is provided by exchanging DVMRP routes through the tunnel, and internally JPL has elected to use PIM. Eventually, all of JPL's internal routers will be configured for PIM, and the RPs will be chosen from the centrally located backbone routers. The backbone technology may migrate from FDDI to switched Gigabit Ethernet or ATM in the future, but the choice of backbone technology is independent of the multicast routing architecutre.

Sparse-mode PIM (actually, a Cisco-proprietary hybrid of sparse- and dense-mode PIM called "sparsedense") has been chosen, with an eventual migration to PIM-SM version 2 once that is available from Cisco. PIM-SM, as an ultimate design goal, was chosen over PIM-DM due to its perceived advantage in controlling traffic to only go where it is required. It integrates well with JPL's metropolitan-area network of leased T-1 and 56 kbps circuits, by not broadcasting traffic unless it has been "subscribed to" in advance. Also, PIM-DM

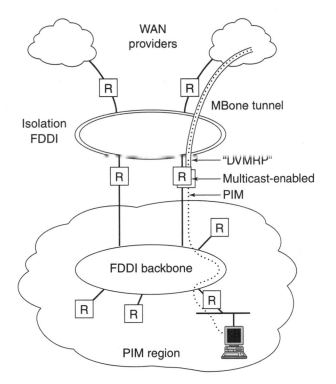

FIGURE 21-1   JPL backbone architecture with multicast overlay

would have caused spurious traffic bursts on some non-member subnetworks during the initial flooding interval (until pruning happens). This "unpredictability" caused some members of JPL's networking community to favor a sparse-mode over dense-mode PIM.

Today's design uses the dedicated MBone router as the RP, but eventually it may make sense to have multiple candidate RPs to divide the multicast forwarding load. The only routers that will be candidate RPs will be attached to the backbone, so they are centrally located within the logical topology. An interim step between full PIM-SM RP bootstrapping and today's single RP design may involve a single "backup RP" to provide operational stability.

Beyond deploying a workable multicast infrastructure, there must be a way to control the applications' traffic so it does not leak beyond its intended audience. The traffic would be broadcast as far as its initial TTL would allow, which could disrupt other MBone events. In most cases, content carried within a JPL multicast session should not be forwarded to the MBone. Of course, events such as the Mars Pathfinder or Mars Global Surveyor missions will probably be specifically targeted at the widest possible audience, but these globally interesting transmissions will probably be rather infrequent. Today, a TTL scoping scheme is in place at JPL and is working well. One reason it works well is that programs like `sdr`, `vic`, and `vat` all support TTL scoping, and early multicast users have been well educated about what TTL levels are to be used with which "scopes."

A NASA-wide administrative scoping scheme is being promulgated by the Ames Research Center. JPL will probably adopt this scheme eventually. One big advantage of admnistrative scoping is that it puts the control of the groups' flooding scope in the routers, instead of relying on the sources to set their TTLs in compliance with the TTL-scoping rules that have been established in advance.

Future Possibilities

Once it is up and running, JPL's multicast infrastructure will likely be used to support further network research. Some areas of future interest include:

- Reliable multicast protocols
  - for software distribution
  - for shared environments such as whiteboards
  - for shared applications/desktops
- Other interactive collaborative applications such as
  - joint document editing
  - multicast-enabled messaging (i.e., multicast "chat")

This is only a short list. Clearly, there will be no lack of further ideas for other ways to use their multicast infrastructure once it is fully deployed. In addition to these new protocols which will be tested and eventually deployed on JPL's multicast infrastructure, there will be new forms of content using applications that leverage the deployed multicast infrastructure.

As users become familiar with the network's new capabilities, their creativity will generate new forms of content that we cannot imagine. Once the tools are in the hands of the users, their creativity will spawn new content, new uses, and new value. Organizations will create unique solutions that match their evolving needs. Ultimately, this is where the true value of IP multicast lies.

PART VIII

APPENDICES

Appendix A is a glossary of terms used in the book. Appendix B is a detailed overview of IGMP's packet formats and protocol operation. Appendix C is a history of the MBone, as excerpted from the "Internet Monthly Reports," a newsletter in which Internet researchers have shared their progress with each other for many years. Appendix D takes a high-level view of multicast routing protocols, summarizing their key similarities and differences. Appendix E contains information on stantards bodies concerned with multicast standardization, and finally Appendix F is a list of references pertinent to multicast IP.

APPENDIX A

GLOSSARY

ANSI	American National Standards Institute
ARP	Address Resolution Protocol. ARP is used alongside IP to discover IP-to-MAC address mappings. ARP is described in RFC-826.
ATM	Asynchronous Transfer Mode
BGMP	Border Gateway Multicast Protocol
BOOTP	Bootstrap Protocol. Designed to help end-stations automatically discover their IP address. BOOTP was specified in RFC-951 and formed the basis for DHCP.
CBT	Core Based Trees. A multicast routing protocol documented in RFC-2189 and -2201.
CIDR	Classless Inter-Domain Routing. CIDR is defined in RFC-1519.
DHCP	Dynamic Host Configuration Protocol. RFC-2131 specifies DHCP.
Distribution tree	A set of routers and subnetworks that allows a (set of) group member(s) to receive traffic from any source. Depending on the algorithm in use by the multicast routing protocol, the tree may be rooted at the source or at some central point in the network.

DLSw

Data Link Switching.   A technique for providing a layer-two bridged service over a layer-three routed network via tunneling. The APPN Implementor's Workshop is developing DLSw and publishing the specification as Informational RFCs. DLSw is described in RFC-1795.

Downstream

Downstream is any direction that is not upstream (relative to any router on a source's distribution tree).

An active downstream interface is a downstream interface that leads to some of a group's active receivers. (Any router that is on an active branch of a multicast delivery tree will have one upstream interface and at least one downstream interface.)

DVMRP

Distance Vector Multicast Routing Protocol.   The DVMRP was the first multicast routing protocol to be widely deployed.

The MBone is built on a DVMRP core today, having been exclusively DVMRP-based at its beginning. The original version of DVMRP is specified in RFC-1075, but a specification representing the up-to-date DVMRPv3 should be out by the time this book is published.

E-IGRP

Enhanced IGRP.   A proprietary unicast routing protocol from Cisco that supports multiple network layer protocols, including IP and IPX.

EGP

Exterior Gateway Protocol.   EGP and BGP-4 are both Exterior Gateway Protocols, though EGP is no longer in widespread use. Besides being the name of a specific exterior routing protocol, EGP may also refer to any non-interior routing protocol.

eLAN

Emulated LAN. Emulated LANs over ATM were the first type of standards-based virtual LANs (VLANs).

FDDI

Fiber Distributed Data Interface.   FDDI is a LAN technology, usually employed in backbone applications. Physically, FDDI is comprised of dual counter-rotating token-passing rings that carry 100 Mbps of data. FDDI was developed by the ANSI's X3T9.5 committee.

GUM

See BGMP

HTML

HyperText Markup Language

IANA

Internet Assigned Numbers Authority
<http://www.iana.org/iana/>

ICMP

Internet Control Message Protocol.   ICMP is specified in RFC-792.

ICMPv6	ICMP for IPv6. ICMPv6 is specified in RFC-1885. ICMPv6 incorporates many functions of ICMP for IPv4, and also includes IGMP's functionality. There is no such thing as "IGMPv6."
IDMR	Inter-Domain Multicast Routing. IDMR is a working group of the IETF. The IDMR WG is standardizing multicast routing protocols.
IEEE	Institute of Electrical and Electronics Engineers, Inc. The IEEE's "Project 802" has defined most of the LAN technologies in existence today, except for FDDI (which was developed by ANSI, but designed to integrate naturally into the IEEE's architecture). <http://www.ieee.org/>
IETF	Internet Engineering Task Force <http://www.ietf.org/>
IGMP	Internet Group Management Protocol. IGMPv1 is specified in Appendix 1 of RFC-1112. IGMPv2 will soon be specified in its own RFC (probably before this book is published).
IGMPv6	See ICMPv6. There is no separate IGMP protocol that operates in conjunction with IPv6: all necessary group-management functionality has been integrated into ICMPv6.
iif	Incoming Interface. The interface on which a packet arrived. In RPF-based protocols, iif is also the interface on which packets from a certain source are *expected* to arrive.
IGP	Interior Gateway Protocol. Examples of IGPs include RIP, RIPv2, OSPF, Integrated IS-IS, IGRP, E-IGRP, etc.
IGRP	Interior Gateway Routing Protocol. IGRP is a Cisco-proprietary unicast routing protocol.
IP	Internet Protocol. IP is defined in RFC-791.
IPng	IP, the next generation. See also IPv6.
IPv6	IP version 6. IPv6 is specified in RFC-1883.
ISDN	Integrated Services Digital Network
ISP	Internet Service Provider

LAN   Local Area Network.   Examples of LAN technologies are Ethernet,
                        Token Ring, and FDDI.

LANE   LAN Emulation.   LANE is a way to emulate Ethernet and token-ring
                        bridging over ATM backbones.

MAC   Medium Access Control.   The MAC sub-layer is the lower part of layer
                        two in the OSI Reference Model.

MAN   Metropolitan Area Network.   A MAN could be a combination of a collec-
                        tion of leased lines, a frame relay-, SMDS-, or ATM-based "cloud" service
                        accessible within a metropolitan area.

MBone   Multicast backBone.   The MBone is a logical overlay which interconnects
                        thousands of multicast-capable "islands" by tunneling multicast packets
                        through unicast-only routers.

MBoneD   MBone Deployment.   MBoneD is an IETF working group in the Opera-
                        tions Area.

MIS   Management Information Systems.   Usually the group of people within a
                        corporation that are responsible for deploying and maintaining the corpo-
                        rate enterprise network, and many of the network-based applications and
                        servers.

MMUSIC   Multiparty MUltimedia SessIon Control is an IETF working group.   The
                        MMUSIC WG is developing Internet standards track protocols supporting
                        Internet teleconferencing sessions.
                        MMUSIC's focus is on supporting the loosely controlled conferences that
                        are pervasive on the MBone today. However, its protocols are designed to
                        be general enough for use in managing tightly controlled sessions.

MOSPF   Multicast extensions to OSPF.   MOSPF is defined in RFC-1584.

mrouted   A UNIX program that implements DVMRP.   This program was the foun-
                        dation of the early MBone, and is still in widespread use. The name is pro-
                        nounced em-rowt-dee.

Multicast routing   Activities performed by IP routers in order to determine how to forward
                        multicast IP packets, either from some particular source to a group, or from
                        any source to a group.

Multicast forwarding   For each multicast IP packet received, a forwarding decision must be made. Typically, each packet must arrive on a specific upstream interface (i.e., incoming interface), and then must be copied onto a (set of) downstream "outgoing interface(s)."

NAT   Network Address Translation.   A technique for translating an intranet-significant private IP address into a globally unique IP address. See RFCs 1631 and 1918.

NIC   Network Interface Card, or
Network Information Center.
[In this book, NIC almost always refers to the former definition.]

oif   Outgoing Interface.   An oif is an interface over which a packet must be forwarded in order to reach some subset of a group.

oiflist   A list of oifs, usually the list of the oifs necessary to reach all of a group's members.

OSI RM   Open Systems Interconnection Reference Model.   A seven-layer framework which may be used to classify and compare existing networking protocol stacks.

OSPF   Open Shortest Path First.   A protocol developed by Proteon and standardized by the IETF. OSPF has been documented in RFC-2178.

OUI   Organizationally Unique Identifier.   The most-significant three bytes in the IEEE MAC address. Sometimes referred to as a manufacturer code.

PIM   Protocol-Independent Multicast.   PIM is actually two protocols: PIM-Dense Mode and PIM-Sparse Mode. Besides sharing some common control message formats, the two protocols are very different.

PIM is so named because neither of its protocols is dependent on any particular unicast routing protocol. Unlike the DVMRP, PIM does not have a built-in unicast routing protocol which it would use to locate itself relative to sources' subnetworks. As long as there is a unicast routing table, PIM can perform its RPF check.

PIM-DM   PIM-Dense Mode.   PIM-DM is a protocol based on RPM, as is the DVMRP. Besides not including a built-in unicast routing protocol, PIM-DM is very similar to the DVMRP. At the time of this writing, PIM-DM has not yet been documented in an RFC.

PIM-SM   PIM-Sparse Mode.   RFC-2117 is the specification for PIM-SM, which
                         uses explicitly joined shared trees emanating from a "Rendezvous Point."
                         PIM-SM has mechanisms whereby source-based trees may be explicitly
                         joined if a threshold is exceeded.

RARP   Reverse ARP

Rendezvous Point   A router in PIM-SM that serves as the "center" of a group. Traffic from
                         sources is conveyed to the RP, and from there is delivered downstream
                         toward known group members. The RP is where senders "meet" receivers.

RFC   Request for Comments

RIP   Routing Information Protocol.   RIP version 1 (RIPv1) is a rather simple
                         distance-vector routing protocol that is classful (i.e., masks are not adver-
                         tised with routes). RIP is specified in RFC-1058.

RIPv2   RIP version 2 is a classless version of RIP, in that it transmits masks along
                         with routes, however RIPv2 is still a distance-vector routing protocol.
                         RIPv2 is defined by RFC-1723.

RIPng   RIP, the next generation.   RIPng is also known as RIPng for IPv6. Basi-
                         cally, RIPng is RIPv2 with bigger addresses. RFC-2080 specifies RIPng
                         for IPv6.

RP   See Rendezvous Point

RPB   Reverse Path Broadcasting was a technique invented by Dalal and Metcalfe
                         to provide a loop-free network-layer broadcasting service. RPB was used
                         as a starting point for the development of a network-layer multicast service,
                         evolving into TRPB, then RPM.

RPF check   Reverse Path Forwarding check.   Used to ensure that packets from some
                         source have arrived on the proper interface.

RPM   Reverse Path Multicasting is the technique upon which both PIM-DM and
                         the DVMRP are based.

SAP   Session Announcement Protocol.   Used to advertise current and future
                         sessions on the MBone.

sd   Session Directory tool (used on the MBone to create and receive informa-
                         tion about multicast sessions). sd implemented SAPv0 and has now been
                         replaced by sdr, which implements SAPv1.

sdr	sdr is just a name for the new version of the session directory tool. sdr has been jokingly referred to as "sd returns," or "sd revisited." It could also be viewed as "Session DiRectory."
SDP	Session Description Protocol
SLP	Service Location Protocol. RFC-2165 defines SLP.
SONET	Synchronous Optical NETwork
TRPB	Truncated RPB. An optimization to RPB in which IGMP Reports are used to ensure that traffic is only broadcast onto LANs that are known to have group members.
TTL	Time To Live. The TTL field in the IP packet controls how far an IP packet may travel. Each router decrements a packet's TTL field by one when forwarding it. The largest possible TTL is 255. If a router ever receives a packet whose TTL equals 1, it cannot forward it further.
Unicast	Style of application in which one end station is directly addressing another.
Upstream	For any router on each source's distribution tree, the direction known as "upstream" is the "best" direction from this router toward that source. Packets must never be forwarded back toward the tree's source, only away from it. In the context of a source-based tree (could be built by either DVMRP, MOSPF, PIM-DM, or PIM-SM), upstream is the direction toward the *source*. In shared tree protocols (CBT, PIM-SM), upstream is the direction toward the *"center" of the tree*.
VLAN	Virtual LAN. IEEE 802.1Q is an emerging standard for defining virtual LANs over IEEE MAC layer protocols such as Ethernet.
VLSM	Variable-Length Subnet Mask[ing]. Classless routing protocols such as OSPF and RIPv2 allow network managers to make subnets as big as necessary for their needs. Such non-uniform subnet lengths within a network number are referred to as VLSM. Classful routing protocols such as RIPv1 require all subnets within a given network number to use the same number of bits.
WAN	Wide Area Network
WG	Working Group. The IETF is composed of various WGs, collected into Areas of related WGs.

APPENDIX B

IGMP DETAILS

IGMPV2 PACKET FORMATS

All IGMPv2 message types use the format shown in Figure B–1 (which is carried inside an IP packet, with the IP protocol ID field set to 2):

```
                       1                   2                   3
   0 1 2 3 4 5 6 7 8 9 0 1 2 3 4 5 6 7 8 9 0 1 2 3 4 5 6 7 8 9 0 1
  +-+-+-+-+-+-+-+-+-+-+-+-+-+-+-+-+-+-+-+-+-+-+-+-+-+-+-+-+-+-+-+-+  \  IHL =
  |Version|  IHL  |Type of Service|         Total Length          |  |   Internet
  +-+-+-+-+-+-+-+-+-+-+-+-+-+-+-+-+-+-+-+-+-+-+-+-+-+-+-+-+-+-+-+-+  |   Header Length
  |         Identification        |Flags|      Fragment Offset     |  |   (usually = 5)
  +-+-+-+-+-+-+-+-+-+-+-+-+-+-+-+-+-+-+-+-+-+-+-+-+-+-+-+-+-+-+-+-+  |
  |  Time to Live |    Protocol   |        Header Checksum         |  \  +-----------+
  +-+-+-+-+-+-+-+-+-+-+-+-+-+-+-+-+-+-+-+-+-+-+-+-+-+-+-+-+-+-+-+-+  =>| IP Header |
  |                       Source Address                          |  /  +-----------+
  +-+-+-+-+-+-+-+-+-+-+-+-+-+-+-+-+-+-+-+-+-+-+-+-+-+-+-+-+-+-+-+-+  |  For IGMP,
  |                     Destination Address                       |  |   Protocol = 2
  +-+-+-+-+-+-+-+-+-+-+-+-+-+-+-+-+-+-+-+-+-+-+-+-+-+-+-+-+-+-+-+-+  |   (0000 0010)
  |                     Options                |::::::::::::   Padding  |  |   and TTL = 1
  +-+-+-+-+-+-+-+-+-+-+-+-+-+-+-+-+-+-+-+-+-+-+-+-+-+-+-+-+-+-+-+-+  /  (0000 0001)
  ::::::::::::::::::::::::::::::::::::::::::::
  .+--------+--------+--------+--------+
  |10010100|00000100|    2 octet value  |   (Value = 0, telling routers to pay attention)
  +--------+--------+--------+--------+

  +-+-+-+-+-+-+-+-+-+-+-+-+-+-+-+-+-+-+-+-+-+-+-+-+-+-+-+-+-+-+-+-+  \
  |      Type     | Max Resp Time |            Checksum            |  |
  +-+-+-+-+-+-+-+-+-+-+-+-+-+-+-+-+-+-+-+-+-+-+-+-+-+-+-+-+-+-+-+-+  >  IGMPv2 Header
  |                         Group Address                         |  |
  +-+-+-+-+-+-+-+-+-+-+-+-+-+-+-+-+-+-+-+-+-+-+-+-+-+-+-+-+-+-+-+-+  /
```

FIGURE B–1   IP Header plus IGMPv2 header

IP OPTIONS AND THE ROUTER ALERT OPTION

IP options serve to extend the functionality of the IP network-layer header. They are attached after the destination address, and once they are complete, enough zero bits are used to pad the IP header to a 32-bit boundary. The maximum size of the Internet header (including options) is 60 octets (15 32-bit words). Some functions of IP options are IP source routing, time stamps, and security labels.

As we have noted already, IGMPv2 packets include the "Router Alert" IP option in the IP header (RFC-2113). To quote the Router Alert RFC, this option exists to provide a mechanism whereby "routers can intercept packets not addressed to them directly, without incurring any significant performance penalty." As we now know, IGMP Host Membership Reports are addressed to the group being reported, not to the router or any other unicast IP address.

Again, to quote RFC-2113:

2.1 Syntax

The Router Alert option has the following format:

```
+————+————+————+————+————+
|10010100|00000100 | 2 octet value  |
+————+————+————+————+————+
Type:
Copied flag: 1 (all fragments must carry the option)
Option class: 0 (control)
Option number: 20 (decimal)

Length: 4

Value: A two octet code with the following values:
0 - Router shall examine packet
1-65535 - Reserved
```

2.2 Semantics

Hosts shall ignore this option. Routers that do not recognize this option shall ignore it. Routers that recognize this option shall examine packets carrying it more closely (check the IP Protocol field, for example) to determine whether or not further processing is necessary. Unrecognized value fields shall be silently ignored.

The semantics of other values in the Value field are for further study.

Obviously, the value field will be set to zero, since IGMPv2 wants the router to notice these packets. According to the IGMPv2 specification, all conforming IGMPv2 routers should be able to process the Router Alert option.

OVERVIEW OF IGMPV2'S MESSAGE TYPES

There are four types of IGMPv2 host-router messages, as defined in the internet draft `draft-ietf-idmr-igmp-v2-07.txt`: Leave Group, Membership Report, version 1 Membership Report (for backward compatibility), and the (two) Membership Queries.

There are two examples of the Membership Query type: a General Query packet, for determining which groups are present on a LAN, and a Group-Specific Query packet, for determining if there are any members of a particular group on a LAN. Both IGMPv2 Query messages use the same message Type: 0x11. The two Query messages are differentiated by the IGMP Group Address field, and by their IP destination addresses. General Queries are sent to the all-hosts group address IP destination—224.0.0.1—with the Group Address field in the IGMPv2 header set to zero. Group-Specific Queries are addressed at the IP layer to the Group being queried, and IGMPv2's Group Address field is also set to the group being queried.

IGMPv2 Host Membership Reports are sent to the IP destination address of the group being reported on, with the IGMP Group Address field also containing this address. Similarly, the Leave Group message sets the IGMP group address field to the IP multicast group address of the group being left. At the IP layer, the Leave Group message is addressed to the all-routers class D address, 224.0.0.2.

At this point, we will illustrate the types of IGMP packets and show exactly how their fields are used. As discussed above, there are four types of IGMPv2 packets: Host Membership Report, Leave Group message, General Query, and Group-Specific Query. The IGMPv2 Type field takes on different values depending on which function is being performed. These values are summarized in Table B–1.

TABLE B–1   IGMPv2 Specific Type Field Values

IGMPv2 Host Membership Query	0x11	0001	0001
IGMPv2 Host Membership Report	0x16	0001	0110
IGMPv2 Leave Group	0x17	0001	0111

It turns out that there is only one IGMP Type devoted to both kinds of Query messages. If an IGMP packet is a General Query, the Group field of the IGMP Header is set to all zeros. If the IGMP packet is a Group-Specific Query, the IGMP Header's Group field is set to the group being queried.

We also show the formats of IGMPv1 Host Membership Reports and Host Membership Queries in Table B–2.

In IGMPv1, the IGMP header began with two four-bit fields, the first being the Version field, the second being the Type field. The IGMPv2 header begins instead with an eight-bit Type field (in IGMPv2, there is no longer a "Version" field.). All IGMPv2 Types (now an eight-bit field) have their most significant four bits set to 0001, which an IGMPv1 implementation would interpret as meaning the packet was version 1.

TABLE B–2   IGMPv1 Formats

IGMPv1 Version field	0x1	0001	: : : :
IGMPv1 Host Membership Query Type field	0x01	: : : :	0001
IGMPv2 Host Membership Report Type field	0x02	: : : :	0010

```
                         1                   2                   3
     0 1 2 3 4 5 6 7 8 9 0 1 2 3 4 5 6 7 8 9 0 1 2 3 4 5 6 7 8 9 0 1
    +-+-+-+-+-+-+-+-+-+-+-+-+-+-+-+-+-+-+-+-+-+-+-+-+-+-+-+-+-+-+-+-+  \   IHL =
    |0 1 0 0|0 1 0 1|Type of Service|         Total Length          |  |    Internet
    +-+-+-+-+-+-+-+-+-+-+-+-+-+-+-+-+-+-+-+-+-+-+-+-+-+-+-+-+-+-+-+-+  |    Header Length
    |        Identification         |Flags|     Fragment Offset     |  |    (usually = 5)
    +-+-+-+-+-+-+-+-+-+-+-+-+-+-+-+-+-+-+-+-+-+-+-+-+-+-+-+-+-+-+-+-+  |
    |0 0 0 0 0 0 0 1|0 0 0 0 0 0 1 0|         Header Checksum        |  \   +-----------+
    +-+-+-+-+-+-+-+-+-+-+-+-+-+-+-+-+-+-+-+-+-+-+-+-+-+-+-+-+-+-+-+-+  =>|  IP Header |
    |1 0 0 0 0 1 0 1 0 0 0 0 0 0 1 0 0 0 0 0 1 0 0 1 1 0 0 1 0 1 0 1 1|  /   +-----------+
    +-+-+-+-+-+-+-+-+-+-+-+-+-+-+-+-+-+-+-+-+-+-+-+-+-+-+-+-+-+-+-+-+  |   For IGMP,
    |1 1 1 0 0 0 1 0 0 0 0 0 0 0 0 0 0 1 0 0 0 1 1 1 1 0 0 0 0 0 1 0|  |   Protocol = 2
    +-+-+-+-+-+-+-+-+-+-+-+-+-+-+-+-+-+-+-+-+-+-+-+-+-+-+-+-+-+-+-+-+  |    (0000 0010)
    |                 Options             |::::::::::::  Padding     |  |    and TTL = 1
    +-+-+-+-+-+-+-+-+-+-+-+-+-+-+-+-+-+-+-+-+-+-+-+-+-+-+-+-+-+-+-+-+  /    (0000 0001)
    :::::::::::::::::::::::::::::::::::::::::::
    +--------+--------+--------+--------+
    |10010100|00000100|  2 octet value  |  (Value = 0, telling routers to pay attention)
    +--------+--------+--------+--------+


    +-+-+-+-+-+-+-+-+-+-+-+-+-+-+-+-+-+-+-+-+-+-+-+-+-+-+-+-+-+-+-+-+  \
    |0 0 0 1 0 1 1 0|0 0 0 0 0 0 0 0|           Checksum            |  |
    +-+-+-+-+-+-+-+-+-+-+-+-+-+-+-+-+-+-+-+-+-+-+-+-+-+-+-+-+-+-+-+-+  >   IGMP Header
    |1 1 1 0 0 0 1 0 0 0 0 0 0 0 0 0 0 1 0 0 0 1 1 1 1 0 0 0 0 0 1 0|  |
    +-+-+-+-+-+-+-+-+-+-+-+-+-+-+-+-+-+-+-+-+-+-+-+-+-+-+-+-+-+-+-+-+  /
```

FIGURE B–2a   Packet format of an IGMPv2 host membership report

The Host Membership Report

For example, if end station 133.2.19.43 (in hex, 0x85.02.13.2B, or in binary, 1000 0101.0000 0010.0001 0011.0010 1011) were reporting membership for the group 226.0.143.2 (in hex, 0xE2.00.8F.02, or in binary, 1110 0010.0000 0000. 1000 1111. 0000 0010), the IGMPv2 Host Membership Report packet would look like Figure B–2a.

The source IP address in the packet is the IP address of this example (133.2.19.43), and the eight-bit protocol field has been set to 2 (0000 0010), the four-bit IP version field has been set to 4 (0100), and the Internet Header Length field has been set to 5 (0101). Finally, the TTL is indicated as having a value of 1 (0000 0001). Note that the IP destination address is the group for which status is being reported, and that this same group address is also written into the group address field of the eight-octet IGMP header.

For both of IGMPv2's non-Query messages, the Max Response Time field is irrelevant. It should be zeroed by senders of non-Query messages, and should be ignored by receivers, regardless of its value.

The Two Query Messages

Now we will describe the detailed structure of the IGMPv2 Host Membership Query messages. First we will describe the General Query, then the Group-Specific Query. The Gen-

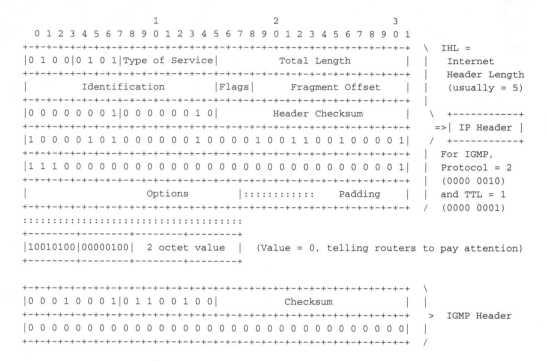

FIGURE B–2b   Packet format of an IGMPv2 General Query

eral Query is sent to the IP "all-hosts-on-this-subnet" multicast destination address of 224.0.0.1 (in hex, 0xE0.00.00.01, or 1110 0000.0000 0000.0000 0000.0000 0001 in binary), while the Group-Specific Query is sent to the class D address of the group being queried.

The IP source address is the elected Querier's IP address on this subnet. For the purposes of this example, we define this to be 133.2.19.33 (in hex, 0x85.02.13.21, or in binary, 1000 0101.0000 0010.0001 0011.0010 0001). Again, the TTL has been set to 1, the IP Version and Internet Header Length fields have been filled in with values of 4 and 5, respectively, and the Protocol field has been set to 2, as in Figure B–2b.

The IGMPv2 Type field for any type of Query is 0x11 (0001 0001). In a General Query, the Group Address field is set to all zeros. The default IGMPv2 Max Response Time is set to a value of 100 (in hex 0x64, or 0110 0100 in binary), which is equivalent to 10 seconds since the Max Response Time field is interpreted in units of 0.1 second. The Max Response Time field of the IGMP Header is only significant in IGMPv2's two kinds of Query packets. Other packets should be transmitted with this field set to a value of zero. If an IGMPv2 implementation receives a non-Query packet with a nonzero Max Response Time field, it must ignore whatever value it finds there.

Now, the format of an IGMPv2 Group-Specifc Query is shown in Figure B–2c. Assume the group being queried is 224.130.45.15 (in hex, 0xE0.82.2D.0F, or in binary 1110 0000.1000 0010.0010 1101.0000 1111). This packet is just like the IGMPv2 General Query, except that the Group Address field of the IGMP header holds the group address being queried (instead of all zero bits).

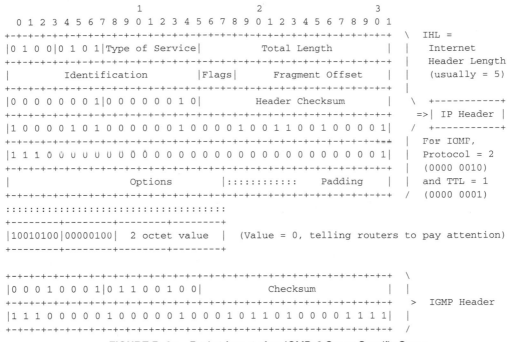

FIGURE B–2c Packet format of an IGMPv2 Group-Specific Query

The Leave Group Message

The final IGMPv2 packet type is the Leave Group message. This message is addressed to the IP "all-routers-on-this-subnet" address (224.0.0.2), as is the Host Membership Report. (Some implementations actually transmit this packet to the group being left, which will probably work most of the time as long as the Router Alert option is used.) The emerging IGMPv2 internet draft seems to prefer using 224.0.0.2.

In this example (see Figure B–2d) we will continue to assume that the source address is 133.2.19.43 (in hex, 0x85.02.13.2B, or in binary, `1000 0101.0000 0010.0001 0011.0010 1011`).

As in the IGMPv2's Host Membership Report, the Max Response Time field should be zeroed by senders of Leave Group messages, and regardless of its value, this field should be ignored by receivers.

The IGMPv2 Type field of the Leave Group message is set to 0x17 (`0001 0111`). The Host Membership Report uses a value of (`0001 0110`). Therefore, these messages can easily be identified as non-IGMPv1 messages. However, both IGMPv2 Query messages do match an IGMPv1 Version+Type combination (`0001 0001`, or 0x11 in hex). See Figure B–3 for a concise summary of usage of relevant IP and IGMPv2 header fields.

IGMPv1 Packet Formats

IGMPv1 is somewhat simpler to summarize than IGMPv2 (see Figure B–4). There is a Version field (always set to `0001`), and the type field is the least significant four bits

```
              1                   2                   3
 0 1 2 3 4 5 6 7 8 9 0 1 2 3 4 5 6 7 8 9 0 1 2 3 4 5 6 7 8 9 0 1
+-+-+-+-+-+-+-+-+-+-+-+-+-+-+-+-+-+-+-+-+-+-+-+-+-+-+-+-+-+-+-+-+   \  IHL =
|0 1 0 0|0 1 0 1|Type of Service|        Total Length          |   |  Internet
+-+-+-+-+-+-+-+-+-+-+-+-+-+-+-+-+-+-+-+-+-+-+-+-+-+-+-+-+-+-+-+-+   |  Header Length
|       Identification          |Flags|     Fragment Offset    |   |  (usually = 5)
+-+-+-+-+-+-+-+-+-+-+-+-+-+-+-+-+-+-+-+-+-+-+-+-+-+-+-+-+-+-+-+-+   |
|0 0 0 0 0 0 0 1|0 0 0 0 0 0 1 0|        Header Checksum        |   \  +-----------+
+-+-+-+-+-+-+-+-+-+-+-+-+-+-+-+-+-+-+-+-+-+-+-+-+-+-+-+-+-+-+-+-+  =>| IP Header |
|1 0 0 0 0 1 0 1 0 0 0 0 0 0 1 0 0 0 0 1 0 0 1 1 0 0 1 0 1 0 1 1|   / +-----------+
+-+-+-+-+-+-+-+-+-+-+-+-+-+-+-+-+-+-+-+-+-+-+-+-+-+-+-+-+-+-+-+-+   |  For IGMP,
|1 1 1 0 0 0 0 0 0 0 0 0 0 0 0 0 0 0 0 0 0 0 0 0 0 0 0 0 0 0 1 0|   |  Protocol = 2
+-+-+-+-+-+-+-+-+-+-+-+-+-+-+-+-+-+-+-+-+-+-+-+-+-+-+-+-+-+-+-+-+   |  (0000 0010)
|                  Options               |::::::::::::   Padding |   |  and TTL = 1
+-+-+-+-+-+-+-+-+-+-+-+-+-+-+-+-+-+-+-+-+-+-+-+-+-+-+-+-+-+-+-+-+   /  (0000 0001)
::::::::::::::::::::::::::::::::::::::::::::
+--------+--------+--------+--------+
|10010100|00000100|  2 octet value  |   (Value = 0, telling routers to pay attention)
+--------+--------+--------+--------+


+-+-+-+-+-+-+-+-+-+-+-+-+-+-+-+-+-+-+-+-+-+-+-+-+-+-+-+-+-+-+-+-+   \
|0 0 0 1 0 1 1 1|0 0 0 0 0 0 0 0|          Checksum            |   |
+-+-+-+-+-+-+-+-+-+-+-+-+-+-+-+-+-+-+-+-+-+-+-+-+-+-+-+-+-+-+-+-+   >  IGMP Header
|1 1 1 0 0 0 1 0 0 0 0 0 0 0 0 0 0 1 0 0 0 1 1 1 1 0 0 0 0 0 1 0|   |
+-+-+-+-+-+-+-+-+-+-+-+-+-+-+-+-+-+-+-+-+-+-+-+-+-+-+-+-+-+-+-+-+   /
```

FIGURE B–2d   Packet format of an IGMPv2 Leave Group messsage

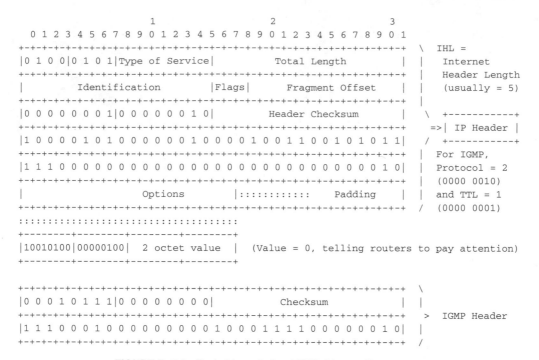

IGMPv2 Messages

IGMPv2 Messages	IP Packet Source	IP Packet Destination	IP Protocol	IGMPv2 Type	IGMPv2 Max Resp. Time	IGMPv2 Group Address
Membership Report	ES	GBR	2	0×12	0	GBR
Leave Group	ES	AR	2	0×17	0	GBL
General Query	Q	AH	2	0×11	100	0
Group-Specific Query	Q	AH	2	0×11	100	GBQ

AH   All-hosts (224.0.0.1)
AR   All-routers (224.0.0.2)
ES   End Station's IP address
GBL   Group Being Left
GBQ   Group Being Queried
GBR   Group Being Reported
Q   Querier's IP address

FIGURE B–3   Summary of IGMPv2 packet types

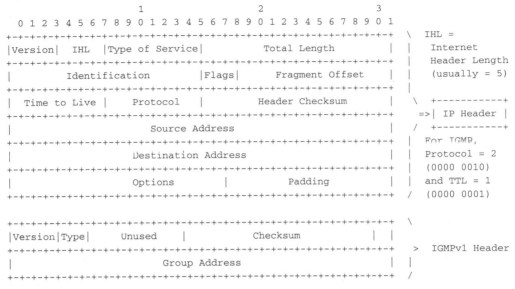

```
                  1                   2                   3
  0 1 2 3 4 5 6 7 8 9 0 1 2 3 4 5 6 7 8 9 0 1 2 3 4 5 6 7 8 9 0 1
 +-+-+-+-+-+-+-+-+-+-+-+-+-+-+-+-+-+-+-+-+-+-+-+-+-+-+-+-+-+-+-+-+  \  IHL =
 |Version|  IHL  |Type of Service|          Total Length         |  |  Internet
 +-+-+-+-+-+-+-+-+-+-+-+-+-+-+-+-+-+-+-+-+-+-+-+-+-+-+-+-+-+-+-+-+  |  Header Length
 |          Identification        |Flags|    Fragment Offset     |  |  (usually = 5)
 +-+-+-+-+-+-+-+-+-+-+-+-+-+-+-+-+-+-+-+-+-+-+-+-+-+-+-+-+-+-+-+-+  |
 |  Time to Live |    Protocol    |         Header Checksum       |  \  +-----------+
 +-+-+-+-+-+-+-+-+-+-+-+-+-+-+-+-+-+-+-+-+-+-+-+-+-+-+-+-+-+-+-+-+  =>|  IP Header |
 |                       Source Address                          |  /  +-----------+
 +-+-+-+-+-+-+-+-+-+-+-+-+-+-+-+-+-+-+-+-+-+-+-+-+-+-+-+-+-+-+-+-+  |  For IGMP,
 |                     Destination Address                       |  |  Protocol = 2
 +-+-+-+-+-+-+-+-+-+-+-+-+-+-+-+-+-+-+-+-+-+-+-+-+-+-+-+-+-+-+-+-+  |  (0000 0010)
 |          Options               |           Padding            |  |  and TTL = 1
 +-+-+-+-+-+-+-+-+-+-+-+-+-+-+-+-+-+-+-+-+-+-+-+-+-+-+-+-+-+-+-+-+  /  (0000 0001)

 +-+-+-+-+-+-+-+-+-+-+-+-+-+-+-+-+-+-+-+-+-+-+-+-+-+-+-+-+-+-+-+-+  \
 |Version|Type|     Unused       |            Checksum           |  |
 +-+-+-+-+-+-+-+-+-+-+-+-+-+-+-+-+-+-+-+-+-+-+-+-+-+-+-+-+-+-+-+-+  >  IGMPv1 Header
 |                       Group Address                           |  |
 +-+-+-+-+-+-+-+-+-+-+-+-+-+-+-+-+-+-+-+-+-+-+-+-+-+-+-+-+-+-+-+-+  /
```

FIGURE B–4   IP header plus IGMPv1 header

of the first byte of the IGMPv1 header. Figure B–4 shows the IGMPv1 header with the IP header (note the lack of the IP Router Alert option, which did not exist at the time IGMPv1 was originally designed).

The IGMPv1 Host Membership Report packet is sent from the end station's source IP address to the group being reported. In this example, we'll assume that the end

```
                  1                   2                   3
  0 1 2 3 4 5 6 7 8 9 0 1 2 3 4 5 6 7 8 9 0 1 2 3 4 5 6 7 8 9 0 1
 +-+-+-+-+-+-+-+-+-+-+-+-+-+-+-+-+-+-+-+-+-+-+-+-+-+-+-+-+-+-+-+-+  \  IHL =
 |0 1 0 0|0 1 0 1|Type of Service|          Total Length         |  |  Internet
 +-+-+-+-+-+-+-+-+-+-+-+-+-+-+-+-+-+-+-+-+-+-+-+-+-+-+-+-+-+-+-+-+  |  Header Length
 |          Identification        |Flags|    Fragment Offset     |  |  (usually = 5)
 +-+-+-+-+-+-+-+-+-+-+-+-+-+-+-+-+-+-+-+-+-+-+-+-+-+-+-+-+-+-+-+-+  |
 |0 0 0 0 0 0 0 1|0 0 0 0 0 0 1 0|         Header Checksum       |  \  +-----------+
 +-+-+-+-+-+-+-+-+-+-+-+-+-+-+-+-+-+-+-+-+-+-+-+-+-+-+-+-+-+-+-+-+  =>|  IP Header |
 |0 0 0 0 1 0 1 0 1 0 1 1 1 1 0 0 0 0 1 0 0 0 1 0 1 1 1 1 0 1 1 0|  /  +-----------+
 +-+-+-+-+-+-+-+-+-+-+-+-+-+-+-+-+-+-+-+-+-+-+-+-+-+-+-+-+-+-+-+-+  |  For IGMP,
 |1 1 1 0 1 1 0 1 0 0 0 0 0 0 0 1 0 0 0 0 0 0 0 1 0 0 0 0 0 0 1 1|  |  Protocol = 2
 +-+-+-+-+-+-+-+-+-+-+-+-+-+-+-+-+-+-+-+-+-+-+-+-+-+-+-+-+-+-+-+-+  |  (0000 0010)
 |          Options               |           Padding            |  |  and TTL = 1
 +-+-+-+-+-+-+-+-+-+-+-+-+-+-+-+-+-+-+-+-+-+-+-+-+-+-+-+-+-+-+-+-+  /  (0000 0001)

 +-+-+-+-+-+-+-+-+-+-+-+-+-+-+-+-+-+-+-+-+-+-+-+-+-+-+-+-+-+-+-+-+  \
 |0 0 0 1|0 0 1 0|0 0 0 0 0 0 0 0|            Checksum           |  |
 +-+-+-+-+-+-+-+-+-+-+-+-+-+-+-+-+-+-+-+-+-+-+-+-+-+-+-+-+-+-+-+-+  >  IGMP Header
 |1 1 1 0 1 1 0 1 0 0 0 0 0 0 0 1 0 0 0 0 0 0 0 1 0 0 0 0 0 0 1 1|  |
 +-+-+-+-+-+-+-+-+-+-+-+-+-+-+-+-+-+-+-+-+-+-+-+-+-+-+-+-+-+-+-+-+  /
```

FIGURE B–5a   Packet format of an IGMPv1 Host Membership Report

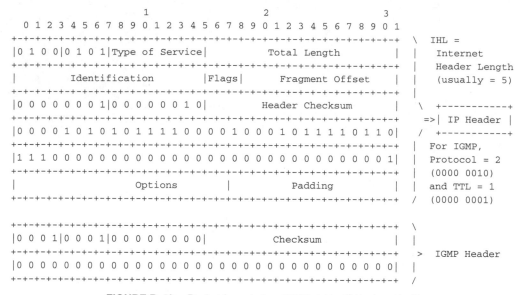

FIGURE B–5b   Packet format of an IGMPv1 Host Membership Query

station's address is 10.188.34.246 (in hex this is 0x0A.BC.22.F6, or 0000 1010.1011 1100.0010 0010.1111 0110 in binary), and the group being reported is 237.1.2.3 (in hex this is 0xED.01.02.03, or 1110 1101.0000 0001.0000 0010.0000 0011 in binary). Besides these address fields in the IP Header, the Version is 4 (0100), the Internet Header Length is 5 (0101), the Protocol is 2 (0000 0010), and the TTL should be set to 1 (0000 0001).

   In the IGMPv1 Host Membership Report's header, the Version field is 1 (0001), the Type is 2 (0010), and the Group Address is the same as the IP destination address. The Unused field should be set to zero, all of which is depicted in Figure B–5a.

   The IGMPv1 Host Membership Query is virtually identical to the Report. There are two differences. First, the IP destination address is the "all-hosts-on-this-subnet" address (224.0.0.1), and the IGMPv1 Header's Group Address field is zero. The really important difference is that the IGMPv1 Type field is set to 1 (0001) as shown in Figure B–5b.

   Figure B–6 summarizes the various values of the IP and IGMP headers as used by IGMPv1.

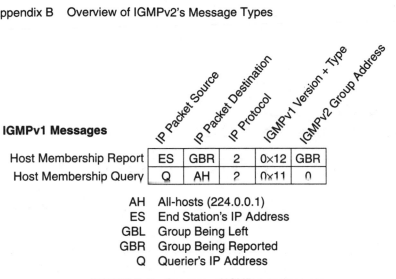

IGMPv1 Messages

	IP Packet Source	IP Packet Destination	IP Protocol	IGMPv1 Version + Type	IGMPv2 Group Address
Host Membership Report	ES	GBR	2	0×12	GBR
Host Membership Query	Q	AH	2	0×11	0

AH   All-hosts (224.0.0.1)
ES   End Station's IP Address
GBL   Group Being Left
GBR   Group Being Reported
Q   Querier's IP Address

FIGURE B–6   Summary of IGMPv1 packet types

HISTORY OF THE MBONE
AND MULTIMEDIA CONFERENCING

The following is a series of unedited excerpts from the Internet Monthly Reports, which have been compiled and transmitted from the University of Southern California's Information Sciences Institute (USC ISI) since approximately 1980. The Internet Monthly Reports are still being produced as of the Summer of 1997. Those since January of 1991 are available from the following URL: `ftp://ftp.isi.edu/in-notes/imr/`.

These excerpts are from the reports "Multimedia Conferencing" section. These sections, from the 1992 through 1994 timeframe, were mainly co-authored by Steve Casner and Eve Schooler, with Joe Touch contributing to three of these sections as well. These excerpts describe much of the early development of the MBone, and capture the excitement of those early years of multicast development and deployment.

```
February, 1992
```

```
MULTIMEDIA CONFERENCING

On February 18, the IETF Audio/Video Transport working
group met via a packet audio teleconference that spanned
three continents and 16 timezones. At least 24 people
participated from 14 different locations. The packet
audio was distributed over an IP multicast topology
spanning 30 network segments. In addition, 5 sites
directly connected to DARTnet also shared packet video
```

via IP multicast. A second teleconference with some
additional sites was held March 5.

The primary purpose of these teleconferences was to
gauge how well UDP packet audio will work over an IP
multicast topology consisting of DARTnet as a
transcontinental US backbone plus multicast tunnels
reaching out to other sites. The results varied
depending upon the paths traversed by the tunnels, but
on the whole it worked pretty well. For large scale use
of packet audio and video, it is clear that resource
management will be required in the network to provide
low delay service.

These teleconferences were also in preparation for a
packet "audiocast" of the general sessions at the March
IETF meeting in San Diego. This first audiocast will be
a small-scale pilot, but may be expanded for future IETF
meetings if successful.

July, 1992

MULTIMEDIA CONFERENCING

At the July IETF in Boston, Internet teleconferencing
continued to break new ground! This time, both packet
audio AND video were "mediacast" to participants
spanning 170 different hosts and 10 different countries
(AU, CA, CH, FR, JP, NL, NO, SE, UK, US). The
configuration supported widescale listening and viewing
of not only the general sessions, but also working
groups pertaining to Audio/Video Transport,
Teleconferencing Architecture, and IP Multicast. The
DARTnet served as the multicast backbone with tunnels
branching out over T3 backbone, lightly-loaded T1's and
Ethernets. We are now coordinating the construction of
the MBONE, the multicast backbone, to expose IP
multicasting to scaling problems of 1 to 2 orders of
magnitude.

September, 1992

MULTIMEDIA CONFERENCING

Organization of the MBONE, a virtual IP multicast
backbone network to support IETF audio/videocasts and
other experiments, is proceeding well. The topology it
taking shape, especially among NSFnet-connected regional
networks in the US. Several networks are ready to
provide multicast tunnel connections for the end-user
sites they serve, and we're hoping to get most of the
sites that would like to receive the next IETF audiocast
hooked up soon to avoid a rush at the last minute.

October, 1992

MULTIMEDIA CONFERENCING

The upcoming IETF meeting will mark the third multicast
of live audio and video across the Internet. This time
we will try to transmit two simultaneous channels of
audio and video during the working group breakout
sessions, and we may be able to demonstrate a return
video stream to IETF.

November, 1992

MULTIMEDIA CONFERENCING

At the November IETF meeting, there were several
advances on the teleconferencing front. This was the
third meeting to be "audiocast" and the second to
include video, this time over the MBONE (virtual
multicast backbone) built up in a more coordinated
manner from the ad-hoc collection of multicast tunnels
used in July.

In the Audio/Video Transport WG chaired by Steve Casner, a draft specification for the Realtime Transport Protocol, based on previous WG discussion, was presented by Henning Schulzrinne. We reached consensus on most of the open issues. A collection of Internet-Drafts will be released very soon. In the third session, we heard presentations on the software video compression algorithms being used in various programs and discussed how we might achieve interoperation among them.

Eve Schooler led two impromptu BOF sessions on Conference Control (sometimes referred to as connection or configuration management). The aim of these discussions was to understand how such a group might contribute to the remote conferencing architecture effort. It was agreed that there is a need for a session layer control protocol to perform higher layer functions than the protocol proposed in the AVT WG. The beginnings of design criteria for this protocol were identified. See the minutes in the IETF proceedings for further details.

December, 1992

MULTIMEDIA CONFERENCING

Slides and annotations on the topic of "A Software Architecture for Packet Teleconferencing" were prepared for the 2nd Packet Video Workshop at MCNC, Research Triangle Park, NC, Dec 9-10, 1992; the presentation itself was given by Fengmin Gong of MCNC, with ISIers listening in and watching over the MBONE.

We were involved in several trial demonstrations of BBN's Synchronization Protocol over the DARTnet. In particular, we served as an endpoint for a distributed music demonstration, performing one of the instrument parts of a Haydn trio in real-time and providing feedback about the sound quality and synchronization accuracy.

January, 1993

MULTIMEDIA CONFERENCING

Internet packet audio and video tools such as INRIA's
IVS, LBL's vat, PARC's nv, and UMass' NEVOT have become
quite popular over the past year. Combined with LBL's
Session Directory tool (sd), these programs implement a
"loose control" style of session management that is
particularly appropriate for large "seminar" events such
as the IETF audio/videocasts. For smaller conferences
with an explicit set of participants, a "tight control"
style of session management that exchanges state
information among the participants can add several
useful services, including:

- an explicit request for participation by a callee,
  perhaps with a small pop-up window, and an explicit
  reply (no answer, busy/refuse, accept);

- key exchange to implement security measures such as
  authentication of conferees and data confidentiality
  and integrity;

- negotiation of session parameters, such as selecting a
  compatible compression algorithm and data rate.

March, 1993

MULTIMEDIA CONFERENCING

At the Columbus IETF meeting, we chaired two
teleconferencing-related groups. The Audio/Video
Transport Working Group is nearing completion in the
specification of an experimental real-time transport
protocol. A second group on Conferencing Control met as
a BOF to discuss the requirements of a session protocol
for multiway collaborations, and particularly to focus on
a suitable scope for this problem to establish a charter

and a working group. The intent is to specify a protocol
to support loose- and tight-control conference styles.

As an example of how such a session protocol might
interact with the already popular tools such as PARC's
nv and LBL's vat, we demonstrated at the IETF an X-based
version of the MMCC conference control tool. MMCC takes
a tightly-controlled approach to session management in
that it explicitly shares full session-related
information among all the participants. In the
demonstration, we used MMCC to invite a specific set of
participants (vs having a wide-open session), to
distribute multicast addresses and a shared encryption
key among those participants, and to initiate as well as
tear down sessions comprised of some selection of
underlying tools. Since MMCC stays "in the loop" after
session initiation, we expect it in the future to
provide a channel for negotiation of quality of service
and configuration parameters as they may change during
the session. We intend soon to release MMCC for more
widespread use.

The Columbus IETF marked the fourth live multicast of
audio and video. A memo on "How to do an IETF A/V
multicast" was written to help the organizers of the
Columbus and future IETFs to set up the necessary
equipment. Also, just before the meeting, Van Jacobson
implemented IP encapsulation for multicast tunnels; with
Steve Deering, we worked to test and distribute that
code as widely as possible since it makes a big
performance improvement.

June, 1993

MULTIMEDIA CONFERENCING

In preparation for a fifth live multicast of audio and
video from the Amsterdam IETF meeting, we have organized
a re-engineering of the MBONE (multicast virtual
backbone). Problems and solutions were discussed in two
teleconferences over the MBONE. A new topology was

designed for the North American portion of the MBONE to more closely follow the physical network topology and to reduce the fanout of the core multicast routers to avoid CPU overload. At ISI, the Sun3/60 mrouter was upgraded to a SPARC 2 clone for more capacity.

July, 1993

MULTIMEDIA CONFERENCING

Two channels of live audio and video were multicast from the Amsterdam IETF meeting, the fifth such multicast. The cumulative total of remote hosts that joined into the audio multicast was 518. For the first time, this was slightly more than the number of people who attended locally (approximately 490). Thanks to the efforts of a number of people, both in Amsterdam and elsewhere around the MBONE, to re-engineer the topology of the MBONE, this multicast was much improved over the previous ones in that both channels of audio and video worked to most places most of the week. However, the quality was often "listenable" but not "good". We need further work on performance monitoring so we can find and fix bottlenecks.

August, 1993

MULTIMEDIA CONFERENCING

On August 17, an MBONE teleconference meeting of the IETF AVT working group was held to review the changes in the "next-to-last call" draft specification for the Realtime Transport Protocol and reach agreement on several questions. One item agreed was to seek "proposed standard" rather than "experimental" status when the draft is submitted to become an RFC. This should happen in September, after the "last call" edition of the draft spec is completed to incorporate the changes discussed

in the meeting and some additional explanatory sections
on usage scenarios.

Our teleconference session orchestration program, mmcc,
was demonstrated at INET'93 with audio/video calls
placed to remote locations such as ISI, where the camera
gave a nice view of the marina. To avoid requiring an
individual to answer the calls, an option was added to
the call setup process in mmcc to allow an automatic yes
or no answer when contacted, rather than ringing.

November, 1993

MULTIMEDIA CONFERENCING

At the Houston IETF meeting, ISI (co-)chaired two
working groups related to teleconferencing. The
Audio/Video Transport Working Group met for only one
session this time since the draft specification for the
Real-time Transport Protocol (RTP) has been submitted
for the first RFC stage. The emphasis of this session
was on implementation experience, with the focus
shifting to companion specifications for profiles and
encodings. The MMusic working group met for two sessions
at the Houston IETF meeting.

The first day was dedicated to a short overview of the
goals and context for the working group and then to a
presentation of an algorithm and framework for managing
shared session state. The second meeting focused on
preliminary ideas on what might comprise shared session
state for a couple of different session types, and then
three short presentations on related work.

The Houston IETF marked the sixth live multicast of
audio and video. The number of remote hosts
participanting was 629, which for the second time was
approximately equal to the number of people who attended
locally.

Eve Schooler gave a presentation "Multimedia Session
Control for Internet Telecollaboration" over the MBone

from ISI to the NASA Science Centers' ICNN/S Conference
in Monterey, CA, Nov 17, 1993.

March, 1994

MULTIMEDIA CONFERENCING

During the MMusic WG meetings at the Seattle IETF, there
appeared to be a convergence of ideas about the general
framework and protocols required for session control in
the Internet, and a readiness to take steps toward
interoperability of existing applications. The group
identified at least two services that we as system
builders might need and use; CCCP, a bus-based protocol
that could provide an API-level messaging abstraction,
and the agreement algorithm on which a session service
could be built. In addition, there was interest in
trying to understand, in the present context of the
Internet/MBone/WWW, what constitutes a session and what
are the functions that can be performed on sessions once
they exist. Thus, a variety of session rendez-vous
mechanisms were described. A final discussion focused on
the relevance of reliable multicast to a membership
management protocol. From formal and informal
conversations with working group participants, it was
clear that these ideas are ready to be codified and
written down.

Eve Schooler's talk, "Evolution of MMCC: Session Control
Revisited", focused on the architectural framework
behind the ISI session orchestration tool, mmcc, and
discussed the ongoing evolution of its session control
protocol. The main goals of the discussion were to
identify similarities and differences among the various
session control approaches, and to suggest a synthesis
of ideas. Several issues were raised: the tradeoffs
between a classic packet format and string-based
messaging, how to characterize media agents, QoS, and
session policies as part of a session description, the
movement toward an adapative soft-state approach
(periodic refresh), building a group consensus service

on top of unreliable transport, options for cross-module
communication, and finally incorporating multicast.

June, 1994

UNRELATED HISTORICAL NOTE: Merit held the first meeting
of the NANOG (North American Network Operators Group)
in Ann Arbor on June 2nd and 3rd.

July, 1994

MULTIMEDIA CONFERENCING

At the IETF meeting held in Toronto this month, there
were several sessions relevant to multimedia
teleconferencing, in particular those of the Multiparty
Multimedia Session Control (MMUSIC) Working Group and
the Audio/Video Transport (AVT) Working Group. The
MMUSIC session focused on reports from implementors of a
range of multimedia conferencing applications with the
goal of identifying common ground for interoperability
of both session managers and media agents. As a result,
there was commitment by several implementors to document
their protocol choices, and to prototype experiments on
interoperation in the near term.

In the first AVT session, rough consensus was given to
submit the revised Real-time Transport Protocol
specification for Area Directorate review and IESG Last
Call as a Proposed Standard. This revision, denoted RTP
version 2, incorporates changes requested by the first
AD review in November 1993. It is the refinement by
Steve Casner, Ron Frederick, Van Jacobson and Henning
Schulzrinne of the rough protocol changes presented and
discussed at the March 1994 IETF meeting in Seattle.
This version of the spec was posted before the meeting
as Internet Draft draft-ietf-avt-rtp-05.txt.

An overview of the revised RTP was presented in the
first AVT session, and the group concurred with the
choices made on all of the previously open issues. It
was agreed that the extension hooks provided were
adequate for planned experiments with mechanisms not
included in the current protocol. A few explanatory
sections of the draft need to be completed, then it will
be submitted. In the second AVT session, video encoding
specifications for H.261, JPEG and MPEG were presented.
These specifications will also be completed as Internet
Drafts and thensubmitted as Proposed Standards.

APPENDIX **D**

HIGH-LEVEL SUMMARY OF MULTICAST ROUTING PROTOCOLS

The five multicast routing protocols we have examined in this book share some similar characteristics. One way to characterize the protocols is by join type. We have seen two broad classes of protocols: implicit-join and explicit-join. As shown in Figure D–1, three out of the five protocols are explicit-join.

Another way to classify the five protocols is by the kind of trees they build, either shared, source-based, or both in the case of PIM-SM, though it builds explicitly-joined shared trees to begin with; see Figure D–2.

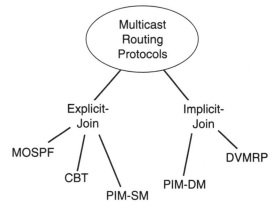

FIGURE D–1   Classification by join type

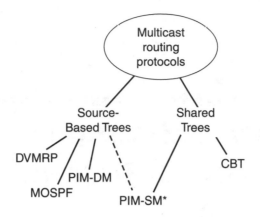

*Even when PIM-SM builds source-based trees, they are still explicitly joined.

FIGURE D–2   Classification by tree type

Remember that upstream and downstream have slightly different meanings depending on the tree type. In a source-based tree, "upstream" refers to the direction toward the source, and conversely "downstream" means the direction away from the source. Shared trees, however, reckon directions relative to the center of the tree. In a shared tree, "upstream" refers to the direction toward the center, and "downstream" means away from it.

APPENDIX E

MULTICAST STANDARDIZATION

IETF

The Internet Engineering Task Force (IETF) is the body that codifies standards related to the Internet Protocol suite. As an integral part of the IP architecture, multicast IP has been and is being specified by the IETF.

The IETF is divided into "Areas" which are in turn subdivided into various Working Groups (WGs). The IETF has two working groups that are primarily concentrating on multicast IP and related issues:

- Inter-Domain Multicast Routing (IDMR), in the Routing Area
- MBone Deployment (MBoneD), in the Operations Area

The IDMR WG has developed the two PIM protocols and the CBT protocol, and has specified the DVMRP (version 3) and the IGMP (version 2, and eventually version 3).

Before the IDMR WG existed, the DVMRP had been specified in Steve Deering's Ph.D. thesis, and in an older specification (RFC-1075). Over the initial several years of its deployment, the protocol evolved to better accommodate ever larger-scale internetworks. The IDMR WG has stepped in to update the specification and to embody these developments as version 3 of the DVMRP. Similarly, the IGMP was originally specified in Deering's thesis and as Appendix One of RFC-1112. The IGMP had also evolved over the years, with new features being added to better accommodate large-scale deployment. A new specification was called for, completely documenting version 2 of the protocol, including its new features.

The MOSPF protocol was a product of the MOSPF working group, closely related to the OSPF working group. A link-state multicast routing protocol was described by

Deering in his thesis, and MOSPF is a concrete example of such a protocol. Certain other working groups are not strictly focused on multicast, but still produce standards which relate to multicast IP. For example, the Internetworking Over Non-broadcast multi-access (NBMA) subnetworks (ION) WG is chartered to develop techniques to allow IP (including multicast IP) to operate over subnetwork technologies such as ATM and X.25.

Development of future multicast IP routing protocols (especially inter-domain protocols!) and related work will probably take place in the IDMR WG. Work on multicast transport protocols will take place in the Transport Area in special, focused, working groups. Currently, there is a lot of interest in "reliable multicast," and the Internet Research Task Force (IRTF) has taken the unprecedented step of opening up their ongoing Reliable Multicast research to the IETF community. The IRTF is the IETF's sister organization, tasked with long-term research projects. The IETF is an engineering group which is chartered with producing workable standards for implementation, incorporating related operational and protocol-design experience.

More information on the current status of these and other IETF working groups may be found on the IETF's world wide web site: http://www.ietf.org/.

IEEE 802.1 Committee

The IEEE 802.1 committee is also actively involved in standardizing techniques for streamlining the operation of multicast IP over switched LANs. The Generic Multicast Registration Protocol (GMRP), part of 802.1p, will allow end stations to notify MAC-layer switches about the MAC-layer multicast addresses they need to hear. Similar to the way that routers use multicast routing protocols plus IGMP to compute multicast delivery trees at the IP layer, the MAC-layer switching fabric will be able to use GMRP-derived information to establish a MAC-layer distribution tree for multicast groups.

APPENDIX F

REFERENCES

IETF REQUESTS FOR COMMENTS (RFCS)

966 "Host Groups: A Multicast Extension to the Internet Protocol," S. E. Deering, D. R. Cheriton, December 1985.

988 "Host Extensions for IP Multicasting," S. E. Deering, July 1986.

1054 "Host Extensions for IP Multicasting," S. E. Deering, May 1988.

1075 "Distance Vector Multicast Routing Protocol," D. Waitzman, C. Partridge, and S. Deering, November 1988.

1112 "Host Extensions for IP Multicasting," Steve Deering, August 1989.

1458 "Requirements for Multicast Protocols," R. Braudes, S. Zabele, May 1993.

1584 "Multicast Extensions to OSPF," John Moy, March 1994.

1585 "MOSPF: Analysis and Experience," John Moy, March 1994.

1700 "Assigned Numbers," J. Reynolds and J. Postel, October 1994. (STD 2)

1812 "Requirements for IP version 4 Routers," Fred Baker, Editor, June 1995.

1889 "RTP: A Transport Protocol for Real-Time Applications," a product of the IETF Audio-Video Transport Working Group (AVT WG), H. Schulzrinne, S. Casner, R. Frederick, V. Jacobson, January 1996.

1890 "RTP Profile for Audio and Video Conferences with Minimal Control," a product of the IETF Audio-Video Transport Working Group (AVT WG), H. Schulzrinne, January 1996.

2000 "Internet Official Protocol Standards," Jon Postel, Editor, February 1997.

2029 "RTP Payload Format of Sun's CellB Video Encoding," M. Speer, D. Hoffman, October 1996.

2032 "RTP Payload Format for H.261 Video Streams," T. Turletti, C. Huitema, October 1996.

2035 "RTP Payload Format for JPEG-compressed Video," L. Berc, W. Fenner, R. Frederick, S. McCanne, October 1996.

2038 "RTP Payload Format for MPEG1/MPEG2 Video," D. Hoffman, G. Fernando, V. Goyal, October 1996.

2090 "TFTP Multicast Option," A. Emberson, February 1997.

2113 "IP Router Alert Option," D. Katz, February 1997.

2165 "Service Location Protocol," J. Veizades, E. Guttman, C. Perkins, S. Kaplan, June 1997.

2117 "Protocol Independent Multicast-Sparse Mode (PIM-SM): Protocol Specification," D. Estrin, D. Farinacci, A. Helmy, D. Thaler; S. Deering, M. Handley, V. Jacobson, C. Liu, P. Sharma, and L. Wei, June 1997.

2178 "OSPF Version 2," John Moy, July 1997.

IETF INTERNET DRAFTS

IETF Statement on Internet Drafts

Internet Drafts are working documents of the Internet Engineering Task Force (IETF), its areas, and its working groups. Note that other groups may also distribute working documents as Internet Drafts.

Internet Drafts are draft documents valid for a maximum of six months and may be updated, replaced, or obsoleted by other documents at any time. It is inappropriate to use Internet Drafts as reference material or to cite them other than as "work in progress." To learn the current status of any Internet Draft, please check the "1id-abstracts.txt" listing contained in the Internet Drafts Shadow Directories:

Africa:	ftp.is.co.za,
Europe:	nic.nordu.net,
Pacific Rim:	munnari.oz.au,
US East Coast:	ds.internic.net,
US West Coast:	ftp.isi.edu.

Accordingly, these cited documents are only listed for your convenience. They are *not* permanent reference documents. Many of these are well on their way to being formalized as RFCs, at which time the Internet Draft will disappear from the online directories listed above. Rather than being published as an RFC, an Internet Draft could expire with no further action taken. Also, an internet draft could be actively revised several times, leading to multiple successive internet draft versions, rendering one of those listed obsolete. If it is revised several times, it could still eventually expire if people lose interest in it, or it could be polished into a form that is suitable for publication as an RFC.

It is guaranteed that after mid-1998 all these documents will have expired. Hopefully, knowing their old names will help you trace their final disposition. Internet Drafts were cited in this book because they were the only sources of certain technical information at the time of the book's writing. Had this information been available in other forms, as RFCs or elsewhere, those references would have been used instead.

> Note: **Not all RFCs are standards;** however, all standards are RFCs. There are several classifications of RFCs: Standards-Track (first, Proposed Standard [PS], then Draft Standard [DS]), and finally just plain Standard), also Experimental, Historic, Informational, and others. Of all these categories, only Standard RFCs are truly IETF standards. As of late July 1997, there are only 53 Internet Standards, but there are over 2100 RFCs.

"Core Based Trees (CBT) Multicast Routing Architecture," `draft-ietf-idmr-cbt-arch-06.txt`, A. J. Ballardie, May 1997.

"Core Based Trees (CBT version 2) Multicast Routing: Protocol Specification," `draft-ietf-idmr-cbt-spec-10.txt`, A. J. Ballardie, July 1997.

"Core Based Tree (CBT) Multicast Border Router Specification for Connecting a CBT Stub Region to a DVMRP Backbone," `draft-ietf-idmr-cbt-dvmrp-00.txt`, A. J. Ballardie, March 1997.

"Distance Vector Multicast Routing Protocol," `draft-ietf-idmr-dvmrp-v3-04.ps`, T. Pusateri, February 19, 1997.

"Internet Group Management Protocol, Version 2," `draft-ietf-idmr-igmp-v2-06.txt`, William Fenner, January 22, 1997.

"Internet Group Management Protocol, Version 3," `draft-cain-igmp-00.txt`, Brad Cain, Ajit Thyagarajan, and Steve Deering, Expired.

"Protocol Independent Multicast Version 2, Dense Mode Specification," `draft-ietf-idmr-pim-dm-spec-05.ps`, S. Deering, D. Estrin, D. Farinacci, V. Jacobson, A. Helmy, and L. Wei, May 21, 1997.

"Protocol Independent Multicast-Sparse Mode (PIM-SM): Motivation and Architecture," `draft-ietf-idmr-pim-arch-04.ps`, S. Deering, D. Estrin, D. Farinacci, V. Jacobson, C. Liu, and L. Wei, November 19, 1996.

"PIM Multicast Border Router (PMBR) specification for connecting PIM-SM domains to a DVMRP Backbone," `draft-ietf-mboned-pmbr-spec-00.txt`, D. Estrin, A. Helmy, D. Thaler, February 3, 1997.

"Administratively Scoped IP Multicast," `draft-ietf-mboned-admin-ip-space-02.txt`, D. Meyer, December 23, 1996.

"Interoperability Rules for Multicast Routing Protocols," `draft-thaler-interop-00.txt`, D. Thaler, November 7, 1996.

See the IDMR home pages for an archive of specifications:
> `http://www.cs.ucl.ac.uk/ietf/public_idmr/`
> `http://www.ietf.org/html.charters/idmr-charter.html`

"IETF Criteria For Evaluating Reliable Multicast Transport and Application Protocols," `draft-mankin-reliable-multicast-00.txt`, A. Mankin, A. Romanow, with the IETF Transport Services Area Directorate, November 1996.

"RMFP: A Reliable Multicast Framing Protocol," `draft-crowcroft-rmfp-01.txt`, J. Crowcroft, Z. Wang, A. Ghosh, C. Diot, March 1997.

"StarBurst Multicast File Transfer Protocol (MFTP) Specification," `draft-miller-mftp-spec-02.txt`, K. Miller, K. Robertson, A. Tweedly, M. White, January 1997.

"RTP Extension for Scaleable Reliable Multicast," `draft-parnes-rtp-ext-srm-01.txt`, Peter Parnes, November 1996.

TEXTBOOKS

Comer, Douglas E. *Internetworking with TCP/IP, Volume 1: Principles, Protocols, and Architecture,* Second Edition, Prentice Hall, Englewood Cliffs, NJ, 1991.

Huitema, Christian. *Routing in the Internet,* Prentice Hall, Englewood Cliffs, NJ, 1995.

Stevens, W. Richard. *TCP/IP Illustrated: Volume 1, The Protocols,* Addison Wesley, Reading, MA, 1994.

Wright, Gary and W. Richard Stevens. *TCP/IP Illustrated: Volume 2, The Implementation,* Addison Wesley, Reading, MA, 1995.

OTHER

Dalal, Y. K., and Metcalfe, R. M., "Reverse Path Forwarding of Broadcast Packets," *Communications of the ACM*, 21(12):1040–1048, December 1978.

Deering, Steven E. "Multicast Routing in a Datagram Internetwork," Ph.D. thesis, Stanford University, December 1991.

Ballardie, Anthony J. "A New Approach to Multicast Communication in a Datagram Internetwork," Ph.D. thesis, University College London, May 1995.

Thyagarajan, Ajit, and Deering, Steven E. "Hierarchical Distance Vector Multicast Routing for the MBone," *Proceedings of the ACM SIGCOMM,* pp. 60–66, October 1995.

S. Floyd, V. Jacobson, S. McCanne, C. Liu, and L. Zhang. "A Reliable Multicast Framework for Light-weight Sessions and Application Level Framing," `ftp://ftp.ee.lbl.gov/papers/srm_sigcomm.ps.Z`, *Proceedings of ACM SIGCOMM '95,* August 1995, pp. 342–356.

Also, a corrected and extended version is available, as submitted to the *IEEE/ACM Transactions on Networking:*

S. Floyd, V. Jacobson, S. McCanne, C. Liu, and L. Zhang. "A Reliable Multicast Framework for Light-weight Sessions and Application Level Framing," `ftp://ftp.ee.lbl.gov/papers/srml.tech.ps.Z`.

Index